Queen of the Clouds
Joan Merriam Smith and Jerrie Mock's Epic Quest to Become the First Woman to Fly Solo Around the World

Taylor C. Phillips

turtle cove press
Tallahassee and Ochlockonee Bay, Florida

Queen of the Clouds
Joan Merriam Smith and Jerrie Mock's
Epic Quest to Become the First Woman
to Fly Solo Around the World

Editor's Note: The author's diligent research revealed inconsistencies with regard to some sources. For example, Joan's writings do not always agree with each other, and occasionally there is a discrepancy over dates, even within a single document. Also, recollections from two or three sources, in print and on the internet, do not match Captain Smith's recall. Wherever there's a disagreement, the author relies on the primary source and shows the alternative narratives and their sources in the text and footnotes.

ISBN: 978-1947536166
Library of Congress Catalog Number: 2022947791

Cover design: Babski Creative Studios, Tallahassee, FL.
Cover photo of Joan Merriam Smith used with permission:
Valley Times Collection/Los Angeles Public Library.
Cover photo of Jerrie Mock used with permission of the National Archives and Records Administration, College Park, MD.

Queen of the Clouds

Joan Merriam Smith and Jerrie Mock's Epic Quest to Become the First Woman to Fly Solo Around the World

as possible. Even inquiries to the US Department of Transportation's National Transportation Library were unable to confirm what the time zones were called in 1964.

Occasionally, dialogue and minor details have been reconstructed based on available sources. Although some details may never be recovered, we have more than enough for a vivid picture of this moment in history and an intriguing story of courage, adventure, and resourcefulness.

I would like to thank many people for their roles in bringing this book to completion: Pilot Garwood Braun for sharing a story about a member of his flight club; Pat Steed, social studies teacher and faculty sponsor of Rho Kappa National Social Studies Honor Society at the Florida State University School, Tallahassee, Florida, Jeanine Meis and Josh Stewart at Leon High School in Tallahassee, Jessica Kimmelman at Cornerstone Learning Community, Tallahassee, and Melissa Willis with the Presbytery of Florida for their heart for bringing living history to students and readers.

I thank my father, Cecil Phillips, for help with the "math homework," calculating distances and times. Thanks to my friend Christopher Linton, Leon County librarians Chris Dueno, Shawna Durtschi, Judi Rundel, Tina Beadnell, Stephanie Moore, and all the helpful staff at the AnswerSquad at the Leroy Collins Leon County Public Library for research assistance. I would also like to thank Adrian Fogelin and Gina Edwards for help with editing on the previous version of this work, *Racing to Greet the Sun*, Florida State University graduate student Shannon Lynch for help with formatting, and my publisher, M.R. Street, for her devotion to this project. Above all, I thank my beloved wife, Pam, for her insight and help with the story and the computer, and for her patience with the author, in general.

–Taylor C. Phillips

Contents

Prologue

From the beginnings of human flight, the world of aviation, like so many other professions, has been dominated by men. This makes it all the more extraordinary that two women embarked at virtually the same time to set the same world record.

Their objective: To be the first woman to fly solo around the world. Amelia Earhart tried (albeit not "solo" as navigator Fred Noonan was also on board) but didn't succeed. Not even Jackie Cochran, who to this day holds more distance and speed records than any other pilot, had made the attempt.[3] And yet, Jerrie Mock and Joan Merriam Smith, among the most important pilots, male or female, ever to "have slipped the surly bonds of Earth,"[4] have never received their full measure of fame.

It's time to correct that.

---

[3] "Jacqueline Cochran," *Wikipedia*, last modified August 30, 2022, accessed Sept. 14, 2022, https://en.wikipedia.org/wiki/Jacqueline_Cochran.

[4] John Gillespie Magee, Jr., "High Flight" (1941).

1930s–1960s:
The Girl Who Thought She Could Fly

Jerrie's love affair with flying began when she was a little girl. In 1931, the year she turned six, her family had moved into a neighborhood in Newark, Ohio, where the only girls Jerrie's age lived across the street.[5] Her mother wouldn't let her cross the street, though, so Jerrie played cops and robbers with the boys on her side instead. By the time she was allowed to cross the street, she had tossed out her dolls. Boys' games were more fun.

When she was seven, her parents took her to see a "barnstormer" air show. After the show, the barnstorming pilot took Jerrie's family up for their first ride in an airplane. Jerrie loved looking down at the rooftops and tiny cars below. As she got off the plane, she told her mom and dad, "I'm going to be a pilot."

"That's nice, dear." Her mother patted her head and chuckled. In 1932, there were fewer than 200 women pilots in the entire country. None of them lived in Newark.

Jerrie's mother forgot about the conversation, but Jerrie did not forget about her desire to fly.

Growing up, Jerrie listened to the big family radio every

---

[5] Mock, interview, July 1, 2007; Betty Vail and Dixon Edwards, "Winner Take All," *Flying Magazine,* July 1964: 60.

night for reports of Amelia Earhart flying across oceans and landing on faraway islands. Her geography book at school gave Jerrie her first glimpses of the world beyond Newark. She looked at pictures of a man riding a camel and an elephant pulling up a tree, and dreamed of seeing these things herself someday.[6] In the 1930s, America still had laws making it hard for women to work at any job, much less become pilots; but if Amelia Earhart could travel to all those exotic places by flying a plane, then Jerrie would, too.

In her high school math class, she got into arguments over algebra with a young man named Russell Mock.[7] Other girls may have been impressed that Russ was tall, with dark blue eyes, long eyelashes, and confidence. Jerrie was more impressed that, at sixteen, Russ had already taken flying lessons and had flown solo.

The admiration was mutual. They became high school sweethearts, going to all the football games and dances together.

Two weeks after Jerrie turned sixteen, Japanese planes bombed Pearl Harbor, and America entered World War II. The next year, high schools throughout Ohio offered a new class in pre-flight aviation. Jerrie was the only girl in her class.[8] One of the tests was the same one given to adults applying to become commercial pilots. Among all high school students in the state,

---

[6] Mock, interview, July 15, 2007.

[7] Mock, interview, Aug. 28, 2007; Vail and Edwards, "Winner Take All": 56.

[8] Mock, interview, Sept. 2, 2007; Amy K. Saunders, "How an Ohio Housewife Flew Around the World, Made History, and Was Then Forgotten," Buzzfeed Big Stories, April 12, 2014, accessed May 8, 2014, https://www.buzzfeed.com/amyksaunders/the-untold-story-of-the-first-woman-to-fly-around-the-world.

Jerrie scored third.

Then the war effort took over everyone's lives. Gasoline and food were rationed, construction of new homes came to a stop, and billboards of Rosie the Riveter encouraged women to work in the factories to support the soldiers. Flying lessons for a teenage girl were out of the question.[9]

When Jerrie went to college, her parents urged her to become a teacher, a librarian, or a secretary. Instead, she majored in aeronautical engineering. At seventeen, Jerrie was the only female aeronautical engineering major at Ohio State. The college boys tried to give her a hard time, until she earned the only perfect score on a chemistry exam.[10]

Russ's parents wanted him to become an engineer, so he was in class with her. Jerrie had not kept Russ waiting for an answer when he "popped the question." They were married in the spring of 1945, as the United States was winning World War II. Jerrie was nineteen.[11] She withdrew from college, and Russ left engineering to become a reporter. Jerrie gave birth to their sons, Roger (1946) and Gary (1947), and much later, to their daughter Valerie (1960).

Russ and Jerrie had fun experimenting with new inventions such as the television. They ran a talk show for a local station in Columbus, Ohio, called "Youth Has Its Say," in which they discussed topics such as "Should Red China Be Admitted to the U.N.?" and "The Woman's Place in the Home."[12] Their show

---

[9] Mock, Sept. 2, 2007.

[10] Mock, interview, Sept. 2, 2007; Saunders, "How an Ohio Housewife Flew Around the World."

[11] Mock, interview, Sept. 2, 2007.

[12] Mock, telephone conversation with author, Aug. 29, 2007.

ran for five years until the Chamber of Commerce got a new boss, who would not allow women in the planning meetings. He cancelled the show.

One night in September 1956, Russ announced that he had signed up to take another round of flying lessons the next Saturday. Jerrie promptly registered to take her first lesson—on Friday.[13] They took lessons together, and while one flew, the other sat in the passenger's seat, learning more. After only nine hours, Jerrie was ready to solo.

Once Jerrie and Russ had both earned their pilot's licenses, they bought their first plane, a Luscomb 8A they named "Tweetie Bird," for $1,200.[14] Tweetie Bird was tied down at Price Field outside of Columbus. When a man named Whitey Jost took over the ownership of Price Field, he hired Jerrie to manage the airport.[15] She became the first woman in the state of Ohio certified to manage an airport. She took advantage of the position to teach herself as much as she could about flying and plane repair, sometimes working on planes at midnight.

In May 1962, Russ found a sponsor for Jerrie so she could afford to enter the All Woman's International Air Race, flying from Houston, Texas, to Nassau, Bahamas.[16] Jerrie had invited a friend, Charlotte Shively, to fly with her. When they encountered a storm, Charlotte was terrified.

The moment the first raindrop hit their windshield, Charlotte let out a gasp. Even though it was only a light drizzle, Charlotte's face and knuckles turned white. Jerrie was forced to

---

[13] Mock, interview, Feb. 28, 2008; Vail and Edwards, "Winner Take All": 56.

[14] Mock, interview, Aug. 28, 2007; Vail and Edwards, "Winner Take All": 56.

[15] Mock, interview, Aug. 28, 2007; Vail and Edwards, "Winner Take All": 56.

[16] Mock, interview, Aug. 28, 2007.

land and wait until Charlotte's color returned. Race rules required that pilots who landed before the finish line had to return to the beginning and start over. Of the forty women pilots in the race, Jerrie finished last.[17] Another pilot who competed in the race was Joan Merriam Smith.[18] Although Joan and Jerrie did not notice or even know about each other then, they would become linked in history less than two years later.

Unfazed by Jerrie's last-place finish in the so-called "Angel Derby," Russ came up with his next big idea: a vacation trip to the island of St. Pierre, a French overseas territory along the Atlantic coast of Canada.[19] Their flight insurance policy covered them for the Western Hemisphere, so he asked Jerrie to fly him from Columbus up to the east coast of Canada, then out to the island of St. Pierre.[20] Russ had every reason to feel happy and proud of his wife and her plane. Jerrie was worried, though. Finishing last in her first race meant she might not get a sponsor for another one. She didn't really care about racing. Nonetheless, she had to *fly*–for real–not just these little vacation trips, but as far out there as she could. If she had to stay on the ground for the rest of her life, her heart might just break.

At the restaurant in their hotel on St. Pierre, Jerrie overheard a familiar sound: the voices of pilots coming over a radio.[21] She excused herself from the table and looked around. Next to the

---

[17] Mock, interview, Aug. 28, 2007.

[18] Tiffany Ann Brown, *Fate on a Folded Wing: The True Story of Pioneering Solo Pilot Joan Merriam Smith* (Reno, NV: Lucky Bat Books, 2019), 23.

[19] Mock, interview, Aug. 28, 2007.

[20] Mock, interview, Aug. 28, 2007; Saunders, "How an Ohio Housewife Flew Around the World."

[21] Mock, interview, Aug. 28, 2007.

dining room, the hotel had set up an overseas wireless room with a radio tuned to the frequency to pick up air chatter. Jerrie listened to pilots talking to each other as they flew over the Atlantic.[22]

Back in Ohio one night after dinner, "up to her elbows in dishwater," Jerrie admitted that she was bored with "laundry, dust mops and school lunches," and she really just wanted to fly as much as she could.[23]

Russ had heard it before. "Maybe you should just get in your plane and fly it somewhere," he said.

"Like where?" Jerrie asked.

"Like . . . like . . . how about *around the world*?!"[24]

Instead of arguing, Jerrie started thinking. *Why not*? Why not fly her little plane, all the way around the world? Why not travel to jungles and oceans as she had dreamed of doing since she was a child? She started asking around.

---

[22] Mock, interview, July 15, 2007.

[23] James Gilbert, "The Loser: An Epitaph to Joan Merriam Smith," *Flying Magazine*, August 1965, 82.

[24] Saunders, "How an Ohio Housewife Flew Around the World."

1940s-1960s: "Let's Go Flying!"

Joan Merriam was born in Oceanside, Long Island, New York on August 3, 1936, less than a year before Amelia Earhart disappeared while attempting to fly around the globe.[25] She grew up in Wayne, Michigan[26] where, as a child, she followed Connie Mack of the Philadelphia Athletics and played baseball ("not softball, but baseball with the fellas"[27]). By age fourteen, she was on an all-boys baseball team. "I was pretty good," she remembered.

From baseball, Joan went on to take baton lessons. "I went through a period of baton twirling where I just had to be a baton twirler."[28]

As a teenager, Joan Merriam was known for the black leather jacket she wore and for her favorite song, Chuck Berry's "Maybellene."[29] When she was fifteen, her father passed away on New Year's Day. That summer, Joan's mother packed up and

---

[25] Bryan Swopes, "17 March-12 May 1964: Joan Merriam Smith," *This Day in Aviation*: Important Dates in Aviation History, accessed February 24, 2022, https://www.thisdayinaviation.com/17-march-12-may-1964-joan-merriam-smith/; "Joan Merriam Smith," Find a Grave, accessed March 2 2019, https://www.findagrave.com/memorial/17235826/joan-smith.

[26] Swopes, *This Day in Aviation*; Smith, interview by author, Prattville Alabama, June 9, 2017.

[27] Gilbert, "The Loser," 80.

[28] Ibid.

[29] Terry Graham, "A Piece of History: Legend Down," accessed August 26, 2020, https://www.wrightwoodcalif.com/forum/index.php?topic=9329.0.

relocated with Joan to South Florida, where they moved in with Mrs. Merriam's sister and brother-in-law. The flight to Miami would change Joan's life. Joan would recall:

> The August day in 1952 when I boarded an Eastern Airlines Constellation for my first flight to anywhere, I was terrified. Fifteen minutes after takeoff, I screwed up my courage enough to ask the stewardess if I could go up where the pilots were. I visited the cockpit for ten minutes, and when I returned to my seat, I was hooked on aviation. I persuaded my mother that I'd rather have flying lessons than continue with baton-twirling lessons.[30]

Joan felt baton-twirling, at which she had won multiple trophies, was no longer a challenge.[31] She convinced her mother that flying lessons would be more cost effective.[32]

Baton lessons cost her mom $6.50 per half hour, while flying lessons were only $12 for a whole hour. Joan gave up the baton in favor of a more exhilarating pastime, flying. "I'd found a new love,"[33] she explained. "I guess it was the feeling of speed–of getting someplace fast–that got me."[34]

One day Joan's Aunt Beryl reached for a book on her shelf and handed it to her niece. *Last Flight* was the diary of Amelia Earhart's attempt to circumnavigate the globe along the

---

[30] Merriam, "I Flew," 78.

[31] Gilbert, "The Loser," 80.

[32] Brown, *Fate*, 22.

[33] Merriam, "I Flew," 78;

[34] "L.B. Flier, Writer Die in Mountain Crash," *Long Beach Independent*, Feb. 18, 1965, accessed March 15, 2018, https://www.newspapers.com/image/17695322.

equator, consisting of entries she cabled or telephoned home from points along the journey. Earhart's husband, George Palmer Putnam, noted that the book "was to have been called *World Flight,* but fate willed otherwise."[35]

In Amelia's words, her flight plan would take her "as near [the Earth's] waistline as could be."[36] Joan would read about Amelia's understanding of "the shadow of danger," as she described it to her husband, of flying for so long, particularly over the ocean.[37] "When I go," Amelia often said, "I'd like best to go in my plane. Quickly."[38]

Despite the risks, Joan told friends and classmates that someday she would fly around the world just as "A.E." (Earhart) had tried to do. They laughed. "They knew I was a baseball-playing tomboy, and [thought] this was a tomboy fantasy."[39]

But Joan knew that, since Amelia disappeared, no other woman had ever attempted a solo around-the-world flight, and that only made her determined to be the first.

At age sixteen, after only nine hours of flight time,[40] and

---

[35] "July 1936. The Round-the-World Flight," PBS, accessed May 19, 2022, www.pbs.org/wgbh/americanexperience/features/earhart-timeline.

[36] "Amelia Earhart, 1897-1937." *PBS*, Public Broadcasting Service, accessed September 3, 2022, https://www.pbs.org/wgbh/americanexperience/features /earhart-timeline/.

[37] Amelia Earhart, *Last Flight,* ed. George Palmer Putnam (New York: Harcourt, Brace and Company, Inc., 1937), xv-xvii.

[38] Ibid.

[39] Merriam, "I Flew," 77.

[40] Coincidentally, both Joan and Jerrie were ready to solo after only nine hours of flight time.

before she even had a license to drive a car, Joan flew solo.[41] Joan remembered her mom as "the bravest passenger" as she practiced maneuvers required for her commercial pilot's license.[42] After receiving special permission because of her age to take the private pilot's license exam, she got her license at the minimum age of seventeen.

Her mother bought Joan her first plane, a Cessna 140.[43] At the time, it was believed that Joan was "probably one of the youngest people in the United States to own a plane."[44] In her senior year of high school, she flew in the Proficiency Air Race out of Detroit, earning third place.[45] For Joan, the scene of Miami in the 1950s offered opportunities. In 1954, she graduated from the Sheffield School of Aeronautics with a certificate as a commercial pilot.[46]

She found employment as a flight instructor and corporate pilot. Evidently, she put her earnings into planes, trying out one after another. In her tape-recorded journal, she reminisced about that first plane her mother bought her, followed by a BT-13 Joan bought for $600, followed by a clip-wing Piper Cub for "acrobatics," another Cessna 140-A, and a Cessna 172 Skyhawk.[47]

[41] Merriam, "I Flew," 78; Claudine Burnett, *Soaring Skyward: A History of Aviation in and around Long Beach, California*, Bloomington, IN: AuthorHouse, 2011: 173.
[42] Swopes, *This Day in Aviation*.
[43] Brown, *Fate*, 93.
[44] Swopes, *This Day in Aviation*.
[45] Beatrice Ann Schubert and Joan Merriam Smith, "World Flight: Joan Merriam Smith" (unpublished manuscript, 1965), shared by Tiffany Ann Brown.
[46] Ibid.
[47] Brown, *Fate*, 93.

She pursued every credential available to her at the youngest possible age, joined the Miami chapter of the Ninety-Nines, and entered one air event after another.[48]

In the fall of 1955, when Joan was nineteen and working as a flight instructor for Avex, Inc., at Tamiami Airport, she met and married Harold MacDonald, a Marine and student in aeronautical engineering, but the marriage was short-lived.[49] By some accounts, there was tension over the desire to have children versus the desire to fly. Capt. Jack Smith also recalled other details that Joan had shared with him. "He was physically abusive. He broke her nose."[50]

In 1956 she was initiated into the Barracuda Flying Club for flying a single-engine plane "across the channel to Cuba five times."[51]

She had to wait until her twenty-third birthday to take the test to earn her airline transport rating, and she passed it on her first try. Passing this test on her birthday meant that Joan had earned every available license and rating at the minimum age.[52] She had soloed at sixteen, earned her private pilot's license at seventeen, her commercial pilot's license at eighteen, and her air transport rating at twenty-three.

In 1959, at the age of twenty-three, she received an award for becoming the youngest person ever to receive the Air Transport Rating, the "world's highest aviation rating." From the age of seventeen to twenty-six, Joan flew in nine air races, including

---

[48] Ibid., 6.

[49] Swopes, *This Day in Aviation.*

[50] Marvin "Jack" Smith, interview with author, Sept. 10. 2020.

[51] Schubert and Smith, "World Flight."

[52] Graham, "Legend Down;" "Joan Merriam Smith," Find a Grave.

three All Woman's International Air Races, remembered as the "Powder Puff Derbies," earned six awards and was recognized as the "youngest" entrant over and over again.[53]

In the aviation world of the 1950s, some doors were closed to women pilots, but not all. A Navy man named Bill Sowell hired her as a corporate pilot for his side business, Sowell Aviation.[54] She became a corporate pilot in 1959, one of only "three female corporation pilots flying in the country."[55] This new position required a move from Miami to Panama City, in Florida's Panhandle.[56]

In 1958, Lieutenant Commander Marvin "Jack" Smith was second-in-command of the USS *Vital*, a minesweeper homeported at Panama City.[57] Jack was also a pilot. Besides flying for work, Jack also enjoyed flying for fun, and he owned and operated a twin-propeller Cessna.[58]

According to Naval Aviator Robert Owen, officers were expected to attend a steady stream of social occasions, and parties on the base were the talk of the town. Pilots liked to drop down as close to the beach as 500 feet and wiggle their wings so that the girls on the beach might wave back. Then at the hangar party, everybody would have fun figuring out who

---

[53] Schubert and Smith, "World Flight." In a list of "Pre-World Flight Races and Honors" included in the unpublished manuscript, Joan records herself as the "youngest entrant" in races in 1954, 1955, and 1959.

[54] Smith, interview, June 9, 2017.

[55] "First Time in Air, She Was Afraid," *Long Beach (California) Independent*, Feb. 18, 1965, accessed Feb. 6, 2023, https://www.newspapers.com/image/719786428.

[56] "L.B. Flier," Feb. 18, 1965.

[57] Smith, interview, 2017; Swopes, *This Day in Aviation*. (Swopes refers to Jack as "executive officer of the USS *Vital*.")

[58] Smith, interview, 2017.

had been waving to whom out there.[59]

Jack, who happened to be single, also made friends with Bill Sowell, the fixed-base operator there. When Sowell mentioned that there was someone he wanted Jack to meet, Jack figured she might be one of those waving girls. Instead, Bill said, "I've just hired a very capable young lady. We're going to have a hangar party for her, and I want you to come and make her feel welcome to local aviation."[60]

Jack said, "Absolutely!"

When they were introduced, her first words to him were, "So you've got a two-prop Cessna. Let's go flying!"

Jack said, "Suits me!"

They made small talk with the people at their table and watched them sip on their Pabst Blue Ribbon beers until he felt it might be okay to ask, "Can we duck out now?" The two of them walked over to his plane, and he took her flying that night.

Panama City was a small town, and it didn't produce much light to guide them. The basic needle-ball instruments on Jack's plane didn't help much over the dark water. He had to navigate by following the direction of the wind.[61] Joan was impressed, and by the time Jack brought the plane down for a landing, the possibility of a future with this "very capable person" was already on his mind.

Yet the tension between career and relationship also emerged, almost immediately. By the 1960s, America's flight schools had only produced a few hundred "lady pilots" across the entire country, yet these select few had even fewer jobs to

---

[59] Robert Owen, interview by author, Tallahassee, FL, Jan. 2, 2020.

[60] Smith, interview, 2017.

[61] Ibid.

apply for. Commercial airlines were not placing women over men in their cockpits, at all.[62]

Jack recalled, "Some people in the aviation community felt that women shouldn't have all the jobs. She fought that all her life. It was really a problem. I didn't feel that way. I had an affinity for women pilots, in fact, I was soloed by a female flight instructor."[63]

Sowell Aviation was a small operation with a contract to fly executives of West Florida Natural Gas Company, a larger company that also operated out of the base in Panama City.[64] West Florida Gas also owned a twin-engine Piper Apache, but they needed a pilot. West Florida Gas soon began offering to let Joan to fly their plane on the weekends, on her own. "We'll pay for the gas," they said. "Take your boyfriend up!" When they asked her to come work for them, she jumped at the chance to fly for a larger company.[65] Sowell was disappointed, but everyone remained friends.

Newspapers at the time reported Joan to be "one of three women corporate pilots in the country."[66] News features described her as a "blue-eyed platinum blonde" and liked to mention "her personal aerodynamic attributes" as well.[67] In an interview, Joan said the major reasons preventing more women from executive flying were "executive's wives and executive's

---

[62] "Women in aviation," *Wikipedia*, accessed June 9, 2022, https://en.wikipedia.org/wiki/Women_in_aviation.

[63] Smith, interview, 2017.

[64] Smith, interview, 2017; Brown, *Fate*, 55.

[65] Smith, interview, 2017.

[66] Swopes, *This Day in Aviation*.

[67] Ibid.

secretaries."

Meanwhile, as the relationship between Jack and Joan was beginning to develop, Jack's career was advancing, as well. He was commissioned as the Executive Officer of the USS *Valor*, a second minesweeper, and then the Navy ordered the *Valor* on a six-month tour to Belgium.[68]

In the 1950s, the United States was reaching out to bolster the defenses of its NATO allies as they all prepared to face the enemy of the time, the Soviet Union.[69] For its part, Belgium needed to bolster their naval strength. In the years following the Allied victory in World War II, the era of the Cold War, the American military and diplomatic leadership promoted a kind of cautious optimism of their capabilities, and their willingness to support their allies. With the launch of Sputnik in 1957, the Russians had beaten the United States into space. However, the National Aeronautics and Space Administration (NASA) was rapidly catching up, and the US military presence was rapidly dominating the globe. The nations of the world were becoming allied with either the United States or the Soviet Union. Belgium purchased American minesweepers, and they wanted a US Navy minesweeper officer to come help them learn how to operate them.

As Executive Officer, Jack was working very closely with the Belgian Force Navale.[70] When it came up in conversation with

---

[68] Dr. Martha Poole Simmons, Honoring Our Heros (sic), "Captain Marvin G. Smith-96, *Alabama Gazette*, December 1, 2019, 2B, accessed July 6, 2020, https://www.alabamamagazette.com/story/2019/12/01/news/honoring-our-heros/1799.html.

[69] "Cold War," *Wikipedia*, accessed Jan. 3, 2023, https://en.wikipedia.org/wiki/Cold_War.

[70] Smith, interview, 2017.

his allies that he was proposing to his girl back home, one of Jack's Belgian colleagues, Commander Andre Schlim, suggested that Jack invite his fiancée to "cross the pond" for a European wedding.[71] A one-star general with the Belgian Force Navale offered to give the bride away.

Jack looked into the particulars and discovered one tradition they would need to follow, called the "banns of marriage."[72] In Europe, he was expected to announce their impending wedding in church in the coastal community of Ostend, Belgium, in perhaps the same way an announcement in the newspaper is customary in America.[73] Being the officer and gentleman that he was, Jack understood that he needed to follow protocol.

Meanwhile, back in Florida, Joan was moving along with her career.[74] It was nice to be offered the little perks, such as getting to fly the corporate planes on her own for fun. Yet the clientele that Joan was transporting were often the executives of other even larger corporations. Early on, these folks began offering Joan better job prospects. As Jack recalled, one company, Green Thumb Nurseries, talked Joan into coming to work out of their Ohio office.[75]

The planning of a European wedding was intended by Jack's Belgian hosts as a way of honoring their American allies. Yet when Jack called Joan to suggest the idea, he encountered

---

[71] Ibid.

[72] Smith, interview, 2017; "Banns of Marriage," *Wikipedia,* accessed March 5, 2018, https://en.wikipedia.org/wiki/Banns_of_marriage.

[73] Smith, interview, 2017; "USS *Valor* (AM-472)," *Wikipedia,* accessed July 7, 2020, https://en.wikipedia.org/wiki/USS_Valor_(AM-472).

[74] Smith, interview, 2017.

[75] Ibid.

resistance he couldn't understand.

Maybe Joan didn't like the sound of her husband-to-be having to make those public declarations. Or maybe she wasn't willing to allow her career to take a back seat to his. Whatever the reason, during those long-distance conversations, Jack began to hear about health problems,[76] and one thing after another, which sounded more and more like cold feet, until Joan actually backed out of the wedding altogether.

Jack had to say no thank you to his colleagues in the Belgian Force Navale.[77] It was all a big embarrassment and setback to him, and his relationship with Joan, already undergoing long-distance stresses, began to dissolve. Jack felt he had little choice but to let Joan go, and turn his attention to his career. He had enlisted in the military back when he was seventeen. Along the way he had begun college coursework in Washington, DC, but now he needed to make it all the way to graduation. When the *Valor* returned to Panama City, it was time for him to finish an undergraduate degree in engineering. The Navy sent him to the Naval Post Graduate School in Monterey, California, where Jack settled into school full-time.

Then one day, just a few months into his course work, Jack got a phone call.

"This is Joan. How are you doing?" She was excited to tell him about the latest high-wing, turbocharged planes she had been flying lately, and as the conversation developed it turned out that she was no longer in Ohio. In fact, she had transferred to for a job with the fixed-base operator, right there in

---

[76] Ibid.

[77] Smith, interview, 2017.

Monterey![78]

Jack couldn't wait to see her again. They picked up where they left off, and this time they made it all the way to a white-uniformed, crossed-swords wedding on September 23, 1960, in Monterey. Jack was thirty-seven and Joan was twenty-four.

When Jack finished college, the Navy sent him to Bay City, Michigan, for a few months.[79] There he served as Operations Officer on the USS *Hoel* destroyer as it was being readied for service.[80] Joan went up the California coast to San Leandro in the Bay area, working as a contract instrument flight instructor at Oakland International Airport for the Sixth US Army, based on the Presidio in San Francisco.[81] For their first few months of married life, they had to put up with a long-distance relationship situation. When Jack returned from Michigan, the Navy sent him to San Diego. His young bride "left her place and moved in with me." Joan would cherish her memories of listening to his Frank Sinatra records with him "in our apartment in San Diego back in 1962."[82]

Next, the Navy sent Jack back up the coast to Long Beach, California, where the USS *Endurance* was homeported, to prepare him to assume command.[83] The new couple bought a

---

[78] Ibid.

[79] Ibid.

[80] "USS Hoel (DDG-13)," Wikipedia, last modified February 10, 2022, accessed July 7, 2020, https://en.wikipedia.org/wiki/USS_Hoel_(DDG-13); Simmons, Honoring Our Heros (sic).

[81] Swopes, *This Day in Aviation*.

[82] Merriam, "I Flew," 82.

[83] Swopes, *This Day in Aviation*.

house on Garford Street.[84]

As Jack and Joan got to know each other, Joan told Jack some of the details about how she grew up. "Joan's dad was her idol," Jack recalled. Yet Joan also told him that she could remember, as a child, walking to the neighborhood bar in her pajamas to ask her mom to come home so that she wouldn't have to be in the house by herself. Despite recollections such as these, Joan and her mother remained close. Jack remembered occasions when Joan would fly home to help her mother get discharged from the hospital.[85]

Early in their marriage, Joan revealed her dream of completing the Amelia Earhart equatorial route around the globe. As unusual as such a goal might be, the idea actually was not new to the flying community in Long Beach.[86] One of the people Joan mentioned in her recorded journal was Dianna Bixby, who had attempted the equatorial flight three times and was killed in a plane crash before she could make a fourth attempt.[87]

In the 1950s, Bob and Dianna Bixby created Bixby Airborne Products, a commercial charter service specializing in aerial transportation of perishables. Dianna's attempts to complete the Earhart route had been impeded by bad weather and

---

[84] Hayley Munguia, "Team rediscovers how a 1964 Long Beach woman was the first to pilot a solo trip around the equator," Press-Telegram, last updated Dec. 18, 2019, accessed Dec. 19, 2019, https://www.presstelegram.com/2019/12/16/a-long-beach-pilot-made-history-55-years-ago-but-she-and-her-beloved-plane-faded-from-memory-until-now.

[85] Smith, interview, 2017.

[86] Burnett, p. 170.

[87] Brown, *Fate*, 6, 94; Tiffany Ann Brown, telephone interview by author, March 12, 2021.

mechanical breakdowns. She was planning to begin the journey for a fourth time in the spring of 1955. However, on a transport run from California to La Paz, Mexico, her plane went down in a storm, and Dianna was killed in January, 1955.[88] Bob remained in air transport, and by the time Joan moved to Long Beach in 1962, his business was named Bixby Air Freight Company, operating out of the Long Beach Airport.

Yet even with the stories of Dianna and Amelia and other pilots in mind, Jack felt confident about Joan and her abilities. She had been flying in Air Races since she was in high school, and moving to California didn't slow her down. As soon as she got settled in Monterey, she joined the Fort Ord Flying Club and the local chapter of the Ninety-Nines.[89] She flew the 1960 All Woman Transcontinental Air Race ("Powder Puff Derby") from Torrance, California to Wilmington, Delaware. The next summer, she flew the 1961 All Woman Transcontinental Race from San Diego to Atlantic City, New Jersey. The *next* summer, she flew the 1962 All Woman's International Air Race from Houston, Texas to Nassau, in the Bahamas.[90] All the while, Joan was talking to Jack about her *ultimate* goal.

Jack watched in fascination as his new bride not only talked about her idea, she persuaded her friends to go out and secure corporate sponsorship for the project. "She was an aggressive little lady," Jack remembers.[91] "Joan and her team could get people to do things." In fact, Joan was able to secure multiple sponsors.[92]

---

[88] Burnett, p. 170-171.

[89] "Joan Merriam Smith," Find a Grave.

[90] Schubert and Smith, "World Flight."

[91] Smith, interview, 2017.

[92] Merriam, "Longest Flight," 44; Merriam, "Tribute to a Star," 12.

For her part, Joan appreciated Jack for being "a real easy-going guy" who "accepts me the way I am."[93]

While other newly married couples drove around looking at cars and furniture, Jack and Joan's top priority was to shop for just the right plane for her special project. After a year, they made an offer on one, but the deal fell through, leaving Joan depressed.[94]

Meanwhile, Jack's career continued to progress. He was the kind of leader that men under his command would remember as an officer "you wanted to work for," Vic Campbell, a member of Jack's crew and lifelong friend, recalled.[95] On November 1, 1963, Jack was commissioned to serve as Commanding Officer of the USS *Endurance*.[96]

Yet he still made time to support his wife. After shopping around for four years, Joan and Jack found a twin-engine Piper Apache, tail number N3251P.[97] On the morning of November 22, 1963, the day President Kennedy was killed, Joan put her life's savings of $10,000 down toward the purchase of the plane.[98] The six-year-old Apache would need to be modified, at a cost estimated to be around $21,000.[99] There was a flight plan to put together, supplies to buy, visas to apply for, and money to raise for it all.[100] Initially, twelve sponsors were found, such

---

[93] Merriam, "I Flew," 79.

[94] Merriam, "I Flew," 79.

[95] Vic Campbell, telephone interview with the author, May 11, 2017.

[96] *NavSource Online: Mine Warfare Vessel Photo Archive*, 3.

[97] Merriam, "I Flew," 79; Joan Merriam, "Longest Flight," *The AOPA Pilot*, Nov. 1964, 44; "Joan Merriam Smith," Find a Grave.

[98] Merriam, "I Flew," 79; Burnett, 173.

[99] Gilbert, "The Loser," 80.

[100] Merriam, "I Flew," 80.

as Buffum's Department Store and the Chamber of Commerce of Long Beach, California. The city council voted–just a week and a half before departure–to offer $1,500, with the idea that private funds would match. If she had felt free to choose, she would have called her plane *Amelia*. Instead, the plane would be named *The City of Long Beach* in honor of her sponsors.[101] She also painted "Long Beach Lady" across the nose of the plane.

Joan found experienced pilots to advise her in the planning stage. Chuck Banfe was a captain with Pan American Airways (Pan Am) and had flown around the world himself. Paul Mantz had helped Amelia Earhart plan her route.

She approached the manufacturers for help. Piper's representative Jake Miller recalled: "She did come to us before she made the flight–about *three weeks* before she left. We didn't want to get mixed up in it. We didn't want her to make the flight."[102]

Miller listed several reasons for Piper's reluctance.

> Her route was not the best route. Hers was an old airplane, of no particular interest to us. It had been converted and reconverted so much we felt she was going to have a lot of problems. We didn't know anything about her fuel system–who had designed it–or her turbochargers. She wanted us to aid her financially. We get three or four such applications every week, and we of course turn most of them down.[103]

---

[101] Ibid.

[102] Gilbert, "The Loser," 80.

[103] Ibid.

She had better luck with the Riley-Rajay Corporation. They came through with some financial backing. They also supplied blowers for her engines, an improvement which offered additional thrust, even though one employee, identified only as "Mr. Keller," said, "we didn't like her fuel system either."[104]

Joan also applied for the around-the-world sanction; or at least, she attempted to apply for it. In an interview with James Gilbert of *Flying* Magazine after the flight, she related:

> Well, let's put it this way. I advised the [National Aeronautics Administration] of the round-the-world flight. They told me what I'd have to do to get a sanction.[105] And they assured me they'd work very closely with me. In December (1963) I sent all my information for a sanction and I did not fill out the sanction forms; but I had done everything up to that point, expecting sanction forms by return mail. They never came. On January 8, which was three weeks after I sent my complete portfolio and life history to the NAA, I then heard about this other girl, Mrs. Mock, flying around the world. I checked with the NAA and they kept me waiting for two days and then advised me they had already granted sanction to another girl and could not give me sanction. So you might say I tried to get a sanction but was denied.[106]

---

[104] Ibid., 81.

[105] Pilots must apply for a sanction for the opportunity to set a world record. If granted, the opportunity is time-limited.

[106] Ibid.

Joan also stated that she had not been aware of Jerrie for very long. "I don't know how long before my flight she was aware of me, but I was first aware of her flight less than five weeks before I actually made my takeoff. You can't throw an around-the-world flight together overnight. I had been planning this in my own mind for ten years and had muffed the chances already, because of lack of expenses and shortage of equipment, airplane and so forth. About five weeks before I was ready for takeoff, after working on this project for over a year, I found out about Mrs. Mock."

In "Joan and NAA," a typed document believed to have been dictated by Joan to her biographer, Trixie-Ann Schubert, a picture is painted of the obstacles Joan faced in trying to get her around-the-world flight sanctioned.[107] She wrote the NAA in August asking if any woman had filed for an around-the-world sanction. In September, she asked about the necessary steps to become sanctioned. In October, she called again and was told it would take about ninety days to process the sanction. Although she was told in October to submit an itinerary of her route, she didn't get the itinerary into the mail until December 17.

In addition to the difficulties in communicating with the NAA, Joan had family situations to deal with, as well. The day after she mailed her itinerary to the NAA, her mother fell and fractured her skull.

On January 3, 1964, Jack was deployed overseas for seven months:

---

[107] Brown, *Fate,* 190.

The last dependent to see her husband off . . . will undoubtedly be Mrs. Joan Merriam Smith.... Mrs. Smith ... will see her husband off at pierside and then will proceed to the Long Beach Municipal Airport and take off at 11 a.m. in her twin-engine Apache for a final salute to the division at sea.[108]

Then, on the same day, Joan's grandmother died. The next day, Joan flew to Miami to be with her mother, who was having brain surgery.

On January 7, Joan reported that she went shopping for a high-frequency transceiver at Sun Aire Electronics and Pan Tronics in Fort Lauderdale. Some of the electronics shop personnel she spoke with became "cagey" and "asked many leading questions." When Joan said she was "planning a trip out of the country," one radio technician responded, "Oh, you must be the girl who's going to fly around the world" and asked, "Are you the girl from Ohio?"[109]

Joan was suspicious. She just made sure that she "played it (the radio system) as if it were the greatest thing since French toast."[110]

Joan also said that she called the National Aeronautics Administration (NAA) that same day and spoke to M.J. "Randy" Randleman. "I had talked with him and written him often before. He told me he had no information regarding another woman's seeking the world flight sanction. I pressed the issue. 'If you're working with another woman, tell me.'"[111]

Randleman responded, "I'm just getting ready to send out

---

[108] San Pedro (California) *News-Pilot,* December 30, 1963.

[109] Brown, *Fate,* 190.

[110] Ibid.

[111] Ibid.

sanction forms." He said the NAA had "received interest" from another pilot "a year ago."[112]

When relating the conversation, Joan noted, "Mock got NAA sanction. Her sanction forms had not yet been received by NAA. She was asking for sanction from February 15 through May 15. Never had the problem of two flights at the same time come up before." She said that Randleman told her, "We'll have to make a decision which one to sanction. We'll look at them together."[113]

Joan replied, "The flights are unalike. How can you measure them as alike?"

Randleman responded that the NAA would "consider which person is better backed, and better experienced pilot, and with a safer plane. . . . All this we consider. Then the papers and check are sent to the FAI (Federation Aeronautique Internationale)."[114]

Joan suggested she fly to Washington immediately to "fill out the papers and give you a $150 check."[115]

By Joan's recall, Randleman responded, "It's not necessary. Even if you're first in with the papers we'd have to make a decision."[116]

Despite what must have been a frustrating conversation with Randleman, Joan worked on every aspect she could take care of on her own. She stretched out charts of the entire route out on the living-room floor, twenty-eight legs of approximately 1,000 miles per leg. When she had the charts all pieced together,

---

[112] Ibid.

[113] Ibid.

[114] Ibid.

[115] Ibid.

[116] Ibid.

they were eighteen feet long. People who came into the room had to take their shoes off to walk around. She had a twelve-foot strip of aluminum floor molding that she used as a straight edge, and she spent about six hours figuring each 1,000 miles–more than 150 hours of plotting in all–marking off checkpoints, double-checking radio frequencies, and looking for errors.[117]

Four of the five seats in her plane were removed to make room for extra tanks. The tanks and other modifications cost more than $7,000, which she had to borrow from friends. In addition, the couple found twelve more sponsors. In February, she wrote to the International Headquarters for the Ninety-Nines, asking for collaboration:

> Dear 99s:
>
> This . . . letter is to announce my plans to you of my forthcoming "Around the World Solo Flight. . . ." I have had this secret ambition, not only to attempt to be the first to fly around the world, but when I did, I would like to fly the Earhart route. . . .
>
> I would like the support of the 99s during this flight and would appreciate any assistance that you might lend after the flight, publicity-wise. . . .
>
> To my knowledge another girl will be attempting to beat me in a single-engine Cessna, along a shorter route to the north of the Amelia Earhart route. She is not a 99, lives in Ohio and probably will be departing about the same time as I will. She made an early press release January 31, and mine will be out this week, so I did want

---

[117] Merriam, "I Flew," 80.

to make sure that you were aware of the two girls attempting this.[118]

She also enlisted promotional help from advertising executive John Sarver, based in Long Beach. She would be sending him telegrams as she went, and he would help promote her flight. [119]

Even though Jack and the *Endurance* were sent on tour, Jack's superior officers were impressed with the accomplishments of this Navy wife. It was made clear to Jack that if, at any point during her flight, the *Endurance* was in port anywhere near where she landed, "we'll fly you" to see her. [120]

All the effort, and the drama that went along with it, brought Joan to departure day in Oakland. She took off twenty-seven years to the day after Amelia Earhart departed from the same airport on her round-the-world-attempt, and she would follow the same 27,000-mile route, wherever possible. Joan said, "I felt I was fulfilling not only my lifelong dream, but Amelia's dream, too."[121]

---

[118] Brown, *Fate,* 39.

[119] Brown, *Fate,* 40.

[120] Smith, interview, 2017.

[121] Merriam, "I Flew," 77.

1960s: The "Flying Housewife"

By the summer of 1962, Russ could see that his wife was serious about flying around the world. Instead of arguing with her, he started helping. They went in with a friend named Al Baumeister to buy a Cessna 180 Skywagon.[122] Jerrie nicknamed their plane "Charlie" after its tail number, N1538C, and pilot shorthand she would use to identify herself and her aircraft over the radio, "November One-Five-Three-Eight Charlie" or "Three-Eight Charlie" for short.

Jerrie figured that someone, such as Jackie Cochran, who in 1953 became the first woman pilot to break the sound barrier, must have already flown around the world. In November 1962, Jerrie wrote the National Aeronautics Association in Washington, DC, to ask about it anyway.[123]

She was astounded to find out that it had not been done. Okay, then, if there was a world record waiting for someone to set, she wanted to find out more about it. She began corresponding with Randleman at the NAA in Washington, DC about the particulars.

Randleman explained the process from the beginning. Whenever someone wanted to attempt any new world flying record, an application had to be filled out and returned along with a fee. NAA rules stipulated that only one person could apply for any particular record at a time. Once granted, the

---

[122] Mock, interview, Aug. 28, 2007.
[123] Mock, interview; Aug. 28, 2007.

sanction was only good for a certain period of time, usually ninety days. This step was mandatory if Jerrie was to be recognized for setting a record.

Jerrie and Russ kept in touch with Randleman every couple of months. In a letter dated January 8, 1963, Randleman told them, "So far, there has been no women's record established for Speed Around the World . . . (A)ny successful flight Around the World by a woman would set a record."[124] Not only would Jerrie fly around the world, but she could become the first woman to do it. Yet Randleman thought they could take their time. "There's nobody else doing this," he told them, "so far as we know."

While waiting for the sanction, Jerrie and Russ tended to other aspects of their project. They called and wrote to friends and experts. They also began looking into airports where Jerrie might land. They searched for sponsorships to enable them to afford this adventure and researched modifications to the plane that would be necessary.

Jerrie flew Charlie all over the country for new parts and a new engine. In March 1963, Jerrie, Al Baumeister, and a woman who was a friend of Al's took Charlie out on a trip to Mexico. They went to a bullfight, dealt with flight maps reading "elevation unknown," encountered airports with nobody answering in the control tower, and had to bypass an airstrip because cows were walking on it, preventing them from landing. [125] It was a glorious trip, and a good warm-up for the

---

[124] Randleman to Russell C. Mock, letter, January 8, 1963, shared with author by Jerrie Mock.

[125] Mock, interview, July 1, 2007; Mock's handwritten notes shared with author.

around-the-world adventure.

By December of 1963, Russ was writing to a friend of his, saying, "Jerrie will be off in nine directions at once . . . Washington, Baltimore, New York, Philadelphia, Wichita, Flint, Chicago and Muskegon . . . not to mention Toledo and Urbana, Ohio."[126]

Sometimes they were delayed by garden-variety human error. On one occasion, Jerrie planned to take off, but the plane wouldn't start. Something had drained the battery. After an hour of "fussing," they discovered the problem. In the work on something else, perhaps the windshield or instrument panel, a screwdriver had fallen onto the master switch, leaving the circuits open over the weekend. That one cost them half a day.[127]

Some of their modifications had never been tried before. They had a friend, Dave Blanton, who had developed the first autopilot for light aircraft.[128] Dave came up with the idea of taking out all of the seats except one, and putting giant gas tanks in their place. The *Dispatch* had Jerrie pose for a photo with the special tanks, joking in their caption that "someone goofed and made the plane's tanks too big."[129]

For a pilot to fly safely, alone, as high as 10,000 feet, and for as long as eighteen hours, some modifications had to be *very* specific. In a letter to a friend only identified as "Ralph" on Feb. 26, 1964, Russ wrote, "Her oxygen bottle is in a sleeve affair on the back of her chair. Fire extinguisher (and urinal) are under

---

[126] Russ Mock, letter to "Ralph," Dec. 9, 1963.

[127] Mock, interview, Sept. 2, 2007; Russ Mock, letter, January 16, 1964; Mock, *Three-Eight Charlie*, 203.

[128] "Alcor Goes 'Round the World," *Flying Magazine*, July 1964: 57.

[129] "Columbus Pilot Jerrie Mock: 14 Photos," *Dispatch*, April 11, 2012.

the seat. (Maybe she could use the latter for non-electrical or non-fuel fires in the event of an emergency.)"

They had to get visas and clearances for every country where she would land or fly over. Russ put his sales skills to work to attract sponsors to help pay the bills. Jerrie pitched the idea of a sixty-day sightseeing adventure, with a take-off date of April 1, sending them stories about her travels to the Columbus *Dispatch*, the local newspaper, along the way.[130]

The *Dispatch* became their biggest supporter when Russ persuaded the paper to pay $10,000 (equal to around $75,000 today) toward the flight, in exchange for exclusive reports along the route.[131] Charlie was officially named *The Spirit of Columbus*.[132]

As word of Jerrie's plans got out, some of the men around town were heard to mutter, "If a housewife can do it, it can't be that complicated." The editors at the *Dispatch* responded by nicknaming Jerrie "The Flying Housewife."[133]

Beyond sponsorship and news coverage, a project this big required real help. And Russ knew whom to ask.

Jerrie mustered up the courage to dial the number Russ gave her. She asked to speak to a Colonel Lassiter at Lockbourne Air Force Base in Ohio.[134] The reason for the call was to request an appointment with Lassiter to help her create a flight plan for a

---

[130] Mock, interview, Sept. 11, 2007.

[131] Mock, interview July 1, 2007; Saunders, "How an Ohio Housewife Flew Around the World."

[132] *Columbus Evening Dispatch*, March 19, 1964, 1; Mock, *Three-Eight Charlie*, 16.

[133] Mock, interview, Sept. 11 2007; "Housewife to Circle Globe in Drip – Dries" *Newark Advocate*, March 16, 1964.

[134] Mock, interview, July 1, 2007.

trip around the world.

"Hmm," Colonel Lassiter said over the phone. "Now *that's* a new one." Still, he gave her directions from their suburb of Bexley over to his office at the base to meet with him one afternoon. He sat quietly as she explained what she had in mind.

When she finished talking, there was a long pause.

Colonel Lassiter got up from his desk. Jerrie thought he looked skeptical. He walked over to a giant globe standing four feet tall, and gave it a spin. "If I were going to fly around the world," he said, "I suppose I would start out by flying from Columbus to Bermuda." He worked his way around his big globe with her. Jerrie could tell Colonel Lassiter didn't believe this trip was going to happen. Still, she left his office with an outline of the complete plan for her long flight.

Dave Blanton flew with her in the plane so he could teach her how to do something scary.[135] She had to prepare for the moment when she might need every drop of gas she could drain out of all the tanks. Her plane, with all its modifications, was designed to allow for that scenario, with one small catch. Jerrie would have to follow a procedure that was simple to do, yet nerve-wracking. She must switch on a transfer pump so that gas from a reserve tank in the cabin would flow into the main tank in the wing.

The way her mechanics had installed everything, Jerrie would have to allow the pump to run all the gas through until, for a few seconds, the engine would pump only air. As soon as she turned off the pump, the engine would crank back up again, on its

---

[135] Mock, interview, Sept. 11, 2007; Mock, *Three-Eight Charlie*, 14, 193.

own. In theory. Plus, she would have to go through this heart-stopping procedure a second time, for the other reserve tank.

Before she left for the trip, she had to practice actually doing all that. With Blanton beside her, she took the plane up over some fields in Kansas. She flipped the switch and sat still, watching the gauge on the first reserve tank drain all the way down, down, down to E. The engine sputtered out–it even seemed to cough. For a moment, the nose of the plane dipped. Only after she was certain the tank was empty could she switch off the transfer pump. Then when the fuel began to flow again, the engine cranked back up, and the propeller began to turn. The plane pulled out of its brief glide, and the pilot went back to breathing. Then she had to go through it all over again for the second tank.

She landed safely in Wichita that day, relieved that Blanton "couldn't tell how scared [she] was."[136] She didn't ask if he noticed how–throughout every millisecond they had glided in silence without the comforting sound of the engine–she had kept her eye on the fields and roads, in case she would need to aim for one.[137]

Preparing for her trip, she met many others who were happy to pass along some of their experience. In Florida, she met Bob Iba, a ferry pilot, who flew planes to different destinations around the world.[138] Bob was particularly helpful with tips about how to find her way across the Pacific Ocean.

As the date to embark approached, Jerrie posed for photographs in a skirt and high-heeled sandals. Front-page

---

[136] Mock, *Three-Eight Charlie*, 193.

[137] Mock, interview, Aug. 29, 2007.

[138] Mock, *Three-Eight Charlie*, 200.

stories quoted her politely downplaying her flying ability. "Except for not wearing high heels, it's just like driving a car."[139]

Russ could see how Jerrie might earn some money with her record-breaking flight, but he also needed her to make it back alive. In a December 9, 1963 letter to his friend "Ralph," he wrote:

> Jerrie has taken over the basement of the house and has ... charts all over everywhere. We have a globe down there and wall maps of the world with all sorts of solid, broken, and colored lines indicating routes and possible routes. ... Putting this together has been a real challenge. My background in advertising and public relations has been a big factor. ... The response we have received has been very gratifying. ... If we could get her around the world, then keep her name hot long enough to knock off a second record, we'll be on the way to having a good commercial property (Jerrie)."

Maybe all their trouble would make some difference in the world. Maybe they would help pave the way for the next young woman to become a pilot, or engineer, or anything she chose. Or maybe her achievement would go unnoticed. Either way, Jerrie would return home with a month of memories to carry her through all the nights of dishes, laundry, and walking their reluctant dachshund when that month was over.

Yet the Mocks began to hear rumors that they might have competition, after all. By December 1963, Russ and Jerrie began

---

[139] Vail and Edwards, "Winner Take All," 59.

to worry that someone else might "beat us to it." In a letter dated December 9, Russ wrote, "We already have a disquieting message from *LOOK* [magazine] that they are presently considering 'similar' material. This, however, I believe is the nomenclature used in most stock disclaimer letters. We are checking with the NAA to see what they know."[140]

As Jerrie pursued state-of-the-art radio equipment, she was asked if she wanted the same thing the other pilot was getting.[141] Russ and Jerrie realized they might have to speed things up. By January 1964, the Mocks had their financial backing, and were ready to apply for the sanction. By Jerrie's recollection, she called Randleman's office on or about January 3, 1964, one year after Jerrie was told she was the only woman going for this world record. Now, Randleman let them know that another woman was considering going for the same record that Jerrie was preparing for. "I told her about you," he said. "Now I'm telling you about her."[142]

In a letter to William A. Ong, President of the National Aeronautic Association (NAA) dated July 10, 1964, Randleman documented that, on Monday, January 6, 1964, he "advised (Jerrie) by letter that she should make formal application."[143]

Regardless of any differences in their accounts, what is clear is that the Mocks took no chances. Russ and Jerrie caught a

---

[140] Russell C. Mock, letter to "Ralph," Dec. 9, 1963.

[141] Mock, interview, Sept. 28, 2007.

[142] Mock, interview, July 1, 2007; Jerrie Mock's notes shared with author.

[143] M.J. Randleman to William A. Ong, letter, July 10, 1964, Smithsonian National Air and Space Museum, (NAA) Archives, Washington, DC., Accession Number: XXXX-0209, Box Number: 139, Folder Number: 6, shared by Tiffany Ann Brown. The date Randleman cited, Jan. 6, does not line up with other records.

commercial flight to Washington, DC, and were waiting for Randleman when his office opened at nine o'clock Monday morning, January 6, to begin the application process in person.

Randleman also documented that on Wednesday, January 8, he got the phone call from Joan. He recalled that Joan asked if she could fly from Miami to Washington to apply for sanction that day. He responded that she could not arrive until "several hours after closing time." Randleman wrote in a letter to Ong, "In my view, it would have been unethical and unfair to the other contestant to have kept the office open to receive Mrs. Merriam's sanction after normal working hours."[144] Randleman wrote that Joan decided to mail the application. "This was her decision, and there was no suggestion on my part that she not fly to Washington to apply for sanction."[145]

Joan was left with the impression that, in her words, "The two requests were never considered side by side."[146]

At some point during this process, Randleman also received other calls from someone else, a male, asking, on behalf of a female pilot for the same application.[147]

When Randleman told the caller he was too late, the caller told Randleman to take Jerrie's application back. Randleman explained he could not do that. The caller told Randleman that someone else would be going for this world record anyway and, if the other person finished first while Jerrie still held the sanction, that would be a mess and Randleman would be responsible. "If Jerrie doesn't finish first," he said, "you will lose

[144] Ibid.

[145] Ibid.

[146] Brown, *Fate*, 190.

[147] Mock, interview, July 1, 2007.

your job."

Randleman did not share these other threatening conversations with Jerrie until years later.

The Mocks made sure to keep moving. In Randleman's account, "On 9 January, Mrs. Mock submitted her sanction requests and check for the sanction fees for Speed Around the World-Feminine, and Speed Around the World, Class C-1."[148]

Then he went on to say, "Later on 9 January, Mrs. Merriam again called from Miami to discuss her flight. I advised her that we had received the sanction requests for the two records above, and that they were under consideration for approval." Randleman also suggested other options, such as to pursue records for a different class of plane, since Joan's plane was heavier, but she declined.[149]

"Mrs. Merriam was dealt with fairly in all respects," Randleman wrote, "and there was no partiality shown toward either prospective contestant. It was simply a case of Mrs. Mock submitting her sanction application first. Actually, Mrs. Merriam never did submit a request for sanction, although she was advised of the open dates available to her."[150]

Meanwhile, puzzling things kept happening to Jerrie and Russ.

The Mocks had a long list of things to take care of, and having competition pushed them even further. Jerrie had to go back to Washington in February to apply for visas and clearances.[151] On this trip she took teenage sons Gary and Roger

---

[148] Randleman to Ong, July 10, 1964.
[149] Ibid.
[150] Randleman to Ong, July 10, 1964.
[151] Mock, interview, July 1, 2007.

with her, and they paid visits to the embassies of Pakistan, India, the United Arab Republic (UAR, what is now Egypt), the Philippines, and Saudi Arabia.

Charlie got a new engine, state-of-the-art radios, and other parts, and Jerrie picked up sponsors and made many new friends in the process. Some of those friends called to tell her and Russ that someone had called them to ask what Jerrie was getting. Champion Spark Plugs told Jerrie, "That other girl's probably going to win."[152]

Others told them that someone had even tried to bribe Champion not to send spark plugs to Jerrie.[153] Russ and Jerrie were told that some mysterious callers didn't want to leave their names. Only one person, their friend Dave Blanton, told them that he was able to get someone who called him, asking about parts and modifications, to reveal who she was: Joan Merriam Smith.[154]

Evidently, Jerrie and Russ were not aware that "fly girls" had been voicing suspicions about sabotage since the first National Women's Air Derby back in 1929, and demanding investigations after subsequent races throughout the 1930s and beyond.[155]

Jerrie went on with all of her other errands. In March, she flew back to Washington.[156] She visited the Libyan and Burmese embassies, but Burma denied her clearance to fly over their

---

[152] Mock, interview, Oct. 11, 2007.

[153] Ibid.

[154] Ibid.

[155] Keith O'Brien, *Fly Girls*, 102.

[156] Mock, interview, Feb. 28, 2008.

country.[157] Turned out, the political situation was changing in that country, and the US State Department didn't even seem to know about it yet.

One of her appointments was with an Air Force officer, the same officer who had looked over his big globe with her, back in Ohio. A year had passed since Jerrie had first visited Colonel Lassiter at Lockbourne Air Force Base. During that time, he had become Brigadier General Lassiter, stationed in Washington.[158] General Lassiter picked Jerrie up at the NAA office and gave her a ride across town in his limousine. She was escorted into the Pentagon and allowed a glimpse of a computer three feet tall while some of the best military strategists in the world helped determine a safe route for her.[159] By contrast, Jerrie's own on-board "computer" would be a Jeppesen computer, a print-out of figures on round, laminated cardboard that she rotated against a set of numbers on round plastic, like a round slide rule, that would help her calculate air speed and travel time.[160] Jerrie's days in Washington would begin at 8:30 a.m. and go on until midnight.[161]

When asked if she planned to take along "pep" pills for the long flights, her response was, "Why?" A Strategic Air Command surgeon urged her to take them as a precaution, but she never used them.[162]

One other medical detail was required: inoculations for

---

[157] Mock, *Three-Eight Charlie*, 174.

[158] Mock, interview, Feb. 28, 2008.

[159] Ibid.

[160] Mock, interview, Dec. 17, 2007.

[161] Mock, interview, Dec. 17, 2007; Vail and Edwards, "Winner Take All," 59.

[162] Vail and Edwards, "Winner Take All," 59.

cholera, yellow fever, and typhoid. She had a reaction – a fever – from the typhoid shot.[163]

She was also required to pass a test to qualify to fly a plane by instrument, since there were parts of the world where she might have no other choice. She took her Instrument Flight Rating test on February 19, and passed it, just in time.[164]

Plus, this project had an impact on their family. In a letter sent in January 1964, Russ wrote that, "today, Valerie went to Kindergarten for the second day . . . the second of maybe 80 or 90 while Jerrie is busy. The little girl puckered up and wanted her mommie. I wonder what it might be like if some day I'll have to explain that Mommie is flying with God forever."[165]

Finally, with all her tests passed, forms completed, a flight plan in place, and international observers notified around the globe, Jerrie was set to make history–if the Mocks could stay ahead. In a letter sent on February 21, 1964 to his friend "Ralph," Russ wrote, "I will die if our competition leaves before us. . . . We have been told [record-setting pilot] Max Conrad is giving a lot of assistance (what kind I don't know) to our competition. . . . I hope they don't know our status."[166]

As each day became more important, Jerrie's husband continued to make the sacrifices he needed to make. Two weeks after Valentine's Day, on February 26, Russ wrote to a friend:

---

[163] Mock, interview, Sept. 2, 2007; Mock's handwritten notes shared with author.

[164] Mock, interview, Feb. 28, 2008.

[165] Russ Mock, letter, Jan. 16, 1964.

[166] Vail and Edwards, "Winner Take All," 60.

It's also difficult [wooing] a mechanic. The other night in Florida, I started turning down the lights in the room, and she said, . . . "Mmm, those dim lights remind me, the airways and inner marker beacon lamps are real weak. We'd better look at 'em tomorrow." I turned the lights back on and poured another drink instead.[167]

Jerrie and her family also had to learn how to talk to reporters "on-the-job."

Daughter Valerie . . . a 3 ½ year-old, likes to fly and "see the little houses and the little people." . . . About the only regret Mrs. Mock has about the trip is that she will not have time for sightseeing. "My husband says that when I get back, I should write a book, 'How to Go Around the World and Not See Anything.'"[168]

Anonymous phone callers pleaded, "Don't go."[169] There was talk of introducing a bill in Congress denying US military search-and-rescue help to anyone who would undertake such an "idiotic" venture.

In California, Joan Merriam Smith announced her intention to go for the record, too. Newspapers and radio stations around the country picked up the story and asked Jerrie and Russ about Joan.

The pressure to get it all done pushed everyone to their limits. In a letter to "Ralph" on March 4, 1964, Russ wrote, "I

---

[167] Russ Mock, letter, February 26, 1964.
[168] Newark *Advocate*, March 16, 1964.
[169] Vail and Edwards, "Winner Take All," 59.

suddenly have the feeling that I want to wrap this up then go away so I am physically as well as chronologically away from it." Yet in the same paragraph, he went on to say, "I have to keep Jerrie's spirits high and on the track."

The editors at the *Dispatch* encouraged both pilots.

> We wish both of these courageous young women well in their respective bids for fame, although quite naturally we hope that our home town entrant sets the new record first. Both disclaim that they are racing against one another and, in any event, there is plenty of glory for both in their hoped-for achievements.[170]

By departure day, the military sent Jerrie on her way with a letter expressing their full endorsement:

> To Whom It May Concern:
> The bearer of this letter . . . is attempting a solo around-the-world flight. We have been assisting her in preparation. . . . It will be appreciated if you can extend any courtesies to Mrs. Mock should she land on or near your base.
> R.H. Strauss, Brigadier General, USAF,
> March 17, 1964[171]

Nonetheless, Jerrie had her doubts. "Are we sure we can stay

---

[170] *Dispatch*, March 19, 1964.

[171] R.H. Strauss, Brigadier General, USAF, March 17, 1964.

in this race?" she asked.[172]

Russ said they were in too deep with their sponsors to back out.[173]

---

[172] Mock, interview, Feb. 28, 2008.
[173] Ibid.

1964: Take-Off

Monday morning, March 16
LONG BEACH, California

Joan Merriam Smith sat in her cockpit, rehearsing the story she was about to tell into her new Norelco tape recorder.

> All was in final readiness. . . . It had taken an hour to load the plane. It had to be done systematically, utilizing every square inch. . . . I was cramped and uncomfortable from the start.[174]

Joan was a five-foot two-inch blonde ball of energy who had been flying–and setting aviation records–since she was sixteen.[175] At twenty-seven years old, she was younger than Jerrie, flew professionally, flew a larger, twin-engine plane, and had 82,000 flight hours against Jerrie's 1,000 hours as an amateur.[176]

Joan got a big send-off, took off, and struggled to gain altitude, fighting a fierce wind.[177] After an hour in the air, she got back to telling her story. "The line from the old song 'five-foot-two, eyes of blue' fits me perfectly," Joan said into her tape

---

[174] Brown, *Fate*, 48.

[175] Claudine Burnett, *Soaring Skyward*, 173.

[176] "Aviation: Shades of Amelia," *Newsweek Magazine*, March 30, 1964, 20.

[177] John Sarver, "Joan Merriam/Around-the-World Solo Flight," press release, April 17, 1964, provided by Tiffany Ann Brown.

recorder. "Though I'm small, the space allotted me in the cockpit isn't sufficient . . . I would eliminate something not vital. When A.E. lightened her load by leaving behind 250 feet of antenna before the fatal last leg of her flight, she cut a critical lifeline to survival over the sea where homing devices were nil, according to some of her biographers."[178]

Joan continued, "The Long Beach municipal band was on the improvised platform to send me winging on my way with music. Mayor Edwin Wade, the California Ninety-Nines, TV, press, and radio, mechanic crews from Aztec Aviation who had worked on my plane, and a crowd of well-wishers waved me off as 51-Poppa skimmed down the runway and lifted off."[179]

By 2:00 p.m. she flew over Vandenberg Air Force Base, then Castle Air Force Base, describing the three-hour flight to Oakland as a rough, turbulent "shakedown cruise."[180] Still, she was completely in her element. Sharing her thoughts with her tape recorder, she went on to say, "Up here is another world, and I belong to it."[181]

Joan listened to weather broadcasts every half hour that included special reports for pilots. On this day, they were giving "severe turbulence warnings for light aircraft," but she was able to fly ahead of trouble, this time.[182]

When she touched down in Oakland, she noticed "a crowd of people on the field." She noted on her recorder, "I will have

---

[178] Brown, *Fate,* 49.
[179] Ibid.
[180] Ibid.
[181] Ibid.
[182] Ibid.

to learn, even when tired and irritable, to treat the well-wishers and the press . . . with courtesy and tact."[183]

Tuesday morning, March 17
OAKLAND, California

"Dawn broke fuzzily" through the California coastal fog to usher in St. Patrick's Day 1964, Joan recorded.[184] It was the twenty-seventh anniversary of the start of the Earhart-Noonan flight and, Joan wrote, "By an interesting coincidence the first world flight of US Army fliers in 1924 also took off on St. Patrick's Day, March 17, from California."[185]

"This morning, early, I bought a smaller suitcase, repacked everything in the plane, and had all in readiness one hour before the press arrived so that I'd have no last-minute worries," Joan recorded. "Mayor Houlihan presented me with the keys to the city of Oakland."[186]

And now, here she was, about to embark on the route "A.E." had attempted all those years ago. After readying the plane, speaking with the press, and accepting the key to the city, Joan handed out magic markers and invited people to autograph the plane. Right from the start the fuselage began to be decorated with names of American, Delta and Eastern Airline pilots and personnel.

"Elmer Dimity, now aged and in crutches, came up to wish me luck. He was friends with A.E.," Joan noted.[187]

---

[183] Brown, *Fate*, 49-50.

[184] Ibid, 50.

[185] Ibid.

[186] Ibid.

[187] Brown, *Fate*, 50.

While she waited her turn on the runway, she took one last look at her supplies. These included:

- 28 manila envelopes containing 100 charts
- Supply of LifeSavers candies and Metrecal cookies
- 2 pairs of sunglasses
- Overnight case containing three days' change of wash-and-wear clothes
- 22-caliber pistol
- $3,000 in cash and traveler's checks
- 2 Thermos bottles
- Camera
- Tape recorder
- Passport with 16 visas
- Kit of survival gear
- St. Christopher medal pinned to the upholstery
- Small, 4-inch-tall stuffed koala bear attached to side window with a suction cup
- Small toy polar bear with rubber claws, a rubber nose, and a purple bow tied around its neck
- Copy of *Last Flight* by Amelia Earhart
- 4-leaf clover from her Irish mother
- Charm carried by astronaut Walter Schirra[188]

Further back in the cabin, back-up and survival equipment included a fire extinguisher, a two-man life raft equipped with rations, a "Mae West" inflatable life preserver–bulky, but required–and a water-activated radio beacon. For the next two months, this cramped little box would be her home. She had

---

[188] List of items compiled from multiple sources: Merriam, "I Flew," 77; Brown, *Fate*, 56; "L.B. Flier," Feb. 18, 1965.

heard of other women who smoked cigarettes to help stay awake on the long night flights. But Joan was not a smoker, so she was going to have to make it mostly on airport coffee.

As she watched the fog dissipate, Joan struggled to find the words to describe this moment.

In a strange way, going down the runway with 51-Poppa had some of the finality, the adventure, the for-better-or-worse-but-forever quality of going down the chapel aisle with Jack. This was it. There was no retreating. The future was committed.[189]

Then she spotted a box she'd had a little trouble convincing someone to sell her. The box contained 100 airsickness bags, an improvised solution for "long flights when I'd be deprived of bathroom facilities," Joan wrote. "I could see the face now of the fellow at Medina Aircraft in Long Beach when I walked into the office before the world flight and ordered a box." The man proceeded to argue with Joan until he realized why she would need so many sick sacks. Joan related that the man's face reddened as he responded, "Sure thing. One hundred sick sacks."[190]

A voice from the control tower came over her radio. She was noticing parallels with Amelia's flight: Her plane had been hangared in number 22, the same hangar which had housed Earhart's plane. Speaking to Joan now from the control tower was airport manager Fred McElwain, the same man who had

---

[189] Brown, *Fate,* 50.

[190] Brown, *Fate,* 91-92.

supervised Amelia Earhart's takeoff in 1937.[191] He told her, "I directed (Amelia) to the same immediate point. We waited to see her back in fifty days." Then, keeping his voice light and bright, he added, "See you back in about six weeks, Joan."

As the hands on her wristwatch ticked to 1:00 p.m., it was time to take off.

The world flight had begun. . . . I had an escort of small planes: Tom Hudson, flying off my left wing in an Aztec, a Cessna 310 and another Aztec carrying airport and city officials, and Fred Goerner . . . in a Sky Knight.[192]

Fred Goerner had investigated Earhart's disappearance and wrote the 1966 book, *The Search for Amelia Earhart*. He was "an acquaintance of both Joan's and Trixie's,"[193] and in the typed line of her transcript following his name, Joan later handwrote that Goerner's "interest in this flight was more than casual."[194]

Within a few minutes, she was settling into life in her cabin, and talking into her recorder. "The Sierras are on my left. Snow crests the mountains on almost all peaks. Off to my right is Monterey where Jack and I used to live."[195]

---

[191] Brown, *Fate*, 50; Merriam, "I Flew," 78.

[192] Brown, *Fate*, 51.

[193] Brown, *Fate*, 141.

[194] Brown, *Fate*, 51.

[195] Brown, *Fate*, 51.

Tuesday evening, March 17
WICHITA, Kansas

As the sun set on the Kansas prairie, Jerrie and a federal inspector performed their final examinations prior to take-off.

When the inspector finished his checklist, he signed the papers and pulled his coat collar up against the biting Wichita wind. He turned to the men who were assisting Jerrie with the flight preparations. "Weren't you boys supposed to be done by now?"

"We got locked out of the hangar last night," one of the men told him.[196] This had caused a delay of several hours.

"Hasn't that other pilot taken off already?" the inspector asked.

Nobody answered. They did not want to waste time talking about the race–which wasn't even supposed to be a race–or their suspicions that somebody might be trying to cheat.[197]

Finally, by 9:00 p.m., Jerrie climbed into the plane's cramped cabin, made one last eyeball inspection of all the modifications that had been installed–from state-of-the-art instruments to a specialized fuel tank–and twisted back around into the single seat. Her ground crew waited as she settled in, turned dials, and called out, "Clear!"

The new engine turned over, then roared to life. Jerrie rolled her plane toward the blue lights lining the taxiway. A voice

---

[196] Mock, interview, Feb. 28, 2008.

[197] Although Jerrie professed that her flight around the world was never intended to be a race, passages in *Three-Eight Charlie,* as well as newspaper articles, indicate that she soon realized that it was, indeed, a race. See Appendix A.

from the tower announced, "Three-Eight Charlie, cleared for take-off."

Jerrie coaxed Charlie into the starry night sky. After a flight of 1,000 miles, she would land the plane in Columbus, Ohio, the official starting point for an epic journey around the world.

Tuesday, March 17-Wednesday, March 18
Over Missouri

Charlie's engine purred along just fine. Still, Jerrie had to watch constantly for warning signs. Landmarks on the ground were not visible in the darkness.

Wait a minute. Her compass wasn't working right. The needle on that compass didn't move. Jerrie had to expect a few issues, but some of the problems they had run into looked suspicious. It was hard to tell the difference and even harder to know what to do about them. Time to test one of the new instruments that her cockpit had been fitted with. She turned a knob, sending out a signal to a radio tower out there.

Jerrie wished she could talk to her family, right then, but there was no way to call or radio them, sitting in the living room in Columbus, from her cockpit. Her stomach growled. She never ate while flying, and tonight she would be in the air for six hours straight.

Jerrie passed the next cloud. The engine sounded okay, nothing smelled wrong, and most of the instruments seemed to be reading right. Soon there was nothing else to do but look at the stars.

Meanwhile, back in Wichita, odd things had continued to happen to the Mocks. Russ had hired a man to install a new radio, but Jerrie caught him putting in an old one.[198] Her crew planned to work all night, until that lockout. With Joan Merriam Smith's declaration to complete the equatorial route, combined with the media attention devoted to both pilots' projects, Jerrie's sightseeing adventure had turned into a race that she hadn't signed up for.

Joan flew a twin-engine Piper Apache, much faster than Jerrie's single-engine Cessna. Originally planning to take off on April 1,[199] Jerrie felt compelled to move up her launch date, but Joan still had a head start.

COLUMBUS, Ohio, 3:21 a.m. (Eastern Time)

Below the night sky, the lights of Columbus were a welcome sight to Jerrie. Time to forget about mysteries and worries. She brought the plane down, down, down, concentrating on the dials and the voice on the radio, feeling the wind whip around the cockpit and over the wings. Charlie's wheels hit the concrete for a perfect landing, and Russ drove her home for a well-earned night's sleep.

TUCSON, Arizona, just after dark (Mountain Time)

Joan landed "alongside the handsome new terminal"[200] at Tucson International Airport as the sun slipped behind the mountains.

She was greeted by representatives of the Chamber of Commerce and several Ninety-Nines. She gulped the coffee she

---

[198] Mock, interview, October 11, 2007; Saunders, "How an Ohio Housewife Flew Around the World."

[199] Mock, interview and handwritten notes given to the author.

[200] Brown, *Fate*, 51.

was handed on her way to the weather bureau to get a report warning about the possibility of ice and turbulence coming up if she didn't leave soon.[201] She was grateful that everyone from air traffic controllers to the Air Force, from meteorologists to fellow pilots supported her and were compiling and relaying helpful information to her. They understood her flight was "not just pleasure flying, but globe girdling,"[202] and they wanted her to succeed.

Still, the social situation was a bit awkward. She knew the Ninety-Nines would understand, but she expected the city officials who had planned welcome festivities in her honor would be disappointed that she could only stay for "a chicken dinner and cake molded in the shape of a plane."[203] During dinner, she overheard a pianist in the adjoining cocktail lounge playing "Around the World" and "Come Josephine in Your Flying Machine," just for her.[204] But the rain was coming in from El Paso, and the low pressure was deepening, so she had to skip a night's sleep and take off again right away.[205]

Wednesday, March 18, just after midnight

She filed a flight plan as fast as she could write and took off again at 2:30 a.m. Weather forced her to fly "north to Phoenix, then to Winslow and east to Zuni and Albuquerque."[206] The Tucson radar operator talked to her for a long time, helping her

---

[201] Ibid., 51-52.

[202] Ibid., 52.

[203] Ibid.

[204] Ibid., 52-53.

[205] Ibid., 53.

[206] Ibid.

stay awake. The clouds moved in, blotting out the horizon until she had to rely completely on instruments. The darkness was broken up only by the red lights on her instrument panel, the lights on the tips of the wings of her plane, and the "swish of the rotating red beacon against the wing,"[207] which eventually made her so sleepy she had to switch on the oxygen.

The heavy clouds kept pushing her north until she landed at Lubbock, Texas, for gas. Airborne once more, she struggled through rain and wind for four hours before finally breaking out of it at Baton Rouge, where she could fly visual, drop down and speed up.[208]

Then she heard a *bang*, and immediately ran through the possibilities of what could have caused it. Baggage door? Landing gear doors? Antenna? She had added some rubber stripping underneath the wing to cut down on wind drag, and she suspected that was it, so she didn't panic. She called Approach Control, but tried to make it clear that she was not declaring an emergency. Another plane flew alongside her, and the pilot told her he could see something long and black flapping against the bottom of the plane. Even though she had told the tower that her situation wasn't an emergency, it had been labeled one, anyway. As she landed at Moissant Field in New Orleans, she was embarrassed to be greeted by four or five fire trucks.

The problem was quickly identified. Sure enough, "part of a fairing, a rubber-covered wing wire . . . had torn loose."[209] It

---

[207] Ibid.

[208] Ibid., 54.

[209] "Mrs. Smith Is Forced To Land," *Palm Beach Post*, March 19, 1964.

wasn't an essential piece of equipment, so it was simply cut loose and Joan continued her flight the next day.

Joan's friend Lillian Huber, a commercial pilot who learned to fly at the same time Joan did, picked Joan up and took her to her home for some much-needed rest. Joan fell asleep as soon as her "head touched the pillow."[210]

---

[210] Ibid.

"That's the Last We'll Hear from Her"

Wednesday, March 18
PORT COLUMBUS, Ohio, early morning (Eastern Time)

Having to leave faster than they had planned forced the Mocks to rush some things. Jerrie hated that, but she just didn't have much choice. One compass still didn't work. Evidently, the metal of the new fuel tanks was attracting the magnet. So, on the day before Jerrie took off, Russ and their mechanic friends took one last shot at getting it to work. He cranked the engine, and taxied, turning the plane sharply to one side, hoping that might "swing the compass,"[211] or break the needle free from being drawn to the metal tank. Yet as soon as he turned, oil poured out of the plane. They opened it up to find a worn-out oil screen installed in her new engine.

If they hadn't tried to swing the compass, they might not have caught this oil screen. Spilling oil over an ocean or a desert could have cost Jerrie more than the race.[212]

After replacing the oil screen, Jerrie was ready to go, albeit with only one working compass. "You'll have to swing the compass again somewhere along the way," Russ said.[213] Their original design had set her up with two compasses, so now she

---

[211] Multiple references to issues with the compass can be found in *Three-Eight Charlie* as well as in Jerrie's handwritten notes which she shared with the author and in the author's recorded interview with Jerrie.

[212] Mock, notes, given to the author.

[213] Mock, interview, Oct. 11, 2007.

would have to rely on the one radio compass, and she would have to keep learning which gauges to believe. Well, she was getting plenty of practice at that.

Thursday, March 19, in the middle of the night (Central Time)
NEW ORLEANS, Louisiana

Joan still didn't get much sleep. With more weather approaching, she had to be up again at 3:00 a.m., and back to the airport by 4:15 a.m. Just before takeoff, at 4:30 in the morning, Joan and her friend Lillian found two teenagers signing her plane, between the signatures of pilots with American, Eastern, and Delta. The girls were in awe that "such a small plane was going around the world."[214] They reminded her of herself at that age, not so long ago. She thanked them, loaded up, and got away by 4:55 a.m.

In the air she started smelling gas fumes, perhaps spilled the night before during refueling. She would have to shut her entire electrical system off to avoid a fire. She also realized that she had left her medicine kit in New Orleans, with vitamins she might not be able to get at upcoming stops. She radioed a station in New Orleans and asked them to call Lillian and ask her to have her medicine kit air freighted to Miami.[215]

PORT COLUMBUS, Ohio, 7:00 a.m. (Eastern Time)

A crowd turned out at the airport to watch Jerrie take off. Along with the usual assortment of well-wishing family, friends, mechanics, police officers, reporters, and photographers, Jerrie had to accommodate a couple of special participants who came

---

[214] Brown, *Fate*, 55.
[215] Ibid.

to see her off, including Ohio Governor James Rhodes and the wives of astronauts John Glenn and Scott Carpenter.[216]

She was bombarded with questions, comments, and requests. Reporters gave directions for photo ops, first giving Jerrie directions for different poses while she sat in the plane, then asking her to get out of the plane so they could get photos of her and the governor in front of the plane.

The reporters' questions ranged from the inane to the personal. They commented on her clothes, high-heel shoes, and "tourist-type straw hat."[217] They asked for autographs. They wondered how her family would feel with her gone for so long. "The barrage of questions had my head spinning," Jerrie wrote in *Three-Eight Charlie*.[218]

These distractions were important for her sponsors, but her pre-flight prep was critical to her safety. Dave Blanton was serious about his last-minute instructions. He obsessively instructed Jerrie about the importance of clean rags. They were needed to keep fuel from sloshing from the filler hole into the plane's cabin. He told Jerrie to insist on a supply of clean rags at every stop, and not to let anyone adjust the fuel system. "Call me if anything goes wrong," Dave insisted. "Let me talk to them on the phone."[219]

Jerrie and her ground crew checked everything from gas gauges to the compass light on the dash. The mechanic reported that he "thought" they had taken care of an oil leak. The mechanic *thinks* the leak is fixed?

---

[216] *Columbus Evening Dispatch*, Thursday, March 19, 1964, 1.

[217] Ibid.

[218] Mock, *Three-Eight Charlie*, 15.

[219] Mock, *Three-Eight Charlie*, 17; Mock, interview, July 1, 2007.

Jerrie was ushered into an office to pose for photos with the astronauts' wives. Then it was time to drive over to the terminal, which meant an escape from all those people. They terrified her more than her upcoming solo flight into the Bermuda Triangle.[220]

The weather bureau gave her a forecast of clear skies, and even tail winds, all the way to Bermuda. She decided to take it as "a good omen."[221] The next stop was the Flight Service Station, a noisy office that Jerrie described as "constant bedlam." Over the racket of the teletype machines and loudspeakers, Jerrie requested, "I'd like to file an International Flight Plan."

The watch supervisor presented her with a stack of forms. Her hand shook as she filled in the necessary information. Then Russ hustled her back to the plane, and the crowd. The photographing started up again, along with the questions.

"Hasn't that woman in California already started?"

Jerrie's two sons, mom, dad, two sisters, and mother-in-law all said their goodbyes. Gary put his class ring on Jerrie's finger, saying, "Don't ever take it off." Her mother-in-law pinned a St. Christopher medal inside her coat and assured her she would take care of Russ and the kids.

Russ stood back a bit for a moment, hands in his pockets, collar turned up against the stiff wind.[222] Then he found his way through the crowd and helped Jerrie slide the yellow life jacket over the corsage of pink carnations she had agreed to wear for the cameras. He helped her step up into her plane and settle onto cushions that accommodated her petite frame, then he

---

[220] Ibid.

[221] Mock, *Three-Eight Charlie*, 17.

[222] Vail and Edwards, "Winner Take All," 33.

stepped up into the cockpit for a last kiss and a last-minute instruction. "Remember the stories for the *Dispatch*." Then he shut the door.[223]

Jerrie called, "Clear!" and pushed the starter button. The propeller began to turn, and the sound of the engine separated her from them all. She had one last chance to wonder what the crowd would say if she admitted that she was so scared, she was shaking. But she was even *more* afraid of what Russ might do if she turned around and taxied back than she was of the unseen world ahead. She called the control tower, trying to sound calm.

"Columbus Ground, this is Cessna One-Five-Three-Eight Charlie. Taxi instructions for take-off."

A voice responded, "Three-Eight Charlie is cleared for take-off."[224]

"Roger. Three-Eight Charlie." Jerrie eased in the throttle. If she and Charlie could make it on their own out there, then "oceans and deserts were waiting." The little plane zipped down the runway, climbed into the sky, and headed east toward history.[225]

As Charlie climbed, Jerrie heard the tower controller and knew the crowd could also hear his voice. "Well, I guess that's the last we'll hear from her."[226]

The words swept away Jerrie's fears. Now she was determined to complete her epic journey.

---

[223] Mock, *Three-Eight Charlie*, 20.

[224] Ibid., 22

[225] Mock, *Three-Eight Charlie*, 21.

[226] Mock, *Three-Eight Charlie*, 22; Saunders, "How an Ohio Housewife Flew Around the World."

MIAMI, Florida

Five and a half hours after taking off from New Orleans, Joan touched down at Miami International Airport.[227]

Her mother lived only three miles from the airport, and was there to greet her, along with her Aunt Beryl and Uncle Frank. The city of Miami treated them all to a big banquet and another key to the city. For the occasion, she said, "I had my hair cut short, sort of Amelia-style, and put on a dress, for the cameras. I certainly didn't feel very glamorous."[228] She would have preferred slacks. But she was "pretty well indoctrinated with the Powder Puff Derby philosophy that women need not be unfeminine to fly."[229] So, she had packed a couple of drip-dry dresses, and a couple of skirts and blouses, all wash-and-wear. Speaking to reporters, she sometimes asked them to write her name as "Joan Merriam," saying it was her professional name. She had to tell everyone, even her mother, that she only had a little time to spend with them on this trip, as there was much to do before her departure for San Juan, Puerto Rico.

"Although the plane is insured, I have no personal insurance on this flight. I didn't have the money for it. What money I could get together is needed for the plane. And anyway, Jack, who would be my beneficiary, says if anything happened to me, he couldn't bring himself to spend the money anyway. So that settles that. "[230]

---

[227] Brown, *Fate*, 55.

[228] Merriam, "I Flew," 78.

[229] Brown, *Fate*, 56.

[230] Ibid.

Somebody Grab the Plane!

Thursday, March 19, 12:50 p.m. (Eastern Time)
NORFOLK, Virginia

It was time for Jerrie to settle in, fly, and try not to think about the other pilot out there. From 9,000 feet, Jerrie watched the mountainous terrain of Ohio and Virginia dissolve into foothills, then the watery reflections of the Great Dismal Swamp sparkling green in the afternoon sun. Ahead lay the Atlantic.[231]

Nobody had mentioned anything to Jerrie about fire engines, or banquets in Miami, or anything else that might be slowing Joan down. All Jerrie knew was that she was busy in her own cockpit. Before she left the continent, she had to get her long-range radio to work right. She switched on an electric motor that reeled out an antenna wire 100 feet from the bottom of the plane for optimal reception. She watched the needle on her new high-frequency long-range radio, waiting for it to start wiggling. It didn't. She tried every knob and switch. Nothing.

She was about to lose all contact with anyone. Should she turn back? Her hand shook as she switched her microphone over to the very high frequency (VHF) radio and picked up the mike. "Norfolk Radio, this is November Three-Eight Charlie. Over."

"Three-Eight Charlie, this is Norfolk Radio. Go ahead."

---

[231] Mock, *Three-Eight Charlie*, 23; Mock, interview, July 1, 2007.

"Norfolk, this is Three-Eight Charlie. Unable to contact New York Oceanic on five-six-one-one-point-five."

Norfolk gave her another setting to turn to on her dial.

She tried. Nothing. "Norfolk Radio, Three-Eight Charlie. No contact. "

"Three-Eight Charlie, Norfolk . . ." but she was losing the transmission. She caught the word "hatbox," but had no idea what that meant. Then the voice from Norfolk faded out.

Now what? Suppose her plane *did* fly along without any problem. If she couldn't communicate with anyone, the Air Force might not identify her, and send a jet to intercept. If the government shot her down, would they send the bill to her husband?[232]

She couldn't give up.

Pamlico Sound glistened below her in the afternoon sun. She crossed a spit of land–Cape Hatteras on one end, Ocracoke and Portsmouth to the south of a narrow pass–and faced the open ocean.

The world was silent except for the reassuring hum of Charlie's engine. She tried another one of the new instruments, turning her twin Automatic Direction Finders (ADFs) to the Bermuda beacon. These two needles were supposed to point in the same direction. At first, they did.

Then, they drifted sixty degrees apart from each other. Without radio contact, she couldn't tell which needle was right. Then she remembered that one of the two dials had been worked on in Wichita–while she was in DC and couldn't stop it–so she decided to trust the other one.

---

[232] Mock, *Three-Eight Charlie*, 25.

Without the radio working, she couldn't ask the tower at Kindley Air Force Base which way the wind was blowing. She tried looking down through the clouds at the waves and taking a guess, but the clouds might be moving with the wind, and watching all that for too long might make her dizzy, anyway. Then the clouds began to close in. She found one gap of blue and descended through the opening.

As she headed down, her instrument needles spun around until they pointed exactly opposite from the direction in which she was flying. She turned Charlie around in a big circle, until she came out of the clouds. Below her lay Bermuda.[233]

A voice from the Bermuda air tower came over her short-range radio loud and clear. "Three-Eight Charlie, radar contact."[234]

She was okay with letting them help her with a surveillance approach. Still, this landing made her nervous. The ocean waves seemed to pound at the runway's edge. The clarity of the water allowed her to see right to the ocean floor. Nice view, but she sure didn't want to get any closer.

She descended straight into a forty-knot wind. Her tires kissed the taxiway, and she rolled to a stop, completing her first overseas landing. She looked around, realizing that she had stopped so quickly, she still had to taxi another mile to the end of the runway, then turn and taxi yet *another* mile all the way to the terminal.

As she crept slowly along the pavement, she had to fight the powerful wind blowing straight at her. She made the first mile okay, but when she turned, the wind hit her sideways,

233 Mock, *Three-Eight Charlie*, 27.
234 Ibid., 27.

threatening to spin Charlie around. Jerrie pushed hard with her foot on the left brake and Charlie inched toward the terminal. But the left brake heated up and wouldn't hold. The two seat cushions behind her along with one underneath wouldn't allow her to stand, so all she could do was push down on the pedal, and still, the left wheel spun faster than the right. Finally, her strength wore out and she couldn't stop the plane from turning. In front of a crowd that had come out to watch–a crowd that had no idea she was having brake trouble–she had to let the plane revolve in a complete circle. She tried again to stop it the next time around but the plane kept rotating. She decided to go off the runway. Maybe the grass would help slow it down.

When Charlie rolled off the pavement, startled airport workers ran to catch this out-of-control plane and rescue the pilot.

The airport attendants held and pushed Charlie up to the terminal. Exhausted, Jerrie just grabbed her high heels and braced herself to face the cameras and questions. She was dutifully posing for a photo in her Mae West when a blast of wind whipped around a corner of the big terminal building, hurtling Charlie toward a stone wall.

"*Help!*" Jerrie screamed. Attendants, photographers, and nearly everyone else out on the tarmac made another run for the plane. They caught Charlie, just inches before the plane would have been crumpled into "useless, twisted aluminum."[235]

When the wind eased off, so did everybody's grip on the plane. "Don't let go yet!" Jerrie said. "Help me roll it into the hangar, quick!"

---

[235] Mock, *Three-Eight Charlie*, 29-30; Mock, interview, Oct. 11, 2007.

"Sorry, ma'am," said a man in a Bermudan air crew uniform, "but the hangar's full. No problem. We can work something out." He turned to another worker. "Get me some rope."

The Bermudan aircrew, reporters, and spectators all worked with Jerrie to tie Charlie down. They used whatever they could find–ropes, concrete blocks, and an oil drum–to secure the plane. Sitting by itself at one end of the long terminal building, Jerrie's little red-and-white plane "looked like a tiny toy," left to fend for itself in the elements.[236]

After all that, the reporters asked only a few questions, then hurried away, until only one woman was left standing with Jerrie.

"Can you sleep on a feather bed?" the woman asked, offering her hand. "I'm Mrs. Bill Judd. My husband is a TWA pilot, and he's flying to London right now, so we have plenty of room at our house."

Mrs. Judd drove Jerrie along a winding road up to their cottage, High Reefs, situated on a cliff overlooking the ocean. After watching the local TV newscaster report Jerrie's trouble landing in the wind, it was time for a long, deep sleep.[237]

---

[236] Mock, *Three-Eight Charlie*, 31.

[237] Mock, *Three-Eight Charlie*, 31-32; Mock, interview, Oct. 11, 2007.

Who Unplugged the Radio?

Friday morning, March 20
High Reefs Cottage, BERMUDA

Jerrie began her day by calling the local weatherman. A sergeant at Kindley Air Force Base read his charts to her over the phone. Winds were expected to build, from spin-a-small-plane-around level up to hurricane strength, within hours. By then, she would be over the open Atlantic.

She dressed, called a cab, and hurried to the airport. She had a lot to do–gas up the plane, file a flight plan, try to get the radio working–before she could take off again, anyway.

Her cab driver pulled up to the main entrance and dropped her off along with all departing passengers. She wandered around until she found Charlie, but the doors were sealed with stickers from Bermudan Customs, and she didn't dare break the rules.

A man in a uniform ran up to her. "Mrs. Mock? You're wanted on the phone."

She followed the man through one NO ENTRY sign after another, up a stairway, down a hall, into an office, and picked up the telephone.

"Joan's on her way to South America!" It was Russ. "You're falling behind already!"[238]

---

[238] Mock, *Three-Eight Charlie*, 34; Mock, interview, Oct. 16, 2007.

The other pilot in this "race" was following a completely different route. Joan Merriam Smith only had to return to California, while Jerrie had to fly all the way back to Ohio. It was going to be hard for Jerrie to estimate how fast she had to keep moving to pass Joan, but Russ seemed to know exactly.

"I can't go anywhere yet," Jerrie said. She tried to explain the approaching storm.

"Well, while you're stuck there, at least take some pictures," Russ said.

"Yes, dear."[239] Talking to her husband didn't help. But when she hung up, Jerrie realized she was sitting right in the middle of Bermuda Air Services. She was able to get a weather briefing, talk to a Customs officer and the air traffic control people, plus they found her a Pan American Airways technician who would look at her radio.

The Customs officer and Jerrie watched as the radio technician climbed around the cockpit until his head was on the pedals with his feet against a gas tank. Everything he could find from there was good, which meant one of the tanks would have to be removed so he could look behind it. Bermuda Air Services found some men that they said could take the tank out.

The Customs officer couldn't stay through all that, so, he climbed in, glanced around at Jerrie's accoutrements– "manuals, tool roll, Kleenex" –and everything else piled around inside the cabin. He decided she wasn't smuggling anything, handed her the key, and wished her luck.[240]

The men that BAS had rounded up helped Jerrie unload some of her stuff then turned to the tanks. Jerrie explained that

---

[239] Ibid.

[240] Mock, *Three-Eight Charlie*, 35; Mock, interview, Oct. 16, 2007.

the seat had to come out first. They decided that couldn't be right, so they tried taking out one of the tanks first. That didn't work, so they had to try doing it her way, and then it began to happen. It was late afternoon before they got the 110-gallon tank out. The men from BAS helped Jerrie go find the radio technician and get him to come back.

The technician climbed into the cockpit, stretched out on the floor, and looked around. Within just a few minutes, he sat right back up, looking perplexed. "The radio wire is disconnected, all right. But it didn't just come off. The raw lead is taped up and tucked away."[241]

"Well, it worked when it was installed," Jerrie said. Who would have disconnected it? She suspected the answer. From the time the new radio was installed in Fort Lauderdale, it had worked fine, until she had the new tanks installed–in Wichita.

The technician plugged in the radio and tested it by talking to the tower on it. Jerrie would no longer be out of contact over the ocean. She wanted to hug the man, but it would have been unseemly to do so. Instead, she simply said, "Thank you."

---

[241] Mock, *Three-Eight Charlie*, 36; Saunders, "How an Ohio Housewife Flew Around the World."

Saturday, March 21
MIAMI, Florida

Joan couldn't get out of Florida until Saturday morning.[242] As she waited to take off, she took her last (for a while) look around at an American airport. In 1964, passenger flying was brand new and exciting, and flying solo pushed the limits even more. With each stop, Joan would leave the known world farther behind. Compared to the "great jets"[243] all around her, Joan's plane looked like "a small, frail bird."[244] The crisp logos of Eastern, TWA, and Pan Am, glittering on airplane fuselages in the rays of the rising sun, advertised the dawn of this new era of travel convenience. These planes would soon fill up with families and tourists bound for San Juan, Puerto Rico. For Joan, San Juan would only be a stopping point. From there, she would fly on, along the edge of the Bermuda Triangle, down to Surinam.

Shortly after dawn, she took off, skirting a few rain showers and testing her special diet.[245] From now on, it would have to be nothing but beef, always well done, vegetables out of a can, vitamins, and snacks out of a package, nothing spicy or unknown. Getting airsick as the only person on board could be more than awkward. It could prove catastrophic.

Joan landed at San Juan without incident, checked into the hotel, and had no trouble falling asleep. Yet, while in the air, an experienced pilot is always listening for any new noise, rattle, or hint of trouble. She must have suspected something, because the

---

[242] Merriam, "I Flew," 78.

[243] Merriam, "I Flew," 78.

[244] Merriam, "I Flew," 78.

[245] Merriam, "Longest Flight," 46.

next day, she asked around about where to find help in the places she was headed next. Pilots in San Juan cautioned her about the shortage of mechanics she might encounter in South America, but should she need work, an experienced repairman would be on hand at Paramaribo.[246]

BERMUDA

In the morning, the men from BAS began wrangling the big tanks back into the plane through a doorway with less than an inch to spare. Jerrie sat on a concrete block, getting "tired just watching" the laborious process.[247] About 10:00 a.m., another man from BAS came out to tell her that she would need to move Charlie out of the way. It was "college week," and several airliners full of tourists were expected. Since the tanks weren't ready, Jerrie would have to wait until the next day to gas up and take off. She couldn't help with the tank reinstallation anyway, so she went to lunch with Mrs. Judd at a place with a nice view overlooking the harbor; she took some photos for Russ. After lunch, she went back to the airport to check the fuel lines and make sure all the little arrows pointed up, like Dave had instructed. Confirming that the fuel tanks had been successfully removed and reinstalled, and knowing that, after filling up in the morning, she would be ready to take off, Jerrie got a rare good night's sleep.[248]

Sunday, March 22, 6:13 a.m. (Atlantic Time)
SAN JUAN, Puerto Rico

---

[246] "Longest Flight," 46.
[247] Mock, *Three-Eight Charlie*, 37.
[248] Ibid., 38.

Joan took off from San Juan at sunrise for a short hop across the south edge of the Bermuda Triangle. For the first time in her life, she looked down into the jungles of South America, which she described as "unpleasant from any altitude."[249]

PARAMARIBO, Surinam

Nine hours of anxiety later, Joan was relieved to spot a clearing below. She said, "I had read A.E.'s description of what Paramaribo would look like from the air: a town squatting at the edge of the Surinam River, lots of red-tile rooftops and some thatched huts. . . . Now, (there was also a) large jet airport, 30 miles out."[250] She was tired and "feeling pretty wrinkled,"[251] took a look at herself in the mirror, combed her hair, put on some lipstick, and then brought the plane down onto the runway at Zandery Airport.

She could have skipped the touch-up. The greeting party for this famous world traveler consisted of the men who helped her fill her main flight tanks, and a man in a uniform who spoke little English. He handed her a stack of forms to fill out, and took his time reading through her information without expression.

Joan looked around at the bare concrete floors and slowly turning fans. Swatting at mosquitoes, she daydreamed longingly about a room and bed. Finally, she was told they were putting her up in their "V.I.P. quarters,"[252] but it was just a small, bare room for transients. She washed what she had worn that day, hung it up to drip-dry in the sink, and sank into sleep.

---

[249] Merriam, "Longest Flight," 46.

[250] Merriam, "I Flew," 78-79.

[251] Merriam, "I Flew," 79.

[252] Merriam, "I Flew," 79.

BERMUDA

In the morning, Jerrie was informed that a front was coming across the Atlantic and was about to hit Bermuda. If she were to take off now, she would be flying right into it. She was on the ground for another day, at least. Russ insisted that she write a story and take a photo every day, then take them to the airport to be flown back to the US.

Mrs. Judd had been sleeping on her own couch, giving Jerrie the bed. Jerrie couldn't stand to see that one more night, so she moved to another cottage, the home of John and Lillian Fountain. John Fountain was Jerrie's official observer, reporting her landing and takeoff from Bermuda to the NAA.

By that afternoon, the weather showed up. Rain hit the island in torrents, slapping against the windows, and the wind howled, keeping her from even thinking about leaving until the system moved on.[253] She celebrated her nineteenth wedding anniversary over dinner with the Fountains,[254] and by a telegram from Russ.[255]

Monday, March 23
BERMUDA

Rain kept Jerrie from going anywhere.[256]

---

[253] Mock, *Three-Eight Charlie*, 38.

[254] Vail and Edwards, "Winner Take All," 33.

[255] Russell Mock to Jerrie Mock, telegram, March 22, 1964, from Jerrie's private collection, copy given to the author.

[256] Vail and Edwards, "Winner Take All," 39.

PARAMARIBO, Surinam

As Joan was filing her flight plan, the local workers called her in a panic. "Gasoline was pouring out of the tanks"[257] at the welded seams. This was devastating on many levels. First, Joan had spent several thousand dollars on high-quality tanks. Second, repairing them would be time consuming and expensive. And third, the leaks posed a potentially catastrophic situation. If the tank had leaked while Joan was in flight, she could have had a cabin full of fumes, without even knowing it, and passed out from asphyxiation. A spark from her electrical system could have started a fire or set off an explosion.[258]

The first step to repairing the tanks would be to remove them. Joan was grateful for help from the manager of the local Pan Am facility, but the tank removal still took six hours.[259] She would spend another night in the "V.I.P. quarters" of Zandery Airport.

Tuesday, March 24
HAMILTON, Bermuda

Bad weather kept Jerrie grounded as well. She told the UPI, "I am just going to carry on as if I never heard of this other girl."[260]

Wednesday, March 25
PARAMARIBO, Surinam

Joan's tanks could not be repaired at the airport. "I pushed everybody as hard as I could, but Surinam was pretty primitive,

---

[257] Brown, *Fate*, 57.

[258] Brown, *Fate*, 58.

[259] Merriam, "I Flew," 79.

[260] "Two Women Fliers Remain Grounded," *Honolulu Star-Bulletin*, Mar.h 24, 1964.

and I was really afraid I was going to have to abandon the trip right there. The tanks had to be shipped thirty miles from the airport to Paramaribo for repairs. Everything moved at a maddeningly slow pace."[261] The tanks were welded, rewelded, wrapped in plywood, and reinforced with metal bands. Gasoline had leaked into her radios.[262] All Joan could do was sip coffee, answer the phone, and wait.[263]

BERMUDA

Rain still kept Jerrie on the ground, as well.

Russ called every day. He said he had heard a report that Joan was slowed by "leaky gas tanks," but he didn't think she would be held up long.

The delays wore on Jerrie's nerves and drove Russ crazy. He accused her of being "slow and inefficient."

"Look, weather can't be that bad for that long," Russ admonished her. "Woman, you have to fly."

Russ warned Jerrie that Joan would "get way ahead" if she delayed any longer. "Remember your sponsors, and take a few chances!"

Jerrie wanted to "bang the phone through the table." When it rang again, she left the house.[264]

She wanted to win just as much as Russ did, but what could she do about a storm? She tried to get used to riding with Lillian along the seaside roads and joining her for English tea at her fireplace in the afternoons. As the days slipped into a week, she

---

[261] Merriam, "I Flew," 79.

[262] Brown, *Fate*, 58.

[263] Merriam, "I Flew," 79.

[264] Mock, *Three-Eight Charlie*, 40.

became sick of the waiting, and tried her best not to let it show.[265]

"Don't Hit the Mountains"

Thursday, March 26
BERMUDA

Jerrie had no way of knowing that Joan was still grounded. All she knew was that on Thursday morning, a full week after landing in Bermuda, she sat at a table surrounded by Air Force officers with their maps and weather charts. In a familiar scene for Jerrie, whether obtaining flight permissions or discussing the weather she would encounter, she was the only woman in a room full of men. They were all waiting for her to speak.

Storms still brewed over the Atlantic, but they had calmed a little. If she left that afternoon, she might make it. If she didn't chance it, the next front was coming tomorrow, and she could be stuck even longer.

Nobody pushed her. Many pilots had flown into iffy weather, only to crash into the ocean. The decision to fly or wait was up to her.

Well, there was no other way back to Columbus. She took a cab up to the cottage, called Russ, and told him it was time to take off.[266]

"Great!" he said. "I'll call the *Dispatch* and get the story in today." Storms didn't scare *him*.[267]

"I love you," she said. "Give Val a big kiss for me."[268]

---

[266] Ibid., 43.

[267] Mock, *Three-Eight Charlie*, 43; Mock, interview, Oct. 16, 2007.

[268] Mock, *Three-Eight Charlie*, 46.

She packed fast and rode on the back of John Fountain's motor scooter down the mountain, politely worked her way through the crowd and reporters who had suddenly showed up, then picked up her flight plan and her bill. Her gas cost her twenty-four cents a gallon, and they asked if ten dollars was okay for the tank removal and installation—work that had taken several men two days, on a weekend. Bermuda had been good to her.

She got the plane loaded and taxied toward the runway, but steered the plane onto the grass to double-check everything. Her cabin gas tanks were full, making the plane overweight by about 900 pounds. Without a mechanism to jettison excess fuel, an emergency landing would be risky until several hours of fuel had burned off. By then, she would be way out over the ocean, with nowhere to land. Finally, she just had to accept that her checklist was complete and it was time to get up the nerve to request clearance.

When the voice from the tower said the words, "November Three-Eight Charlie is cleared for take-off," she pointed her plane toward the end of the runway and pushed in the throttle. As the plane reached ninety miles per hour, Jerrie pulled the controls toward her and felt Charlie leap into the sky "like a restless, excited bird." The airspeed indicator ticked over to 120 miles per hour. Charlie handled the extra weight just fine as Jerrie pulled the plane to cruising altitude of 9,000 feet.

4:56 p.m. (Atlantic Time)

When she reached cruising altitude, Jerrie flipped the switch to unreel the special antenna that trailed out 100 feet from the bottom of the plane. When she turned on the new radio, multiple languages filled the cabin. One voice came in all the way from Santa Maria, the island among the Azores that was her destination, 2,100 miles ahead.

The sun slipped down the sky at her back, and she could turn the plane just a little to watch the last splashes of the sunset reflected on the water. Then she switched on the navigation lights and tried to tidy up the cabin.

She struggled to find a place for all the charts, food, gear, and doodads piled all around her. A heavy, black, manual typewriter, lent by the *Dispatch* to type stories while she flew, kept sliding around. She would have to find a better place to stow it.

The only clouds were far below, and the stars began to come out. Without the haze and city lights of civilization to obscure the view, more stars appeared than this girl from the suburbs had ever seen.

The moon rose nearly full that night. With her cabin awash in moonlight and voices wishing her luck from all over the Atlantic, Jerrie realized that "dreams really do come true."[269]

However, staying on course was tricky. She had to check the readings from all of her different instruments, guess at which ones were accurate and which might be off, estimate her location without any landmarks down there, then follow her hunch as to the best direction to take. If she wandered too far off course, she might never be heard from again.

The time came for her to make sure she wasn't lost by tuning in one of the five different types of radios on board. The US Coast Guard positioned ships called Ocean Stations throughout

---

[269] Mock, *Three-Eight Charlie*, 47-48; Mock, interview, Oct. 16, 2007.

the North Atlantic, and an Ocean Station named *Echo* was expecting to hear from her.

Out over that dark ocean, the one instrument she wanted to work right was the Consolan radio. Consolan radio stations all over the world sent out a continuous signal of dots and dashes, or *dit*s and *dah*s. She searched for a signal from the *Echo*, which would be halfway between Bermuda and the Azores. She listened for the reassuring sound of a steady *dah-dit-dah-dah, dit*, Morse Code for "Y E" or "Yankee Echo." She began to pick up a signal. As it grew louder, she listened more closely. *Dah-dit-dah-dah, dah-dit-dit-dit*, "Yankee Bravo." Ocean Station *Bravo* would be to the north around Greenland. Could she be *that* far off course? She shifted course to the right and picked up a faint *dah-dit-dah-dah, dit*. "Yankee Echo." Better.

She never saw the *Echo*. She reported to them that she was "abeam *Echo*, a little to the north," but she never heard back. She corrected her heading by ten degrees, hoping that would get her in sight of the Azores.

Clouds, lit by the moon, drifted in beneath the plane. The dark ocean below faded out of sight, and then the cloud layer slowly rose until Jerrie was surrounded by an eerie gray. A red beacon on the top of the plane rotated around and around, making the fog blink gray- pink, gray-pink. The lights from the dials in the cockpit cast a comforting red glow onto her maps and charts. Turbulence knocked the Cessna around, but the autopilot held it upright and level. Jerrie was flying by instrument, completely blind, trusting that everything would work right.

Then the plane started slowing down and losing altitude. Was the carburetor freezing up? No, the instruments indicated that the engine was warm and running fine. What was wrong?

She grabbed a flashlight and aimed the beam at the strut supporting the wing. *Ice!* An inch thick, along the front edge of the wing strut. That meant the ice would be even thicker up where she couldn't see it, on the wings. Charlie struggled against all the added weight.

Jerrie had to do something about it, fast. She had to get out of these clouds, either by going down or up. Flying down would take her right into the storm they had warned her about, but she couldn't go up without clearance or she might hit another plane. She got on the radio.[270]

"Santa Maria, Santa Maria, this is Three-Eight Charlie. Over."

No answer. She waited as long as she could stand it and tried again.

"Santa Maria, Santa Maria, this is Three-Eight Charlie. Over."

No answer. She was about to try again when her loudspeaker crackled. "Three-Eight Charlie, this is Santa Maria Radio. Go ahead."

"Santa Maria," she said slowly, "Three-Eight Charlie has ice, wing ice."

"Three-Eight Charlie, Santa Maria. Please repeat."

"Santa Maria, Three-Eight Charlie has ice. Repeat–*ICE*. Request clearance to flight level one-one-zero!"

"Three-Eight Charlie, Santa Maria," the man answered. "Understand you have ice, are requesting flight level one-one-zero. Is that affirmative?"

---

[270] Mock, *Three-Eight Charlie*, 49-52; Mock, interview, Oct. 24, 2007.

"Affirmative. Affirmative!"

"Three-Eight Charlie, Santa Maria. Stand by one."

So, he got the message, but he still wanted her to wait a minute. She pointed the flashlight beam at the strut. Now the ice was an inch and a half thick, at least. How much weight could Charlie hold, and still make the climb all the way up to 11,000 feet? Too much ice could bend the wings enough to make the plane uncontrollable. Santa Maria, hurry *up*.

That one-minute wait dragged into two. Then three. Four. She picked up the mike. "Santa Maria, Santa Maria, Three-Eight Charlie."

"Three-Eight Charlie, Santa Maria."

"Santa Maria, Three-Eight Charlie requests clearance to flight level one-one-zero. I have ice!"

"Three-Eight Charlie, Santa Maria. Stand by."

"Santa Maria, please hurry. I can't hold altitude much longer." She knew the controller was checking for any other planes out there, but if he didn't clear her to get out, the plane would head down anyway.

Ice piled up on the strut, twice as thick now. Even without clearance, she would have to head toward the top of the clouds while the plane could still climb, and look out for other planes herself.

The loudspeaker came on again. "Three-Eight Charlie, Santa Maria. You're cleared to climb to flight level one-one-zero. Over."[271]

She shoved the throttle all the way to the firewall and set for a climb. That new engine began to deliver Charlie out of the

---

[271] Mock, *Three-Eight Charlie*, 52-53; Mock, interview, Oct. 24, 2007.

freezing mist. The sky up there was clear, except for a few "cumulus balloons," taller than the rest, off in the distance.[272]

Charlie gradually settled back to flying level. Charlie's pilot sank back in her seat, exhausted. After a long, anxious night, the rays of the sun began to reach through the clouds, and ice dripped off the struts. It might still be rainy and freezing below, but in the cockpit, it was the dawn of Jerrie's next day.

Breaks appeared in the clouds below her and she spotted land. There wasn't supposed to be land yet! Then the clouds closed in, just before she caught sight of a mountain. What *mountain*? Seeing anything this close meant she was too far north.

"Santa Maria, Three-Eight Charlie. I just passed over an island."

"Three-Eight Charlie, Santa Maria. Understand you just passed over Pico Island?"

She hadn't said the name. She must be on their radar. "Affirmative."

"Roger, Three-Eight Charlie. You're cleared to Santa Maria." As she approached the island, the clouds closed over everything. He called her again. "Three-Eight Charlie, can you see the island?"

"Negative. No land."

"Three-Eight Charlie, Roger. You're cleared to descend." Then he added, "There are mountains." He sounded nervous. "Don't hit the mountains."

"Roger," was all she could think to say to *that*. As she dropped below the cloud ceiling, she spotted an airport.

---

[272] Mock, *Three-Eight Charlie*, 53.

Charlie's wheels hitting pavement was a big relief, until the tail bounced. What was wrong with those brakes? She taxied slowly, making sure the crosswind wouldn't send the plane spinning like it did in Bermuda.

A crowd had gathered around the terminal, including lots of US Air Force personnel. Wasn't this supposed to be a civilian airfield? As she taxied in, she could tell they looked happy. Okay, so they weren't waiting to arrest her for trying to make "an unauthorized landing at a military field."[273]

---

[273] Mock, *Three-Eight Charlie*, 54-57; Mock, interview, Oct. 24, 2007.

"Try Not to Use the Brakes"

Friday, March 27
PARAMARIBO, sunrise (Atlantic Time)

Joan was up with the rooster, cows, and everything else, ready and waiting–for the coffee to percolate, the office to open, the phone call to go through, the person on the other end to tell her that her tanks would be ready the next day, *"quizas,"* (maybe). The waiting went on, pushing every one of her clearances and visas for every stop around the world, one more day closer to expiration.[274]

SANTA MARIA, Azores, 8:21 a.m. (Azores Time)

The next round of camera flashbulbs going off in Jerrie's face and people gathering around were distracting. Her life jacket got hung up on something, and she stumbled out of her plane onto wet pavement. Still, setting foot on solid ground was a relief. Some people were talking in Portuguese, a subtle reminder that she was already far from home.[275]

A General Boylan explained that he had received a message from General Strauss back at Lockbourne about her arrival, so these Air Force men had flown over from another island to

---

[274] Merriam, "I Flew," 79.
[275] Mock, *Three-Eight Charlie*, 58.

greet her. Jerrie was grateful that Strauss was working behind the scenes for her, as he had said he would.[276]

The people in charge and the crowd swept her toward the terminal and into the expansive office of the airport manager, Alexandre Negrao. Coffee appeared, along with tropical fruits, eggs, and ham, but reporters surrounded her, as well. One official insisted on walking off with her passport, and there was too much going on to argue. She tried to eat and answer questions all at once.[277]

When the reporters' questions let up, an Air Force doctor had another one.

"Aren't you sleepy?"

"No, I'm wide awake."

"How about a sleeping pill?"

"No, thank you. I'm just fine." She had never taken one before.

Negrao gave her a ride to the Terra Nostra Hotel, the only hotel on the island. As soon as she got into a room, "twenty-four hours without sleep caught up," no pill required.

A "shrill blast" jerked her awake, followed by feet thundering down the hall. As she blinked at the daylight, she realized it was just children going to lunch. Jerrie may have been flying over the ocean all night, but for everyone else, this was just another day. By eleven a.m., she had only been in bed for two hours, but she was awake now. May as well come out for lunch.

A massive stone fireplace with a roaring fire warmed her up nicely. Negrao escorted her to a large table with lots of people

---

[276] Mock, *Three-Eight Charlie*, 58; R.H. Strauss, Brigadier General, USAF, "To Whom It May Concern," letter, March 17, 1964.

[277] Mock, *Three-Eight Charlie*, 59.

for a lunch that was long and social. Polite boys in white gloves brought "*sopa a paisana*, fish, meat, cheeses, fruit, coffee–and wine with every course."

After lunch, she struggled to keep her eyes open as Negrao took her to meet a mechanic with Pan Am to talk about those brakes.

"Ma'am, your brakes are so badly scored that adjusting them won't help."

"How can that be? They told us they put in brand new brakes!"

He shook his head. "I don't know when you put them on the plane, but they've had a lot of wear. The only ones we have will fit a 707, not a Cessna. You need to have new ones shipped immediately. Until then, try not to use the brakes."[278]

She was left to puzzle over what to do about the brakes while Negrao took her sightseeing. He drove her up a misty, winding mountain road into a world where people had carried on without airplane parts for 500 years. A farmer led oxen, pulling a small wooden cart piled high with branches, slowly down the hill. When Negrao crested the next rise, Jerrie took in the view. "It's a valley full of churches."

He laughed. "Those white spires aren't steeples. They're chimneys."

"Every house has one," Jerrie said.

"They're for bread ovens."

"No wonder the bread at lunch tasted so good."[279]

Negrao then drove her to an actual church. Our Lady of the Assumption, with its white stucco walls and red-tiled roof, stood on a hilltop overlooking the ocean.

---

[278] Ibid., 61.
[279] Ibid., 62.

"Christopher Columbus came to visit once," he said, opening the wooden door for Jerrie. "After discovering the West Indies, his ships stopped here on their way back to Spain."

Jerrie looked around at the burning candles and into the polished wooden faces of Jesus and Mary. She was awed by the thought that Christopher Columbus and his men had stood on this same stone floor.

"The conquistadors didn't get to finish Mass," Negrao said. "Their lookout spotted enemy ships, and they all had to rush back to theirs. They didn't even have time to haul anchor, but had to chop it free."

Jerrie smiled. If Christopher Columbus and the *Santa Maria* left Santa Maria with brake trouble and still made it home okay, then maybe *The Spirit of Columbus* would, too.[280]

PARAMARIBO

Joan was *still* stuck, and it was driving her crazy. The days kept going by and the rain kept coming down. The tanks were still getting fixed, far away. There wasn't much she could do except try to keep an eye on the plane and sit around at the airport, drinking "gallons" of black coffee.[281]

She was introduced to a local pilot named Marian Ziel, who broke the monotony a bit by talking with her about flying, and she decided to sponsor Marian as a Ninety-Nine when she returned.[282]

---

[280] Mock, *Three-Eight Charlie*, 62; Mock, interview, Oct. 24, 2007.

[281] Merriam, "I Flew," 79.

[282] Merriam, Long Beach Chapter, "Tribute to a Star," *Ninety-Nine News* (Aug.-Sept. 1964), 12.

Champagne, Couscous, and Tea

Saturday, March 28, 9:19 a.m. (Azores Time)
SANTA MARIA

Icy wind whipped trees, flattened grass, and went right through Jerrie's light jacket and skirt.

More importantly, the wind blew directly across her runway. With weak brakes, a crosswind might send Charlie spinning again. Jerrie and the airport officials stood out on the wet concrete, talking it over, until somebody got an idea. Instead of taking off from the runway, they could try using a big ramp, built during the military days for larger planes. From the ramp, Jerrie could take off straight into the wind, if she dared.[283]

The men pushed Charlie up to the ramp. Jerrie squeezed into her cabin and tried to make sense of the big weather folder the men had drawn up for her. Some clouds were drawn and colored green; others red. *Turbulencia moderado* meant "moderate turbulence," okay, and *borrasco* must mean "squall," but she had no idea what the word "RISK" was supposed to tell her. Well, the airport people seemed sure that the cold front coming in would be weak, and she would have five hours to figure out where any dangerous squalls might be. Unless one found her first.[284]

---

[283] Mock, *Three-Eight Charlie*, 66.
[284] Ibid., 67.

As she reached for the door, Negrao ran up to the plane to hand her a huge cardboard box. "We noticed that you have no food. So we fixed a little something."[285]

The "little something" turned out to be a stack of thick sandwiches, cans of tomato juice, a can opener and a souvenir doll for Valerie. She thanked him and looked around for some place in the little cabin to put it. On top of that typewriter, for now.[286]

With everything done, all the goodbyes said, and her passport returned, she could shut her door. At 10:22 a.m., Santa Maria time, only twenty-four hours after touching down in the Azores, she flew Charlie directly into the wind and quickly climbed above the "angry" waves. As she banked left, the wind came in behind her, helping to push her plane toward Africa.[287]

She took it on up to 9,000 feet, above clouds that looked like harmless "whipped cream," but the clouds kept growing taller, as well. Thunderheads began to build, turning bluish-purple, followed by "orange fireworks." That "weak" cold front in her weather folder was building up.[288]

Charlie and Jerrie skimmed over "ripply white cloud waves" and swung around a giant "cloud mushroom." The temperature outside was close to freezing, but inside the cockpit, she stayed warm, ate a big roast beef sandwich, and drank a can of tomato juice.

The clouds kept climbing until she was surrounded again, and getting knocked around. Her instruments kept the plane on

---

[285] Ibid.

[286] Ibid.

[287] Ibid., 68.

[288] Ibid.

course, and she tried to relax. It felt odd to sit in clouds, with nothing to see past the red nose of the plane, and trust this autopilot that Russ found to deliver her. In her head, she knew it was okay, and yet she still began "feeling creepy."[289]

She sensed a "quiver," as the airspeed started to drop again. Out on the strut, more ice.

She grabbed the mike. "Casablanca Radio, this is November One-Five-Three-Eight Charlie. Over."

A "crisp voice with a French accent" came back. "November One-Five-Three-Eight Charlie, this is Casablanca Radio. Go ahead."

"Three-Eight Charlie is picking up wing ice. Request clearance to climb."

"Three-Eight Charlie, Casablanca. Stand by a few minutes."

Helplessly, she watched the ice build up, maybe even faster this time. She pushed in the throttle, making the engine work harder to overcome the extra weight, until she refused to wait any longer. "Three-Eight Charlie needs clearance. I have lots of ice. Please."

The controller calmly told her, "Stand by a few minutes" yet again, but, finally, clearance was granted. She pulled Charlie up to 11,000 feet and sunshine, watching the ice drip and dribble away.[290]

After five hours of flying, she should be within 135 miles of Casablanca, but the white sandy edge of Africa's coastline showed up in the windshield far too soon. That tailwind must have been stronger than the forecast she had been given. She

[289] Ibid., 69.
[290] Ibid., 70.

grabbed the mike to call Casablanca, embarrassed that she was calling in late, by now.[291]

"November-One-Five-Three-Eight Charlie, you're cleared to descend," was all the man said.

Below and straight ahead lay a city that looked white and clean, just like its name. She circled Anfa airport and touched down gently, until the tail vibrated; "up, down and sideways." Another bouncing landing by the "Flying Housewife," in front of another crowd. She was mortified.[292]

But when she got out of the plane, nobody said a word about her rough landing. Instead, she was led quickly into a huge room and seated at a giant table, surrounded by reporters and flashing cameras.

"Do you think it's good for your children for their mother to be gone this long?"

"Do you really think your plane can make it around the world?"

"Do you like the color blue? You wear the same thing in every picture."

She felt like an "animal in a zoo." When she'd had enough, she stood up. "Okay! Can someone direct me toward Customs and Immigration?" She wasn't letting go of her passport this time.[293]

"Mrs. Mock? We got word from Lockbourne Air Force Base that you were coming. Perhaps we could be of some assistance."

A man with graying temples and the corner of a handkerchief in the breast pocket of his suit offered his hand.

---

[291] Ibid.,71.

[292] Ibid.,72.

[293] Ibid.

"I am Henri Richaud, and this is my wife, Renee. Would you care to be our guest in Casablanca?"

Her husband and their associates in the State Department and the military had reached out to people to meet her at her scheduled stops, but she never knew for sure when someone would be there, or if the people would be of any help. Henri's calm voice and elegant French accent sounded promising.

"Can you tell me where to find Customs?" she asked.

Henri smiled. "Allow me to escort you."

The crowd cleared out of their way as Henri and Renee led Jerrie through the airport. "Henri is the control-tower operator," Renee explained. "He'll take you around to all the right people."

The Richauds walked Jerrie through lots of offices, including the *policia*, which made her nervous. But the *policia*, in their little caps and badges, asked only the usual questions:

"Where did you come from?"

"How long will you be staying?"

"Do you know anybody in Casablanca?"

"Are you transporting anything illegal?"

Then they released her. She must not have sounded like a big threat, but it still felt Hollywood-creepy.[294]

Henri and Renee escorted her to their car, which *almost* had room inside for everybody plus everything. They drove through streets *almost* wide enough for the car, plus all the men in turbans and boys on motor scooters honking their horns, along with women walking or riding on the backs of the scooters in tan robes covering everything except their eyes.

---

[294] Ibid.

First stop: the Richauds' home, to celebrate her landing by clinking glasses of French champagne.

Next: out to a restaurant, for a real Moroccan dinner. Dusk was settling in when Richaud opened the car door for her onto a deserted street with no neon or lights in sight. They led her toward a boring office building, indistinguishable from all the others. But once inside, Jerrie stood on a floor of shining black-and-white tile admiring carved Moorish pillars. A string trio played, and one player sang. The music and voice struck Jerrie as a strange blend of Chicago jazz and a scene from a movie she had seen portraying a priest calling the faithful to prayer from a tower.

She sat with the Richauds on silk couches for a dinner of soup, pigeon pie and couscous served on a knee-high table. After dinner, it was off to the airport for a party given in her honor by the Aero Club of Morocco. Henri introduced Jerrie to the president of the Aero Club, a distinguished-looking, white-haired gentleman who was also Jerrie's NAA observer.

After the party, the Richauds drove Jerrie next to the Aero Club president's home for tea, which, Henri Richaud explained in the car, more than once, was an "unusual and great honor."

The president's house was filled with "soft rugs, silk-covered couches and hammered-brass trays." Yet, their host greeted them in his Western-style business suit, same as back at the Aero Club. As they sank into the upholstery, a barefoot servant girl brought tea and cakes.

"When the next reporter asks me why you're doing this," the president said, "what should I tell him?"

She had learned to have an answer ready. "You can tell him I am making this journey to remind everyone not to overlook the little pilot in this jet age that we're in now," Jerrie said. Her host seemed to like that.

The men stood up when the president's wife came in to meet their guests. This striking woman with jet-black hair and amber eyes wore a scarlet satin gown embroidered in gold. She didn't say much, or even make eye contact, and she didn't stay.

When the president's wife left and nobody sat back down, Jerrie said, "It was nice to meet you."

"You must return to Casablanca," he responded.

Everybody seemed to be okay with saying goodnight, and she was relieved to finish socializing.

As they were leaving, Jerrie spotted her hostess, now wearing the customary tan robe. She wondered how many women on the street wore red satin or gold or lace under their tan robes, too.

Back at the Richauds', she was shown to her guest bed in Renee's art studio. Jerrie lay down on the bed surrounded by veiled ladies and dancers who looked as if they had stepped out of a painting by Henri de Toulouse-Lautrec. She quickly slipped into sleep, unbothered by nightmares of thunderheads at sea, but dreamed instead that, "dressed in red satin," she "danced in marble palaces."[295]

---

[295] Ibid., 73-74.

"You Want Me to Fly Through Mountains I Can't See?"

Sunday, March 29, 6:00 a.m. (Greenwich Mean Time)
CASABLANCA, Morocco

In Jules Verne's novel *Around the World in Eighty Days*, Phileas Fogg thought he had failed in his quest to travel around the world in eighty days. He got off the bus in London and walked home in defeat until he saw the day's date. He realized that he had crossed the International Date Line, so he had returned one day ahead of his calculation, and he had actually succeeded.[296]

On this morning, Jerrie woke up at 5:00 a.m., having to remind herself of several things to keep up with, starting with the time.

First, she had to remember that Morocco was on Greenwich Mean Time. To file her flight plan, she could simply write her estimated time of take-off to be the same as theirs, 10:30 a.m., and put the letter "Z" beside it, the shorthand for Zulu, or GMT.

Second, when she filled out the flight plans required at every stop, she would have to write her estimated arrivals and departures in the GMT time zone, but also in military time, so 1:00 p.m. in civilian time would become "13:00 Z."

Finally, she also had to keep in her head that, back in Columbus, Russ was still on Eastern Time, five hours behind

---

[296] "Around the World in Eighty Days by Jules Verne: Plot," *Wikipedia*, 3.

her this point. As she entered each new time zone going forward, he would fall one more hour behind her for most of the rest of her way around the world.

All of that was almost too much to keep up with, and it was only going to get harder. Never mind also trying to guess where Joan might be.[297]

Richaud called the weather bureau as the sun rose out the window. Jerrie eavesdropped from the doorway, trying to follow his end of the conversation, recalling what little French she had picked up in high school. As she recognized the French words for "squall line," "heavy icing," and "severe turbulence," she knew what the verdict would be.

Richaud hung up and shook his head. "I'm very sorry, madam. Not even the commercial planes are taking off today."

Losing an entire day would hurt her in the race, but she could sleep in and then go out and see Casablanca! Getting to sightsee was what she wanted most anyway, even if she could never say that out loud.[298]

But before she could get back in that warm bed, Russ called. "I'm glad I finally got you. When I tried to reach you on the Azores, I got an operator who asked just what part of the Ozarks I thought Santa Maria was in. How is the airplane doing?"

"Fine, except for the brakes," she said. "I thought new brakes were put on the plane in Wichita. At Santa Maria, a mechanic said they looked real old and bad."

"I guess I forgot to tell you. The new wheels couldn't be put on because the axles had been changed. So they just put tires on

---

[297] "NAA: Summary;" Mock, interview, Dec. 3, 2007.
[298] Mock, *Three-Eight Charlie*, 75.

the old wheels. But didn't they change the brakes? They knew you needed them."

"I'd sure like to know what happened in Wichita. Now every little bit of braking is gone."

"Maybe you can find parts someplace," was all Russ said about that. "I was so worried when you were out over the ocean," he went on, "but the Air Force kept track of you. Some guys took me out to dinner to calm me down with martinis, and when I got back, my mother was sitting up in her robe and said General Strauss had called to tell us you passed by *Echo*. Every hour after that, Dick Lassiter at the Pentagon called with a new position report."

"Those poor people! I don't like to cause so much trouble," Jerrie said.

She realized now that the ocean station *did* track her on radar, as they should have. But instead of answering her on the radio directly, they had reported her whereabouts to her husband. So she was being watched, all along the way. Evidently, they only talked to her when they felt like it.

"Just get going," Russ urged, as usual. "Joan's on her way to Africa."

"Then let me get off the phone, so I can go back to the airport."[299]

The Richauds drove her along a broad street, passing by the surf as it pounded onto white, clean sand she had never pictured before as a part of the landscape of Africa.

---

[299] Ibid., 75-77.

At Anfa airport, everything was closed, and they couldn't find a mechanic. Even in this country that she had thought was Muslim, they were celebrating Easter Sunday.[300]

Monday, March 30, 8:00 a.m. (GMT/"Z" Time)

Next morning, the clouds were still building up out there.

"Perhaps it is possible to fly to Tunis," Richaud told Jerrie.

She rode with him back to the airport to see if anyone could come up with a safe route through the clouds and passes in the Atlas Mountains.

The weather station was set up with state-of-the-art equipment, and full of busy men. She was handed a weather map with wind speeds and directions marked by "little purple flags." Richaud helped translate their French coming out thick and fast. The more she heard, the less she liked. It sounded as if their weather report included severe turbulence, a squall line headed directly across her flight path, and–

"Henri, did he say ice?" Jerrie asked. "I don't like the sound of that." When she spoke, everybody looked up. If they didn't understand English, maybe they heard the tension in the American woman's voice.

"Yes, but you won't be in ice all the time," Henri said. "The freezing level is about 9,000 feet."

"I'll have to fly pretty high to clear the mountains," Jerrie said. "I had enough ice out over the Atlantic. At least out there, you don't have anything to run into. I won't fly by instrument, either, not through mountains I've never seen before. What is the visibility ceiling under the clouds? Can I fly visual?"

---

[300] Ibid., 77.

Richaud looked over the charts, maps and figures. "Well, maybe yes, maybe no. They have radioed to Taza, the highest part of the pass." He pointed out a river valley zigzagging between mountain ridges. "If it's okay there, you can go."

Jerrie looked over all his maps and charts, and paced and worried, until one man got up from the radio and walked over, talking and nodding.

Richaud translated. "It's okay. The cloud ceiling is 1,000 feet. You'll be all right."

"Wait a minute, now," Jerrie said, putting her finger on his chart. "There at the station, by the river, it's 1,000 feet. But the ground rises on both sides, so the ceiling is lower around the high ground. Just one narrow part has 1,000 feet. And what if some clouds are lower than others?"

"Then fly lower," Henri said.

"Too many unknowns here," she said, getting worried again. "Using your method, I'm liable to run into a mountain!"

"You'll be flying visual. You can *see* them."

"Look." She commanded the attention of a roomful of men who had never seen a female pilot before, had never taken orders from any woman, and couldn't understand a word she said. "Sometimes it can be clear to 1,000 feet, and then just a few miles later the clouds can be back down to 500. And I don't have a co-pilot or all the instruments that the big commercial planes have. It's just me. I know of pilots back home who are dead because they trusted a weather report. I'm not afraid to make a 'one-eighty' because of weather, but not into a mountain I can't see!"

Richaud translated her concerns into French. Everybody tried to think of something. She thought she heard somebody call her a *"froussard"* (chicken). Good thing Russ wasn't with her.

Then one of the weathermen started talking. If not the mountains, then what about heading north to the Mediterranean and then along the coast? She might hit rain, but not ice.

"Fine. I'll try that."

Everybody looked relieved. Jerrie hurried off to take care of last-minute errands at Customs and Immigration.

Just when she thought everything was ready, a man ran up to her. "Mrs. Mock? The man must speak with you, *si vous plait*?"

Jerrie went back to hear what the meteorologist had to say this time.

"It is not possible to fly to Tunis over the ocean VFR [visual flight rules]. You will not arrive until after dark."

Flying at night meant she would have to navigate by instrument again, and tonight, it also meant flying through thunderstorms, over mountains, and into heavy ice. Refusing to risk all that might force her to cancel and lose yet *another* day.

He continued, "But let me show you something else." He pointed to a name on his map: Bône, Algeria. If she rushed through filling out a new flight plan, packing, and pre-flighting her plane, she could just barely make it before sunset to some airstrip she "had never heard of," landing conditions unknown.[301]

PARAMARIBO, Surinam, 7:12 a.m. (Atlantic Time)

Finally, after six days and 300 precious dollars, the tanks were replaced and filled up, and Joan was ready to get going– except for one thing. Making her pre-flight inspection, just before sunrise, she noticed that her fire extinguisher was missing. It wasn't as if she could just go pick one up at the store.

---

[301] Ibid., 81-83.

She would have to find one somewhere at another stop.[302] She took off at dawn and flew straight into the next trouble.[303]

She was flying into the rainy season of South America. She had determined all along to follow Earhart's route as closely as she could. This meant she would fly through the Intertropical Convergence Zone. Along the equator, the weather would be the worst.[304]

The weather reports she got for that day had forecast only light activity. Yet after only an hour in the air, visibility directly ahead began to disappear into a jungle fog. The clouds steadily grew and became more distinct, extending from her windshield in both directions.

As Joan watched the clouds grow larger and thicker, she knew that flying by sight would get harder, and so would maintaining radio contact. Her little twin-engine plane would get knocked around, and crashes were common. Best to fly under or over a cloud, if she could.

As she flew into the airspace of French Guiana, a front of boiling thunderclouds reaching 50,000 feet blocked her path, and her plane could only climb to 25,000. First, she tried zigzagging under them. She took the plane down to 500 feet, racing against time, never knowing when the rain and lightning would hit her. Through the rain slamming onto the windshield and the gray fog beyond, the horizon ahead kept disappearing, yet she couldn't afford to lose track of that vague, distant line.

By now, she was flying by instrument and watching each needle, second by second. If anything failed, there was no place

---

[302] Brown, *Fate*, 125.

[303] Merriam, "I Flew," 79.

[304] Merriam, "Longest Flight," 46.

to set down for miles. At 300 feet, she could see the green jungle below. No landing strips anywhere in sight, of course. Not even any open space. "I knew that if I were forced down here, my chances of getting out alive were awfully slim."[305]

CASABLANCA, Morocco, 10:02 a.m. (GMT/"Z")

Jerrie ran back to the airfield, threw everything on board and made a hasty preflight inspection. Okay, ready to skip town. Except, where was Henri Richaud with her papers? The president of the Aero Club had to sign her papers for the NAA. She had last seen Richaud and his wife in the terminal. She ran back there. Nowhere in sight. Finally, she walked back to the plane, and sat down, fighting back tears. If they didn't show up, she wouldn't even make it to Bône. But she *had* to have those papers.[306]

Over northern BRAZIL, 11:40 a.m. (Atlantic Time)

Across the Atlantic, Joan had no way of knowing about Jerrie's next impasse, and even if she had, she wouldn't have wasted a second thinking about it. She was busy bringing her plane down, down, down until she was flying just above the canopy of the Amazon rainforest and just below the clouds, fighting to see through the rain, and trying to figure out how to get out of this mess, *now*.[307]

---

[305] Merriam, "I Flew," 79.

[306] Mock, *Three-Eight Charlie*, 83.

[307] Merriam, "I Flew," 79.

CASABLANCA, late morning ("Z")

Jerrie was about to give up when she spotted Richaud, walking across the pavement with the president of the Aero Club and James F. Green, the American consul general.

"We've been waiting by the car," Richaud explained.

"Mr. Green, I'm pleased to meet you," Jerrie said, handing him the typewriter. "Would you send this home for me?"

The Aero Club president had her papers ready. She said her goodbyes, and took off.[308]

Over BRAZIL, 12:26 p.m. (Atlantic Time)

There was no way Joan was going to get through this storm, all the way to Natal. She flew along the Amazon River, so wide that it sometimes looked like a lake. She followed its lazy, brown curves downstream, then angled right to follow the south fork toward the big Brazilian city of Belem. Her charts said it was ahead somewhere.[309]

As she descended out of the thunderclouds and drew closer to her destination, the humidity grew worse until sweat took over every inch of her body. She couldn't get a full breath without coughing so hard it felt as if her lungs were ripping out. She tried taking shallow breaths instead, but that made her dizzy.[310] Somewhere along the way she crossed the equator, but at the moment, she didn't notice. She was too busy keeping an eye out for where she might have to make a forced landing, and

---

[308] Mock, *Three-Eight Charlie*, 83.

[309] Merriam, "I Flew," 79.

[310] Merriam, "Longest Flight," 46.

the river looked like her only choice. "One thing never left my mind: those alligators."[311]

Over the MEDITERRANEAN, 10:43 a.m. (Z)

Jerrie flew along the African coast in bright sunlight, passing over the city of Rabat, followed by green fields, villages, mountain ridges and terraced vineyards. Then heavy mist moved in, blotting out the sunshine, forcing her to turn out from land, and drop low over waves that seemed to build and grow darker with each mile. She flew close enough to the mountains to double-check her position, but stayed far enough out to avoid any surprise peaks in the mist.

The Sahara had to be just a few miles off her right wing, but all of that was hidden by fog. She counted each dip and bend in the shoreline and kept a finger on her position on one of her charts. Her radio picked up the signal from Bône, *dah-dit-dit-dit, dah-dah-dah,* or "Bravo Oscar." She only had to bank around the next ridge to come in view of the airport.[312]

COLUMBUS, Ohio, 11:38 a.m. (Eastern Time)

When Russ couldn't get in touch with Jerrie, he tried sending telegrams to destinations ahead of her:

AMERICAN EMBASSY NEW DELHI – JERRIE MOCK BEHIND SCHEDULE BADLY AROUND THE WORLD FLIGHT **STOP** CAN YOU ARRANGE PERMISSION FLIGHT DIRECT KARACHI **STOP** NO LANDING DELHI

---

[311] Merriam, "I Flew," 79.
[312] Ibid.

STOP CAN ANYTHING BE DONE EXPEDITE CUSTOMS **STOP** MUCH AT STAKE **STOP**[313]

Over the coast of ALGERIA, mid-afternoon (Z)

That next airport was so close, yet, oh, so far away. A "purple-black thunderhead" sat right in Jerrie's flight path, with lightning flashing in her windshield. All she could do was close her eyes through each crackle of lightning and fly in a big loop around the cloud, waiting for the storm to move on. It didn't. She circled the storm cloud again. Then, again. No matter how many times she circled, the storm still kept her from getting through to the airport. The sun would be setting soon. After dark, she would lose sight of the shore.[314]

She circled the bay and the cloud for forty-five more minutes. She had been in the air over five hours. This day was getting "long."

Finally, the heavy rain and lightning inched just a little farther along the coast. She could bank the plane around the last hills and follow the needles toward Les Salines Airport.

"Three-Eight Charlie, you are cleared to land." The magic words came through with a pleasant French accent. As she approached the airport, the last rays of the setting sun broke through the dissolving clouds, giving the coastal town a soft glow. "White ships in the harbor, shiny tin rooftops, and bright green palms shimmered against a dark purple sky. The rain-swept runway looked like a golden finger."[315]

---

[313] Russell Mock to American Embassy New Delhi, telegram, March 30, 1964, from Jerrie's private collection, copy given to the author.
[314] Mock, *Three-Eight Charlie*, 85.
[315] Ibid.

Without *too* many bumps, she brought the plane down, then taxied to a terminal that looked calm and quiet; no crowds or reporters or cameras, only a couple of men showing her where to park.

A Shell truck pulled up and pumped in gas right away, but the driver had to fill out a form about her international flight, saying where she had come from and where she was going. What he put down was "Vertical Tunis (Cairo)," which made no sense to her. "Maybe someone in some grubby bureaucratic office got a feeling of deep satisfaction out of it."[316]

Then she looked around and discovered that there was no hangar, and no place to tie Charlie down. The two men who guided her in had an anxious debate about how to secure her light plane against the wind. She was relieved they knew to be careful about that. Plus, she had learned to bring something along for this situation.

On that flight into Mexico, years before, she needed ropes to tie her plane down in Acapulco, so she asked for *"ropas,"* but nobody got her any; they just stood there looking lost. Pointing to her plane and shouting *"Ropas!"* eventually produced some *"cordas."* Next day she saw the word *ropa* translated on a laundry list at her hotel. She had been shouting for clothes. [317]

Still, that episode also taught her to bring her own tie-down ropes and three rods to hold the plane down. The catch was, they didn't have any open ground. The only available dirt was covered by a metal ramp with some openings in its latticework on the side.

---

[316] Ibid.
[317] Ibid., 86.

One man tried to stick Jerrie's rod through a hole in the latticework of the ramp. The rod bent, then broke. He tossed it away, picked up a second rod and tried again. Eventually, he got it through a hole, bent it under a metal strip, and up through another hole. They tied two ropes to the plane and held the tail rope down with a rock. Now her plane would stay put tonight, but with only one straight rod left for every other stop around the planet.[318]

With the plane secure, she was off to Customs and Immigration and to find out how the next round of rules and questions would be different in *this* country.

Somewhere over BRAZIL, early afternoon (Atlantic Time)

Joan finally started picking up the control tower of Belem on her radio. Through the drenching rain, she spotted a small, light-colored airfield completely surrounded by jungle.[319] "The runway was pitted with holes, but it seemed like the sweetest airport I had ever seen." She landed just minutes ahead of a downpour that closed the field.[320]

---

[318] Ibid.

[319] Brown, *Fate*, 59.

[320] Merriam, "I Flew," 79.

We Don't Take American Express

Monday, March 30, evening (West Africa Time)
BÔNE, Algeria

Jerrie was handed a stack of forms to fill out. She dutifully told the good men of the Customs and Immigration Department of Algeria whatever they wanted to know. She was asked to divulge everything from the maiden name of her grandmother to her occupation. For occupation, she wrote "housewife."

As she handed each form back, it was read, then handed over to someone else, then someone else. Most of it was quickly skimmed, until the three men got to the word "housewife." That seemed to be a problem. A couple more guys came over to discuss it. She couldn't tell what they thought she said she was, but they did not like that word.

One official hurried off and came back with another man in a khaki uniform spoke enough English to point to "housewife" and ask, "Madam, don't you want to change this?" Somehow, "housewife" kept getting re-interpreted as "madam of the house," and that phrase just wouldn't do. She changed it to "mother," and that seemed to be the end of it.[321]

The official at the next table waved his hand at Jerrie's purse until she opened it. He kept waving until she started pulling things out, then he looked over every item. He shook his head at her lipstick and hairbrush, but he nodded at her wallet, so she

---

[321] Mock, *Three-Eight Charlie*, 86-87.

pulled out money. He shook his head at the francs and the marks, but nodded at a US dollar bill. He waved his hand until she counted out the American dollars in her pocketbook. Nobody had ever asked that before, but okay, fine. The total–she counted as he watched–came to thirty-six dollars.[322]

Her new translator offered her a ride to a hotel, and she was happy to accept. He drove along the only street with lights, so she didn't get to see much, to the Grand Hotel d'Orient. He escorted her into the lobby, and explained in French who Jerrie was to an elderly gentleman sitting at a table.

The man at the table handed over some papers, and her airport companion helped her sign in. Then he asked for her Algerian currency.

"I don't have any," she said, "but I can cash a traveler's check."

As she pulled out her American Express traveler's checks, the older gentleman behind the table said, "No." He only had enough money to exchange five dollars, but the smallest American Express check was for ten.

"But madam," her translator said, "you must eat dinner. And there is no food here." He waved across the empty lobby and shrugged. "You see. So you *must* have money."

Jerrie looked around. The only people around were this old man and a small boy standing beside him. Travel on this side of the world wasn't turning out quite the way it looked in the travel posters.

"Madam, you must have some francs to buy food," her translator said, "and the banks are all closed. But I will help

---

[322] Ibid., 87.

you. If you have some American dollars, I will give you francs. Only enough for dinner. Even for one dollar I could go to jail. But you must eat. Yes?"

He must be planning to sell any dollars he got from her on the black, or "informal," market. Some countries were more stringent about that than others, and she didn't want any trouble, but she *was* starving. She found three dollars U.S to give him. He handed over a few francs and said goodnight, leaving her alone with people who spoke no English at all, in a hotel showing no sign of having any other guests.[323]

The little boy picked up her overnight bag and led her up a flight of stairs to a room with an old-fashioned toilet with a box above it and a cord she had to pull to make it flush. She went to the sink, splashed some water on her face, and tried to get up the nerve for the next adventure of the evening. To find food, she would have to go back out, act confident, walk, and see if she could recall any French from high school.

She tried asking the old man in the lobby. *"Où se trouve un restaurant?"*

He glanced in her general direction, nodded, stood, walked across the lobby and out the same door that she had come in, then waved vaguely down a street.

She took a deep breath and set out in that direction.

At the next corner, she spotted a "Café" sign in a window and walked in. Every seat in this café was occupied by a man wearing a turban and robe, sipping a drink. No food, or women, in sight. The manager spotted her immediately and walked her quickly back out to his front door. When she tried her French,

---

[323] Ibid., 87-88.

he seemed relieved to hear that all she wanted was dinner. Evidently, a woman walking alone in the evening had aroused his suspicion.[324]

The manager pointed around a corner and down the next street. It looked dark, but she gathered her courage and walked, straying farther and farther from the lights of the boulevard, or any restaurants. The people passing wore robes and veils, and they all ignored her. Each street she crossed looked narrower, still.

Two boys, maybe ten years old, began tagging along behind her, whispering excitedly in French, evidently fascinated by this American woman in a blouse and skirt. Eventually, they tried to talk to her. She tried to respond. *"Où est un restaurante?"*

Recognition appeared in their faces. They turned a corner and walked down a side street. After a few *more* turns, they led her right to the Café Moulin Rouge. She found an American dime to give to each one.

In this café, people were actually eating, including a woman who didn't wear a veil. Jerrie took a seat and looked over the menu. She could recognize the words for a couple of the vegetables and meats, but she had no idea how the chef had prepared them. She tried asking for a recommendation, but couldn't get that idea across, so she just pointed to items on the menu and took her chances. What she got was "mystery soup, meat, fish, vegetables and sauce." It wasn't bad. She couldn't trust the water, so she tried a little *vin rouge* instead, and she must have had enough francs.[325]

---

[324] Ibid., 88.
[325] Ibid., 89.

After dinner, she somehow remembered her way through the shadows back to the Grand Hotel d'Orient. She washed out her same old white blouse and blue cotton skirt, and hung them up to drip-dry, which was the best she could do to be ready for the next photographer. She took one last look at the empty street out her window then quickly fell into a deep sleep.

A harsh ring went off in the dark. Ignoring it didn't do any good. She stumbled out of bed and slapped around for the light. High up on the wall, almost out of reach, was an old-fashioned black telephone with a big annoying bell.

"Mrs. Jerrie Mock, please?"

"Huh, what? Yes."

"Mrs. Mock, this is the overseas operator in New York. Please hold the line. I have a call from Mr. Mock."

"Jerrie, is that you?"

"Oh! You! What do you want at this time of night?"

"Jerrie, what are you doing in Bône? Why didn't you go to Tunis?"

"What am I doing in Bône? Trying to sleep!"

"Well, give me a story. The papers say Joan's covering 2,000 miles a day. You have to go farther."

"Look, after the day I just put in, I wish I never had to see an airplane again. And I don't care *where* Joan is. The weather's not fit for flying over here, they do everything wrong, and if you call me again to talk about Joan, I'll come home on an airliner!" She slammed the receiver as hard as she could, but it was so high on the wall, she couldn't get real muscle into the bang.[326]

---

[326] Ibid., 90.

BELEM, Brazil

The *Honolulu Advertiser* ran an article two days later.

Belem (UPI). Joan Merriam Smith made an emergency landing here Monday (March 30) because of bad weather over the Amazon jungle. She had planned to land in Natal. When surprised citizens learned she was here, a rally quickly formed in her honor and she was accorded a heroine's welcome. "This adventure is one of my biggest dreams," she told the cheering crowd. She said the emergency landing was the twenty-eighth she had made in her career.[327]

---

[327] "Girl Fliers Slowed by Setbacks," Honolulu *Advertiser*, April 1, 1964.

Smells Like Something's Burning

Tuesday, March 31, 5:30 a.m. (West Africa Time)
BÔNE, Algeria

"Naaa!" The complaint of a goat pulled Jerrie out of what could have turned into a good, deep sleep. Last night, the street below her window had looked like a "black, empty canyon." Now it sounded full: salesmen shouting, bicyclists ringing their little bells, car horns honking, chickens clucking. She staggered out of bed to pull back the curtain and blink at crowds of vague silhouettes, jostling back and forth in the gray dawn. Naptime was over.

As she dressed, a question floated into her head: Just how, exactly, had Russ found her? If Russ got his last word from the Pentagon, then they must have found her here, too. Hmm. She was thankful for all the help from the US Air Force, but she wasn't sure just how they kept track of a traveling woman's hotel room, or why.

Downstairs, her translator was up and waiting to give her a ride to the airfield. As he drove, the dark city gave way to countryside. Palm trees, flat-roofed houses, men walking donkey and wooden cart at sunrise looked like a "Christmas card," and she felt as if she had "been there before."[328]

At the airport terminal, her translator gave her the bill for all of her airport fees, plus the hotel bill. She owed him a grand

---

[328] Mock, *Three-Eight Charlie*, 91-92; Mock, interview, Dec. 11, 2007.

total of nine dollars US. Again, she tried to write a traveler's check for ten dollars, and again he tried to refuse it.

"I could go to jail for this, you know," he said. "But I had to help you." All she knew was that when he said "jail," other people could hear. She insisted he keep the ten-dollar traveler's check. From his disappointed face, it looked as if he had rather have gotten the nine American dollars.[329]

Time to move on to her next obstacle: the bureaucrats of their Flight Service Station. Her translator escorted her into a big room with a long, high counter and five men sitting up behind it, talking in French. Her companion helped interpret, but some things got "lost in translation."

The man in charge had his own ideas about where this foreign pilot ought to land and how much gas she ought to carry. Then they wanted her to tell them exactly how long her flight would take. She responded that depended on the weather. A tailwind would speed her up; a headwind would slow her down.

Checking the weather appeared to be a novel idea to them. Evidently, in this part of the world, pilots just filed a flight plan, took off, and showed up late or early, depending on the wind. Then her translator smiled. "*Oui*, madam, what an excellent idea. We go to the meteorology."[330]

He led Jerrie down the hall to the meteorology room. They arrived just as the weathermen were showing up for work. Men came in shaking hands and saying their good mornings. People kept coming in, and everybody asked about everybody's health, while Jerrie could only sit and watch the sun climb the sky.

---

[329] Ibid., 93.
[330] Ibid., 94.

Eventually this new group seemed to grasp the idea that the American woman wanted the weather report from Bône to Cairo. Once they understood, they settled down to work, drawing clouds and diagrams of wind currents at different altitudes and checking ground stations on her flight path. They all thought the weather would be fine. Even some sandstorms coming up were "nothing to worry about."

Sandstorms? She had been warned that sandstorms could peel the paint off a plane, reduce visibility from 100 miles to zero, blast her windshield to an opaque "milk-glass white," or clog her air intake until her engine quit in mid-air. Jerrie had never heard of a "good" sandstorm. Maybe this was another day to sightsee. The delay would mean getting yelled at over the phone again, but Russ was 5,000 miles behind her. Those sandstorms were straight ahead.

Despite the language barrier, she figured out that they had no weather report for Cairo. She was told they didn't get weather from that far away.

Yet her translator didn't seem bothered. With "a smile like a connoisseur approving a vintage wine," he simply said, "Ah-h-h, Cairo. She is *always* good." Then he took her by the arm. "Come, madam. Now we finish the flight plan." They said their goodbyes to the weather staff, and returned to Flight Service.[331]

At the Flight Service Station, the head Air Traffic Controller of Bône, Algeria, dictated what he wanted her to write on her own flight plan. If she didn't see the sense of it, well, *"C'est la vie."*

---

[331] Ibid., 95-96.

She had to play along, so she started writing. He told her to put Tripoli as the next place she would land.

Jerrie looked up. "No, I want to go to Cairo."

"But first you go to Tripoli."

"I don't want to go to Tripoli."

"Everyone goes to Tripoli."

"But I want to go to Cairo."

"You can get gasoline in Tripoli."

"I have plenty."

The head Air Traffic Controller scratched "his gray, curly head," evidently wondering "what to do with this strange female" who wouldn't cooperate. He looked at the five men sitting behind him, as if hoping they had any ideas, but nobody said a word.

"Tell you what. You go to Tripoli. If you don't want to land, you call the tower and tell them you are not landing. *Then* you go to Cairo."

He looked so happy with his plan that she "gave up arguing." Her flight plan for this trip over the desert got written up, down to the listing of the life raft and life jacket as "emergency equipment."[332]

Everything was just about to get moving when a tall young man walked in. He wore sunglasses and a leather jacket, like an old-school pilot. Whoever he was, he walked up to Jerrie, looked over her shoulder, pointed at the sandstorms on her papers, and shouted "*Madame! Non, non, non!*"

The man who had said there was nothing to worry about began arguing with the man in the leather jacket. They walked

---

[332] Ibid., 96.

to a corner of the room for a heated, hand-waving discussion about sand. Eventually, the "nothing to worry about" guy seemed to win and they all wanted her off to Cairo. After all that, Jerrie wanted to go back to her hotel room.

She tried not to think about sandstorms as she boarded the plane and made all the adjustments to her wing angles and everything else, pre-flight. She was reaching for the starter button, when her interpreter rapped on her door.

"Madam, you can *not* go to Cairo. Very bad sandstorms. You must land in Tripoli."

Now she really wanted to go back to the hotel. Maybe she *should* take a jet home. But if she left the country without her plane, she could be questioned for attempted smuggling.

"Okay, okay, OKAY! I will go to Tripoli! I will land at Tripoli! I will not go to Cairo! Tell Cairo to forget me!" She was "almost screaming" at the man as the propeller kicked over.[333]

BELEM, Brazil, in the middle of the night (Atlantic Time)

Joan sat up in bed. *That* was a party. The good people of Belem had pulled out some of their headdresses and drums from last month's Carnival, poured into the street, and danced in the rain, just because some California girl had dropped in on them.

Now she just had to figure out what woke her. The only sound was a parrot or some bird she had never heard before, but it was away from her window, out in the trees beyond her room and the airstrip, not annoying at all.

---

[333] Ibid., 97.

That was it: What had awakened her was that the rain had actually, finally come to a stop. After six days, she just might get to leave the continent.[334]

Over ALGERIA, 9:29 a.m. (West Africa Time)

After Jerrie got up in the air, things began to look better. As she angled away from the Mediterranean Sea to head over the Atlas Mountains, she got sunshine, cliffs and terraced vineyards. Then all signs of life faded away until there was nothing to see except "rocks and sand."[335]

Checking her instruments, she caught that the radio antenna had trailed out all 100 feet. She must have bumped the switch with her knee, getting in. She hit the switch to reel the antenna in and went back to looking over the desert, daydreaming about spice traders and caravans, and wondering when she would get that camel ride she had wanted since poring over those pictures in her first childhood geography book.

Wait! What was that smell? *Smoldering rubber insulation.* While she was daydreaming, the motor to the antenna kept turning, trying to reel in the wire long after it had been rolled up tight. She fumbled for the switch and turned it off, but the overheated antenna motor would still need to cool off, and it was situated right next to a tank full of gas and fumes. Were there sparks? Burning wires? How much heat could the thin aluminum wall of the tank absorb before those fumes ignited?

---

[334] "Girl Fliers Slowed by Setbacks," Honolulu *Advertiser*, April 1, 1964.
[335] Mock, *Three-Eight Charlie*, 97.

"The airplane could blow up at any second. Charlie and I would be scattered over the Libyan desert. Nobody would ever know what happened."[336]

She fought the panic. "If I had had a parachute, I probably would have jumped."[337] Trying to land in the sand could set off an explosion. Even if she made it, the plane might sink into sand over the wheels. She couldn't touch anything electrical, including the radio, and without the trailing antenna, nobody could hear her call. Even if someone heard, how could they help?

She forced herself to sit, keep flying, and hope that everything would simply cool off. Doing nothing was hard. "The Lord is my shepherd. . . ." Out came as many of the words of the Twenty-Third Psalm as she could remember.[338]

Little by little the burning smell began to fade away. Charlie went on flying, the sun went on shining, and Jerrie went on breathing.

Repairing the radio would require taking a gas tank back out again, and that would have to wait until she got American help, which wouldn't be until Manila, still a week ahead, at least. The antenna motor might not be salvageable. But those worries would still be there tomorrow. Today, it was enough to be alive.[339]

NATAL, Brazil, 10:00 a.m. (Atlantic Time)

With the sky over Belem clearing out and with help from several cups of locally grown coffee clearing her head, too, Joan

---

[336] Ibid., 98.

[337] Ibid., 99.

[338] Ibid; Mock, interview, Dec. 17, 2007.

[339] Ibid, 100.

was in the air again and headed for Natal.[340]

After flying around a few storms, she approached Natal with great expectations. In Natal, Pan Am had built some nice hospitality quarters for their pilots and flight attendants. A girl might get a hot meal, a conversation with someone from the States, maybe even a chance to do laundry. That was her hope, anyway, until that afternoon, when the airfield came into view.

At Agosto Severo Airport, she spotted planes on the ground that were not private planes or regular commercial aircraft. Large and dull green, with swivel guns mounted in the nose and tail, they bore the blue circle and yellow-green star of the Brazilian Air Force. Other aircraft were scattered around the field. Married to a military man, Joan recognized an old B-25 from World War II as well as P-38 and AT-6 aircraft. What were all these military aircraft doing there?[341]

---

[340] Merriam, "I Flew," 79.
[341] Merriam, "Longest Flight," 46; Claude Meunier, "Joan Merriam Smith: 2. The Flight," Soloflights Around the World, accessed October 1, 2013.

The King's Pajamas

LIBYA, 1:00 p.m. (West Africa Time)

With the smell gradually clearing out, Charlie kept flying along just fine. Jerrie passed over a rocky coastline, the "deep blue water" of the Gulf of Gabes, the island of Djerba Mellita that Odysseus was said to have visited, and on to Tripoli.[342]

Coming in to the airport of the co-capital of a country, she braced herself. More crowds, reporters, and questions would be coming at her soon.

Yet the British-sounding air traffic man from the Tripoli tower talked to Jerrie over her radio often and without hurry, as if he had not much else going on. She landed and turned into the parking area. There was only one other plane out there.

She shut off the engine and opened her door. Across an empty stretch of concrete stood a few buildings and the control tower, nearly a mile away. Beyond them, only flat sand. Everything was still, even the air.

She was afraid to step onto foreign soil without an okay from anyone official, but the sun bearing down on the metal plane quickly rendered the cabin uninhabitable. She climbed down, but stayed put in the shade under the plane's wing. Time for that world-famous blue skirt to "attract some attention."[343]

---

[342] Mock, *Three-Eight Charlie*, 100.

[343] Mock, *Three-Eight Charlie*, 101; Mock, interview, Dec. 17, 2007.

NATAL, Brazil, 3:00 p.m. (Atlantic Time)

When Joan stepped down from her plane, she was escorted by an armed guard into the terminal. Brazilian soldiers marched around in all directions, looking important and yet distracted, in their helmets, greens, and boots. Something was up, but it didn't seem to have much to do with her.

"Mrs. Smith?"

A gentleman wearing a badge with the American flag and eagle clipped to his lapel walked up. "Frank Walton, US Consulate."[344]

"What's going on?"

"President Goulart is reconsidering his future." Walton's fingers at Joan's elbow guided her gently around a corner and over to a wall, where he leaned in and spoke softly. "And the military has agreed to assume command."

"This is a *revolution*?"

"You need to leave Brazil immediately."

So much for a real dinner or a hotel bed. Joan was allowed to walk through the cafeteria line in the officer's quarters at the airport and was escorted to another small room. Armed guards stayed posted outside her door all night.[345]

TRIPOLI, Libya, 1:47 p.m. (West Africa Time)

No response from any direction. Jerrie walked around Charlie, sipped some very warm water, and wiped the sweat off her face with tissues.

Okay! Time to go someplace. She gathered up her papers, purse and walked. The only signage in sight seemed to be in

---

[344] Merriam, "I Flew," 79.
[345] Merriam, "I Flew," 79; Brown, *Fate*, 59.

Italian. The voice from the control tower had spoken English. May as well try there.[346]

After a hike across blistering concrete and a climb up three flights of stairs, she found a room full of men. A tall one with a neatly trimmed moustache turned to her. "Can we help you?"

"Good afternoon. Could you gentlemen direct me to Customs and Immigration?"

Everyone stopped what they were doing, looking puzzled, until the tall one said,

"Would you care to sit down?"

Only then could she begin finding out what was going on. The ATC man told her what he knew. Bône, despite their insistence that she go to Tripoli, had never transmitted her flight plan on to them, so nobody in Tripoli had been expecting her. She hadn't faced Customs or Immigration yet because they hadn't been told that she had crossed a border. And, "the sandstorms still ahead are indeed bad. You should spend the night here."

"Can I at least get an oil change?"

"We can find someone to look over your plane for you," the ATC man said. "Now come with me."

He gave her a ride in a jeep over to Immigration, where it took him a while to explain her situation, in Italian, to the officer.

She passed through Customs and Immigration to be led next to a man who wanted to count her money. Not just American money, this time, but every "dollar, pound, peso, franc, piaster, escudo, traveler's check, and letter of credit."[347] But, he couldn't

---

[346] Mock, *Three-Eight Charlie*, 101; Mock, interview, Feb. 18, 2008.
[347] Ibid., 102.

write any of it down, because he didn't seem to have a pen. Jerrie handed him one. When he was done, he put her pen in his pocket. Jerrie didn't say anything.

The ATC man called a cab and gave the driver the name of a hotel. Although reluctant to be separated from him, all Jerrie could do was thank the man for his help and get in the cab.

The cab driver took off *way* too fast, just missing people and carts on either side of the road. Jerrie held on and kept her mouth shut. When the driver came to a stop, she quickly paid what he asked and got out.

The Libya Palace Hotel looked brand new. The man at the desk spoke English, and he accepted her traveler's check. Her upstairs room turned out to be spacious and it had a bathroom with no surprises. Out the window, giant freighters and elegant yachts sat in a harbor. The next building over had a walled-in garden, where Jerrie could see down onto flowers and a pair of bright red pajamas hanging out to dry. Within the wall, soldiers walked sentry duty.

Jerrie went downstairs and asked. "Could you please tell me, what is this building between the waterfront and the hotel?"

"That is the palace of the Rey."

She went back to her room, snapped a photo of the King's pajamas, then changed out of her skirt into a short-sleeved, sheer green dress she had packed for an occasion such as this warm day. She came back downstairs, determined to sightsee, and maybe even find a market.

From the hotel, she guessed left and started walking past the waterfront. Within a block of the hotel, the pavement of the sidewalk and the street gave way to sand and gravel. The street narrowed, becoming a tiny alley, with sand crowning in the middle, perhaps for rain runoff, and lined with wooden stalls offering food that didn't smell right. The women kept their bodies and faces covered with a big white sheet they held together with both hands. Whenever Jerrie approached a Libyan woman, she pulled her sheet tight over her face.

Yet when men walked toward Jerrie, "they insisted on [taking] their half out of the middle"[348] and *also* around a pile of sand crowned down the center, besides. *She* had step aside for *them*, edging her into the next smelly stall. When one man riding a horse pulled the reins to guide his mount around the sand and straight toward her, she gave up her shopping day and went back to the hotel.[349]

In the lobby, Jerrie spotted a woman in a sleeveless blouse and big sunglasses, drinking a Coke. She and Jerrie recognized each other as Americans right away.

"The men out there are trying to run me into the gutter!" Jerrie blurted.

The woman in sunglasses laughed. "They just don't like women who don't wear sheets. I tried driving out there, but they force me off the road."

So much for sightseeing, Jerrie thought.

"My husband has another one of his business trips, and he brought me along," the woman said. Jerrie was invited to join a group of American oilmen and wives for dinner at the hotel. Over her first meal in forty-eight hours, Jerrie listened to stories of how these men had survived in the desert, answered their questions about her journey, and listened to their opinions

[348] Mock, *Three-Eight Charlie,* 103.
[349] Ibid.

about how she should manage things. They insisted she had overpaid for her cab ride to the hotel, and they also insisted she shouldn't fly over water on her route the next day.

She thanked them all, said goodnight, and went upstairs to sit by her hotel room window for moment before getting into bed.

The phone did not ring. She watched the King's guards swing their lanterns along their walk, and the gently swaying lights of the ships in the harbor, until sleep took over.[350]

---

[350] Ibid., 102-104.

I Know I Packed That Thing

Wednesday, April 1, 4:30 a.m. (West Africa Time)
TRIPOLI

If Jerrie got out of bed early enough, maybe she could get all the paperwork done and still manage her earliest take-off yet, and today, it mattered.

As fun as it was to admire the silhouettes of the ships on the horizon and daydream about the warships throughout history weighing anchor in this harbor, Jerrie faced a seven-hour flight, and she needed to land before dark. She didn't want to fly by instrument in a part of the world where people on the ground sometimes wandered out of the control tower or forgot to turn on their equipment. The bellboy's rap on her door broke the spell, and it was back to facing whatever obstacles she might encounter this morning.[351]

In the lobby, the taxi driver from the day before waited for her again this morning.

"Uh, thank you, sir, but yesterday you charged me three pounds. I am told the fare to the airport should really be only two pounds."

At that, the man growled something she couldn't understand and turned red in the face. The line of drivers behind him looked long. Why not just take the next cab? Oh,

---

[351] Ibid., 105-106.

quit worrying about the extra dollar or two. The main thing was to get to the airport. She handed him her bag.

Maybe she had annoyed him, or he didn't like uncovered women, or he was in a hurry. Whatever the reason, this guy didn't wait for cars ahead of him. He simply went around them, into the oncoming lane, keeping his hand down on the horn all the way. "Trucks, taxis, horses, donkeys and carts" all just had to swerve out of his way. Jerrie resisted the urge to shut her eyes and say her prayers again. When he stopped at the airfield, still a long walk from the terminal, she was grateful to escape.[352]

Since she was at the plane, she checked it first. Charlie had fresh oil, but she couldn't tell who she was supposed to pay. She walked around asking, but nobody knew, and she lost a precious half hour. By the time she walked to the terminal, then to the far end to the control tower, then climbed the stairs to the weather room, the sun was already high in the blue and white sky. The day's forecast was obvious: *Hot.*

"Good morning, Mrs. Mock!"

Once she made it into the weather room, the British men helped her get things done promptly, the same as the day before. The ATC man signed her NAA form, verifying her stop in Tripoli.

"Can we send a telegram for you?"

"Thank you. Please send my take-off time back to Lockbourne Air Force Base in Columbus." She hadn't heard from Russ since Bône, and the only possible explanation was that America may have lost track of her out there. The ATC man

---

[352] Ibid, 106-107.

gave her a ride to Customs and Immigration in his jeep and walked her in.[353]

The tiny Immigration room was packed with "white–robed pilgrims carrying babies and baskets of food," waiting for their flight to Jedda so they could go on to Mecca.

"Mrs. Mock, if you will excuse me, I have to get back," the ATC man said.

Jerrie thanked him, said goodbye, and was again left on her own. While she waited for the faithful to board their plane, she walked back to the hangar area to pay for the oil, but she still couldn't find anyone who knew who she needed to speak to. She returned to Immigration. By then, the plane for Jedda had taken off, and the room was empty. No more passengers, but no officials either. She opened doors and walked through off-limit areas, until she spotted a man in uniform, walking away.

"Please, sir, would you sign my visa so I can go on to Cairo?"

"Come back later, lady," he said, brushing past her. At least he spoke English. She followed him.

"But I have to take off now!"

"The next flight doesn't leave -" he started to say.

"But my plane is right out there. Please! Look!" She took him by the arm, "pulled him to the door," and pointed to her little single-engine plane across the pavement.

The man stared at the tiny plane with his mouth open. Then he relaxed, as it sank in that he wasn't talking to another lost passenger, but to a pilot.

---

[353] Ibid., 107-108.

With her visa signed, she was free to walk back to the service area and find that, by now, the mechanic who had given her fresh oil had come in to work. He explained why nobody could find a bill for the oil: he had never written one. "Forget it! One of our planes uses that much oil just taxiing out to the end of the runway."[354]

Then he told her about all the parts needing to be replaced and everything else that concerned him about the engine and the plane. She was well aware of the parts that weren't working, and, that there was nowhere to get them. She politely thanked him for his input, headed for her plane, and started to climb in.

Oh, not so fast–a man was running across the concrete to catch her. The official who made her count her money yesterday was telling her today that she was supposed to come back and sign her copy of the form he gave her, the day before. Nobody had told her that one. She had to go back to the terminal, and go through everything until she found the form in her overnight bag. This time, she didn't have a pen. She noticed hers, still in his shirt pocket from the day before.

"Oh, I'm sorry," she said. "I don't have a pen." She "could almost see the wheels going around in his head." Then, he handed over her pen. She signed his form–and then gave him back her souvenir pen from Columbus, Ohio.[355]

By now, it was eight o'clock. She hadn't gotten away early, but at least she was about to get away. She clicked her seat belt and gave the starter button a push. Nothing. No kick from the engine, not a turn of the propeller. A few lights came on across the instrument panel and that was it.

---

354 Ibid., 108-109.
355 Ibid., 109-110.

She jumped down and ran to find that mechanic. She had to talk him into coming back to the plane and listening, while she tried again.[356]

"Sounds like your starter solenoid."

"Thank the Lord," Jerrie said. "That happens to be the one and only spare part I brought with me. Just give me a minute to find it." She had kept it on a shelf above the kitchen sink back home, but where had she packed it in the plane?

She pulled things out of the cabin and set them out on the pavement. No. She pulled everything from under the seats. No. By now the pavement was "shimmering in the fantastic heat." Her mechanic walked off.

She had hung some bags behind the cabin tank, and she would have to start on them. She pulled on a rope and something started coming up. Then it got stuck. She tried another cord. Whatever was jammed back there blocked everything. She would have to climb onto the tank somehow and pull things free.

There were only a few inches between the ceiling and the top of the gas tank. Going to find somebody to help her wouldn't do any good since she was the only person small enough to even try squirming around up there, anyway.

She wriggled her way on top of the gas tank. Wedged between the ceiling and the tank, she couldn't move much at all. The sun heated up the metal plane and sweat poured off her. She got one arm down the back of the tank, and ran her hand down the cord until she found an oil measuring can with a long spout that had everything stuck. She could just barely touch it,

---

but he could *not* get it to budge. Pulling out the tanks to get to it might cost another day, even two. She laid her head on the tank and started to cry.

The heat became suffocating. She couldn't just lie there. She backed out, took a screwdriver from her toolkit, climbed back up, twisted around, and banged on the can, wham, wham, wham, until it dropped free.

She pulled a bag up, crawled out of the plane, and dumped everything out onto the blistering concrete. The solenoid wasn't there. She went back in, got another bag, and did it all again. Nope. A third one. No. Had she even brought the thing? At the bottom of the last bag, there it was.[357]

Now she had to go find the mechanic again. He replaced the part while she loaded all her bags back in the plane.

Installing the new solenoid didn't take nearly as long as it took to find it. Still, it was after nine when she was free to get moving on the runway, and she couldn't help worrying about the failing light waiting for her at the end of today's flight. She was "seething."

Then as the plane gained altitude, she began making herself start trying to let it go. Idris Airport might have been the only place within "thousands of miles" with a mechanic who could work on a Cessna. If the solenoid had chosen somewhere else on her route to conk out, what had cost her an hour could easily have taken a week.[358]

---

[357] Ibid., 111-112.
[358] Ibid., 112.

NATAL, Brazil, 7:00 a.m. (Atlantic Time)

Breakfast for Joan was again served in the officer's quarters. She was the only woman in sight, and she felt like a goldfish in a bowl. She gobbled her food and left quickly. It was time to get a weather report, file a flight plan, and leave South America behind.[359]

Not so fast. No one gave complete answers to anything. They didn't seem to know much themselves. They all appeared to be listening to a steady stream of rapid-fire Portuguese coming in over the radios in their jeeps. Whatever was going on, it was for real, it had nothing to do with her, and yet she was stuck in it.[360]

Over NORTH AFRICA, around noon (West Africa Time)

In the air, Jerrie daydreamed about the pyramids, waiting for her on the other side of the next 900 miles of sand and salt water.

She flew along the shoreline of the Mediterranean, getting to see the "golden desert come all the way to the blue water," uninterrupted by even a speck of green. She made it to her next milestone, a town named Misurata with a radio beacon.[361]

At this point, she recalled the well-meaning advice of last night's dinner company, cautioning her not to fly over the open water of the Gulf of Sirte. Compared to the Atlantic, the gulf below her looked calm, it was dotted with ships of all shapes and sizes, and it probably didn't have as many sharks as the ocean, either. She reached Benghazi, and headed over the desert

---

[359] Brown, *Fate*, 59.

[360] Merriam, "I Flew," 79.

[361] Mock, *Three-Eight Charlie*, 112.

for 200 miles. When she crossed the border into the air space of the UAR, she was supposed to notify them, but she couldn't call in without her trailing antenna.

Along the coast of Egypt, she picked up a good strong signal from the next radio beacon, coming from the small town of Mersa Matruh. Then as she flew over the buildings below where the beacon should be, the needle kept pointing ahead, as if the beacon itself had been moved out of town. The needle actually pointed her toward a designated "prohibited area," but she stayed away from that. Wandering north out over the ocean seemed preferable to "getting chased by a reconnaissance plane, or anti-aircraft gunfire."[362]

She relied instead on other charts and good visibility on this clear day, and arrived next at the Rosetta Radio Beacon. She reported her position, and turned Charlie toward Cairo.

In a few minutes, her loudspeaker crackled to life. "Three-Eight Charlie, this is Approach Control at Cairo. Do you have the airport in sight?"

It was a relief to hear a voice she could understand, but the question seemed early.

"Not yet," Jerrie replied. She couldn't be that close, could she? Maybe they were used to the big jets traveling twice as fast as her single propeller, or maybe she wasn't used to being able to see so far ahead. She checked her charts for the airports, then looked around. Nope, just more desert. Wait. There was an airport, maybe ten miles ahead.

"Affirmative, Cairo. Three-Eight Charlie has the airport in sight."

---

[362] Ibid., 113-114.

"Roger, Three-Eight Charlie, continue approach for runway five," came the answer. So far, so good.

As she approached the airport, she pulled out one of her charts with a diagram of Cairo International Airport. Landing on the wrong runway might set her up for one more question from reporters for the "Flying Housewife" that she would rather avoid.

She flew one circle around the field, compared the picture in the book with the airport outside her windshield, and picked out what must be runway five.

"Cairo Tower, Three-Eight Charlie is on downwind for runway five."

"Roger, Three-Eight Charlie, continue approach for runway five." He gave her the altimeter setting in millibars, requiring her to make a hasty conversion to inches of mercury, as well as wind direction and velocity, and she adjusted her course.

Not so fast. She could see no number painted on the runway below her and the location didn't seem to match her chart, so, it wasn't looking like runway five.

She circled the airfield, checked her readings, lined up on another one, and called in again. "Cairo Tower, Three-Eight Charlie is now on downwind for runway five."

"Three-Eight Charlie, continue approach," came the answer.

She descended cautiously toward *this* runway, spotting a big number five painted on it, still trying to shake the feeling that something was wrong.

She was afraid of another bouncy landing, but this time the wheels touched down just fine.

"Three-Eight Charlie, what is your present position?"

"Three-Eight Charlie's on the ground." If the man in the tower had to ask, then something was off.

She spotted a taxiway angling to the left. She headed that way to get the plane off the runway so she could assess this situation. The tower controller called her, and she was calling him back, as she made the left turn.

That's when three trucks carrying armed soldiers came speeding around a corner from somewhere and slammed to a halt, bumpers just short of Charlie's propeller.[363]

NATAL, Brazil, 3:00 p.m. (Atlantic Time)

Frank Walton, the nice man from the Consulate, patiently explained to Joan that the Goulart government was tottering. Communications throughout the country were uncertain, and she needed to leave as soon as possible.

"Mr. Walton, with all due respect, you're asking me to fly over 1,900 miles of the South Atlantic to Africa. Reliable weather information might help."

"Mrs. Merriam, I'm afraid, on this day, you may not get it in Brazil."

Joan spent the day getting her plane gassed up and as ready as she could get it.

She found a fire extinguisher, only to discover that now the plane's tow bar was missing.[364]

---

363 Ibid., 115-116.
364 Brown, *Fate*, 103.

Charlie, I Don't Think We're
in Kansas Anymore

April 1[365]
Somewhere in the UNITED ARAB REPUBLIC

"Guns in hand," soldiers jumped out of their trucks and surrounded Jerrie's airplane.[366]

This did not look like a drill.

An officer motioned for her to shut down the engine. She had to ignore the panicked tower operator still coming through the loudspeaker and find out what these gentlemen wanted. She tried not to notice if those guns were pointed in her direction. She opened the door.

The officer stuck his head in. Politely, and in clear English, he said, "Madam, you are not in Cairo."

"What do you mean, I'm not in Cairo?" Okay, so maybe she had the wrong airport, but she couldn't have the wrong *city*.

"Madam, you are not in Cairo."

"Okay, then if I'm not in Cairo, where am I? Here. Show me." She "shoved a chart in his face," clearly showing only one

---

[365] Jerrie's official summary of arrival and departure times omits her layover at Inchas. She lists departure from Tripoli as March 31 and arrival in Cairo as April 1. We know she was detained at Inchas until after nightfall, which in that part of the world was approximately 6:30 p.m. She would have arrived in Cairo approximately 7:11 p.m.

[366] Mock, *Three-Eight Charlie*, 117; "Oops! Wrong Airport," Honolulu *Advertiser*, April 2, 1964.

airport within miles. She could not let them intimidate her. At least, she couldn't show it.

He pushed her map back. "Madam, turn your plane around and follow me."[367]

She cranked up the engine. Soldiers approached, then trucks and jeeps pulled around, until vehicles pinned her in from the front, behind, and on either side of the plane.

With soldiers pushing and pulling, the plane was turned around and rolled back onto runway five. This parade of trucks, plane, and men in uniforms inched along the airstrip for a mile. They seemed to be leading her in a particular direction, so she must have been headed toward something they didn't want her to see. As she taxied her plane, she was careful to keep looking straight ahead. In this era of the Cold War, she wasn't sure whether the UAR was allied with the US or the USSR.

They stopped where they wanted her to park, and she climbed out. Two soldiers took a seat under her plane. She was escorted toward a large, stone building.

"I must call Cairo airport," Jerrie said.

The officer kept walking.

"People are expecting me," she said. "I must tell them where I am."

Now the officer seemed to have forgotten English. He wouldn't even look at her. The men on all sides of her made sure she kept walking.

As they entered a hallway, a phone on the wall rang. The officer marched straight to it. She need not worry about calling Cairo. They were desperately looking for her. For over an hour,

---

[367] Mock, *Three-Eight Charlie*, 117.

the phone was ringing or somebody was talking on it, and all because of her.

Even though Jerrie didn't speak a word of Arabic, it appeared that this officer wasn't sure what to do with her. Evidently, he wasn't going to simply give her directions to Cairo and wave goodbye. The phone calls, meanwhile, were coming, not only from the control tower operator and her NAA observer, but also from the press. By the annoyed look on the officer's face, she guessed that the television, radio, and newspaper people had all come out to greet her at the Cairo airport, wherever it might be. The longer the military kept her, the more awkward things might get for them.

While the men in charge sorted it out, another soldier spoke to Jerrie, also in understandable English. "Madam, may we show you around?"

She tried to relax and followed the soldiers. One of them managed enough English to admit that she had actually landed at a military base–she would find out later that it was called Inchas–that she was in what the American Air Force would call their officer's club, and that it had originally been one of the palaces of King Farouk. She was invited to a lounge to watch the news on television.

"Tomorrow, you . . ." Her escort nodded awkwardly at the TV.

Okay, so they knew who she was, but how was the Cairo television station going to run their story without her?

"Madam, would you care for cider or tea?"

"Oh, tea would be lovely. Thank you!"

"I'm afraid the cider is ready, but the tea is not."

"Well, then, cider would be lovely. Thank you!"

Cider; cold, sparkling and delicious, was served at a table on the terrace beside the King's empty swimming pool. Every minute or two, a soldier came out and asked her some question, such as, could she fly at night? Every time she said yes, they seemed "puzzled." Apparently, they didn't fly much at night themselves. One soldier admitted that when they first spotted her coming in, they had wanted to send up a red flare to warn her not to land, but nobody could find the flare gun. They must not have radio either, or they would have shown up on her chart of radio tower locations.

One by one, men in khaki kept coming to the terrace door to peek at the "lady pilot." Turned out, she was not the first pilot to visit this "secret" base unintentionally. In fact, an airplane of one type or other landed every other week or so, sometimes an international airliner. "Whenever someone comes here," one soldier explained, "they must spend the night."

Would they release her to face the crowd and reporters in Cairo any time soon? Would she get to eat any time soon? What about a hotel? No way to tell.

Suddenly, the commanding officer came out to the terrace. "Okay, madam, now you can go to Cairo."

She just stared at him. "But where is Cairo?"

"Oh, you just come with me, madam, and I will show you."

They all marched through the palace, out the front door and down the road. By then it was completely dark. Evidently, they had held her until she couldn't see anything–possibly a particular *some*thing–on their base, or nearby.

The guards at the plane had fallen asleep. At the approaching noise, they scrambled to their feet, and the officer gave orders. Charlie was pushed and pulled until it faced a runway, in the darkness, without a single light. Satisfied with the position of the plane, the officer turned to Jerrie.

"Now, Madam, you take off on this runway. It's the wrong runway, but you use it anyway."[368]

She must have allowed the perplexity to show in her face, because he said, "You do understand? It's the wrong runway, but it's all right."[369]

The officer continued giving her directions. "You will see the lights to an airport on your left. Don't land. Military. On your right, you will see the lights to another airport. Land. That's Cairo!"[370]

Okay! Maybe they thought she couldn't find Cairo unless she was "pointed at it." She "shook hands all around" and boarded her plane. Everybody smiled, and the officer invited her to "hurry back." As she eased in the throttle and the plane picked up speed, a green flare arced from the tower. Oh, good. She was "glad that they had found their flare gun."[371]

Charlie lifted off and climbed to 1,000 feet, and she spotted lights. She had to double-check which way was left and which was right, to make sure that she got the right airport this time. She called the Cairo tower, approached runway five, and was cleared to land at a complex much larger than her last stop.

She landed to face a huge swarm of people, and the next two hours passed in a blur. She dutifully answered questions and posed for a photograph with a group of Egyptian flight attendants. She sent a cable to Ohio attempting to get some help ordering

---

[368] Ibid., 121.

[369] Ibid.

[370] Ibid.

[371] Ibid.

parts. She found out later that the cable that arrived was unreadable, as if perhaps some censor thought that "rocker arms" and "valves" were code for something, and scrambled them up. A tall American couple introduced themselves as Peter and Marlin Barker and took her to their apartment for a drink, dinner, and a deep sleep.[372]

CAIRO, 12:01 a.m. (Eastern European Time)
COLUMBUS, Ohio, 5:01 p.m. the night before (Eastern Time)

Russ could not have known how the military episode was working out, partly because Inchas, the Soviet-built base Jerrie had landed on, did not officially exist until 1972. All Russ could do was send his next telegram:

AMERICAN EMBASSY CAIRO – PLEASE RELAY TO JERRIE MOCK. . . . ALL FAMILIES AND SPONSORS SCARED TO DEATH BECAUSE NO WORD FROM YOU **STOP** AIR FORCE SPENT HOURS LOCATING YOU FROM THIS END **STOP** YOUR MOTHER IN TEARS **STOP**[373]

---

[372] Ibid., 117-121.
[373] Russell Mock to American Embassy Cairo, telegram, March 31, 1964, photocopy given to author by Jerrie Mock.

A Camel Ride to the Sphinx

Thursday, April 2, 8:01 a.m. (Eastern European Time)
CAIRO

Jerrie *tried* to sleep in. The authorities of the United Arab Republic weren't going to let her take off until they were sure she hadn't been "spying" on them, and that could take all day. She kept her eyes closed through the crow of a rooster, but the "tantalizing aroma of strong coffee" was too much.[374]

She got up, dressed, and went down to breakfast. It felt almost like being back in America when Marlin Barker served up fresh scrambled eggs and ran her skirt and drip-dries through their washer and dryer.

Peter Barker drove her along the eastern bank of the Nile back to the Cairo airport. Across the brown river, between antennas and billboards, outlines of the pyramids peeked through a haze of dust and pollution. Since she was flying out the next day, today was her one chance to visit them. But first, she had business to take care of, as always.

At the airport, she followed Barker through large glass doors and down an overcrowded escalator. Beneath a loudspeaker booming out the departures and arrivals in five languages, surrounded by jet-set tourists with their lipstick and sunglasses, Jerrie felt as if she had just jumped into a different century than the one she left back in Tripoli, with the faithful pilgrims in

---

[374] Mock, *Three-Eight Charlie*, 124.

white, hanging on to their babies and food baskets, waiting for their ride to Mecca.

Peter led her through the crowds until suddenly he was introducing her to a young-ish looking Egyptian man in a business suit, and explaining that he was with AID (Agency for International Development) or FAA (Federal Aviation Agency)– the story seemed to change–and was there, courtesy of the UAR government, to "help us with translation," Peter said, walking them both through the airport.

"Gas," Jerrie said. "Flight plan . . ." she tried to explain what she needed, and the new man seemed to listen, but for someone from the FAA, this guy didn't seem to know where to file a flight plan or anything else about aviation. They both had to scramble to keep up as Barker led them through the crowd and down a flight of stairs to the bottom level of the airport and into a tiny office. They all shook hands with some new older gentleman, in a black suit with a somber face, who looked like a funeral director.[375]

Barker and their translator sat down, so Jerrie did, too. While Barker smoked cigarettes, they all sat.

Jerrie was asked to pay her fees, and she quickly took care of that.

Then they sat some more.

She couldn't understand the language or the diplomacy game. The three men kept making small talk, evidently waiting for something, but nobody bothered to clue Jerrie in as to what. All she could do was politely ask for gas. The three men went on talking, but at least "gasoline" was mentioned.

---

[375] Ibid., 124-125.

Every few minutes, the man in black picked up a phone on his desk, listened to it, then hung up. Then, he opened a desk drawer, pulled out a second phone, this one so old-fashioned that he cranked it by hand, listened to it, then put it back in the drawer. The phone checking and chatting went on for another hour.

Then, the man in black wrote a note and sent yet another man out, to take his handwritten message "upstairs." Then, the first phone rang. The man in black spoke in Arabic for a while, then he said something to Barker, who finally let Jerrie in on the news. "We're expected at the Aero Club of Egypt for a reception and to meet your NAA observer, a General Attia, this afternoon. Would you please speak to him?"

"Of course!" But by the time Jerrie was handed the phone, it had gone dead again.

"When does he want to see us?"

"We're not sure," Peter said. Then, he put out his latest cigarette and stood up. "Now we can go file a flight plan and gas up the plane." Why it was suddenly okay to get moving, Jerrie couldn't tell, but she didn't dare question it.[376]

For that, Barker, Jerrie, and their translator had to walk some more stairs and elevators to pick up the necessary forms, then get back in Peter's car, pull out from the big modern terminal, and drive across the pavement and out a service road to find Charlie's propeller peeking out from a hangar.

A truck with a Shell logo promptly pulled up, and four men in yellow uniforms got out. But they wouldn't pump her gas. They stood there as if needing someone's okay, which seemed

---

[376] Ibid., 126-127.

never to come. The group was stuck, standing under the hot sun, with more unexplained waiting.

"Why won't they get on with it?"

"The 'man' is not here."

More waiting, until Jerrie asked, "Okay, where is he?"

"We will call him."

One of the crew walked over to another building, but he never came back. "He must have been trying to call 'the man who wasn't there' on another phone that didn't work."[377] Everybody paced around in the sun with their pretend smiles for a while. She had arrived at the airport at 10:00 that morning. Now it was after 2:00 p.m.

Eventually, they spotted a man walking the two miles or so across the concrete. His update: "If you wait about two hours, then taxi the plane to the terminal, *probably* you can get gas."

"PROBABLY?!" Jerrie had had enough. "Please explain that it is impossible to wait two more hours. General Attia is expecting me later today. I will try to get gasoline again tomorrow."[378]

Barker drove Jerrie as fast as he could through the Cairo traffic to meet his wife Marlin and her driver at the American Embassy, where they had been waiting for hours. "Now we have an hour and a half for the pyramids," Marlin said to Jerrie. "Let's go."

Marlin's driver took off. They crossed the Nile, drove into the desert, and stopped when the road dead-ended at the top of a small sand hill. No pyramids anywhere—only some parked

[377] Ibid., 127.
[378] Ibid, 128.

cars, a few camels, and men wearing what looked like striped nightshirts.

The camel drivers hustled over to Marlin and Jerrie, pulling their camels behind them. One of the men spoke to these two American women, who seemed to be the only tourists around.

"They want to know if we want to ride the rest of the way," Marlin translated for Jerrie, and then started to shake her head "No."

"Tell him yes!" Maybe Marlin had taken this tour already, but Jerrie had waited thirty years for hers. The driver guided the camel to a kneeling position, and Jerrie climbed up between the hump and the neck. She tried to remember what to do from a description in a book she had read years ago. As the camel straightened its rear legs, Jerrie leaned back. When the front legs came up, she leaned forward. The driver prodded the camel into a trot, she struggled to keep from swaying, and bouncing on the saddle was uncomfortable.

This brief ride down a tourist trail over some sand was not exactly the days-and-nights sojourn across a desert she had counted on since childhood. Still, the path took her around a dune until she looked up at the Great Sphinx of Giza. For a precious few minutes, she could lose herself in the peace and quiet of the ancient past.

The large, "haughty" face of the Pharaoh Khafre looked past Jerrie toward the timeless Nile, quietly reminding her of the relative insignificance of one little "Flying Housewife," dropping in for an afternoon. Nearby, the Pyramid of Cheops rose 500 feet, dwarfing the Sphinx. She only had minutes to paint a mental picture to keep with her for a lifetime, so she tried to play this scene in slow motion.

Another group of tourists, climbing and complaining up the staggering height of the pyramid, was transformed in her mental camera into slaves, struggling to inch gigantic blocks of stone up the incline.

But the modern world back in Cairo wasn't going to slow down just for her, and with one last look at the great ancient monuments, she turned to go.[379]

Then it was off to her evening's social engagement. The Barkers had some trouble finding the Aero Club, which turned out to be "in the penthouse of a modern skyscraper." Jerrie was one of the honored guests of the party, along with a Boy Scout troop from England. Next, they had to step into General Attia's office and fill out forms. He wanted to fill in the blanks for how much gas she would be carrying. But, since she didn't get filled up that day, she didn't know yet. The general became "indignant," as if she was responsible for the long morning with the gas crew that wouldn't pump her gas. She caught a break when the local news came on, so all the guests and the Boy Scouts watched the plane land in Cairo the night before. Maybe her new buddies back in Inchas got to see that, too.[380]

NATAL, Brazil, 5:00 a.m. (Atlantic Time)

Joan awakened to learn that she *still* couldn't find out anything definite about this revolution. Each delay cost her a day in this race. The intense Portuguese voice coming over the radio seemed to pick up the pace and volume. Everyone in sight stopped what they were doing to listen. Then they all cheered.[381]

---

[379] Ibid., 128-130.

[380] Ibid., 130-133.

[381] Merriam, "I Flew," 79.

"The Goulart government has fallen," Walton said.

The next news they got was that all domestic and international flights from the next closest airport in Recife had been canceled.[382]

"I still have no way to know if there is a hurricane out there," Joan said.

"If you wait much longer, it won't matter." Walton tried to smile, but it was one of those tense little diplomat's smiles and not very convincing. "Perhaps you can get a forecast in the air."

Joan took a deep breath. All she could do was take off early the next morning and search one radio frequency after another until she picked up some guidance from the African side of the ocean.[383]

---

[382] Brown, *Fate*, 59.

[383] Merriam, "Longest Flight," 46.

You Can Yell at Me, But You Can't Make Me Go Away

Friday, April 3, 3:35 a.m. (Eastern European Time)
CAIRO

Cock-a-doodle-do!

Jerrie opened one eye. Nope, no light in *this* room. She closed her eye.

Cock-a-doodle-do!

The Barkers' alarm hadn't gone off yet, so she tried to close her eyes again, but instinct made her look around for her wristwatch. Three thirty-*five*. Their alarm was supposed to go off at three *thirty*. Saved by the rooster.

Barker drove along the highway to the airport at full speed, using only his parking lights, like every other car on the road. Egyptians seemed to flick their headlights only to flash each other or a pedestrian, even though it was pitch-black. She never did get what Peter's job was, exactly. Supposedly, he did something with the American Embassy, but that sounded sketchy. Last night she had given him her roll of film with her pictures of the Azores, the King's pajamas in Tripoli, and her perch on the camel, but by this morning she suspected that he really worked for the Central Intelligence Agency (CIA).

Peter stopped suddenly at an apartment building and flashed his headlights. Jerrie recognized General Attia from the Aero Club the night before, but the general slipped into the back seat next to Marlin without saying a word. Next stop: a street corner, where their AID/FAA translator waited, awake and dressed for work. It was all very James Bond.[384]

At the airport, they got through the lines and paperwork okay at first, and everybody relaxed. General Attia started talking to someone and fell behind the rest of the group. When Jerrie stepped up to the Immigration counter to have her passport stamped, the Immigration officer looked down at her and said, "Lady, go get your ticket."

She did not back up.

"Lady, get out of here. I'm busy. Go buy a ticket."

Her translator explained that she didn't need a ticket for her own plane.

The Immigration man started shouting at her translator. He ran out of words in English, and both men reverted to Arabic. Other travelers closing in to get their visas stamped gave Jerrie dirty looks. She was holding up everybody. In mid-argument, the Immigration man waved toward another man in a different uniform. Was she about to be removed from the line by force?

General Attia left the person he was talking to and ran over to the group. He got Jerrie's passport stamped, plus permission for Jerrie and her group to pass through the barrier. The Immigration officer's bewildered face revealed that he never did understand why Jerrie didn't need a ticket.[385]

It was time again for Jerrie to deal with the annoyance of getting gas.

Mrs. Mock," her translator explained, "the gas truck cannot drive to the plane. You must taxi the plane back to the terminal building."

---

[384] Mock, *Three-Eight Charlie*, 134; Mock, interview, March 16, 2008.
[385] Mock, *Three-Eight Charlie*, 135; Mock, interview, March 16, 2008.

"But they drove to the plane yesterday!" Jerrie said. Jerrie, Barker, and their translator drove out to the plane, and Jerrie got in. A black jeep pulled up, with five or six men inside, and a "Follow Me" sign on the back.

"They will lead you," her translator explained. Then he got back into Peter's car, and he pulled up behind Jerrie.

Jerrie thanked him and shut her door. She knew not to move her plane without clearance from the control tower, "Follow Me" or not. The jeep didn't seem to have a radio, and those men weren't talking to anybody, so she called Ground Control.

"Three-Eight Charlie," Ground Control answered. "Affirmative, you are cleared to taxi."

Okay, she could start her plane, and taxi along behind the jeep. When "Follow Me" turned left, Jerrie turned left.

The controller came through Jerrie's speaker. "Three-Eight Charlie, negative. Please make a right turn."

Jerrie followed instructions.

The "Follow Me" driver spun around and pulled in front of the plane again. The men in the jeep waved and jumped onto the ground, all trying to get her to turn back around. She pointed to the loudspeaker over her windshield, held the microphone up to her mouth, and pointed toward the control tower. The driver looked lost, then pulled "Follow Me" around, and reluctantly followed Jerrie.

Her speaker came on. "Three-Eight Charlie, go to Gate Number Four."

"Is this where I get fuel?"

"You may park there for twenty minutes," was the only answer she got. Then the controller added, "The next plane coming in to Gate Number Four will be a Caravelle."

The Caravelle was one of the largest jets in the world. He was telling her that she would not want to be in the way when it landed.

Jerrie taxied to Gate Number Four, stopped the plane, and climbed out of the cabin. The "Follow Me" guys didn't look happy, but they didn't seem to want to argue with the control tower either.

Along came a jeep towing a trailer, carrying a barrel with a hand crank.

The men pulled a wooden scaffolding out of the jeep and asked where she wanted her gas. Jerrie unscrewed the cap on the tank next to her seat, and a man started pumping, until he got tired. Then another man took over for him. Then another man after him. Then another one.

She stood under a wing of her plane for shade, talking with Peter Barker and their translator, trying to act relaxed, but really checking her gas gauge every so often. The gas seemed to be going in *really* slowly. She listened wistfully to the flight announcements coming from the main terminal, with their "air-conditioning and silver jets."[386]

Twenty minutes of pumping didn't move the needle on the gas gauge at all. The "Follow Me" guys stopped cranking, dismantled the pump, got it all put back together, and tried again. Nothing, like yesterday's phone. They formed a huddle.

Then a new man walked up. He unscrewed the nozzle, lifted a screen out of it, banged it up against their wooden scaffold, and screwed the nozzle back into the hose. He fitted the nozzle into the hole to the tank and cranked. This time gasoline

---

[386] Mock, *Three-Eight Charlie*, 136-138; Mock, interview, March 16, 2008.

spurted out, not only from the nozzle, but also out of the fittings holding the nozzle on, like a garden hose loose at the faucet. Gas poured into the tank, across the top of the tank, and down the sides, all over her charts, clothes–everything.

"STOP! Rags! I need some rags!"

A single, greasy rag was handed over. Peter and their translator each pulled a handkerchief out of their pockets. Jerrie grabbed her last box of Kleenex. She could barely stand to stay in the fume-filled cabin, but she had to pull things out, wipe up gasoline, and wring it out of handkerchiefs onto the ground as fast as she could, all under the card Dave Blanton had Scotch-taped to the tank: *Clean rags should be wrapped around the neck of the tank to prevent dripping.*[387]

Eventually, the tanks were filled, the cabin was cleaned up as much as it could be, and nothing had caught on fire yet. Jerrie tried to calm down. She started wiping off her belongings, which, even though she had scooted them under a wing of the plane, *still* got dripped on.

One of the men stepped down the scaffolding, backing away from the nose of the plane with an empty oil container in his hand. She was scared to ask how much oil he had poured into her engine.

"Half an imperial gallon," was the translation she got. "That's the closest we had to the two quarts you wanted."

Imperial gallons, liters, quarts. There was no way to figure out exactly how much oil the Cessna had in it now. Oh, well. Gasoline still ran over the cabin floor, and when she cranked the engine, oil would spill inside the engine compartment, too.

---

[387] Mock, *Three-Eight Charlie*, 138-139; Mock, interview, March 16, 2008.

Then as they were getting the last gas cap back on, another man came running toward them, shouting and waving his arms. The other guys picked up what he was saying and they all started shouting, too. "The Caravelle! The Caravelle, she comes!"

Now they were all in a hurry. Still, Jerrie didn't dare take off until she attempted a pre-flight inspection. Everyone "pointed in different directions." They still didn't seem to know where to tell her to go.

Well. "It was fun to watch the show," but somebody had to take charge. "You," she said, "load my bags. You, load my life raft. You, pick up this equipment."

With a lot of hand–waving, she managed to direct each man as to what to pick up and where to put it. They seemed relieved to be told what to do, and her gear was reloaded, or at least, it all seemed to disappear from the pavement, anyway. She crammed her life raft, thirty pounds of dusty, smelly rubber, in behind her head cushions. Then she pushed the starter button, shouted "Clear," tried not to laugh at the men jumping back from the propeller as it came to life, pulled out of Gate Four, and onto a stretch of concrete off to the side. She tried to air out the cabin, pre-flight the plane, adjust wings and check instruments, at least a little.

She never saw the Caravelle. Maybe it visited Inchas, too.[388]

As she headed down the runway for take-off, a calm voice came over her radio. "Three-Eight Charlie, this is Captain Bill Judd, wishing you a good flight."

---

[388] Mock, *Three-Eight Charlie*, 140; Mock, interview, Mar. 16, 2008.

The name sounded familiar. The fireplace. "Bill Judd! Where are you?"

"We're taking off from Cairo just now, headed for Rome."

The sound of his American voice, coming from his big, quiet, clean cockpit of a TWA airliner that probably didn't smell at all like gasoline hit Jerrie with a wave of homesickness. She remembered the plaque on the mantle at the Judds' cottage in Bermuda, recognizing him as the "First Man after Lindbergh to Fly the North Atlantic between New York and Paris." Bill Judd had made that flight in a Cessna 180, the same model as Charlie.[389]

NATAL, Brazil, 4:00 a.m. (Atlantic Time)

Getting up with the rooster in the village beyond the airstrip, Joan took off at dawn for a flight of at least thirteen hours. Her tanks were topped off at twenty hours' worth of fuel.[390] That was all they could hold, and she just had to hope it would be enough. *If* she got enough radio contact, nothing leaked, the headwinds weren't too strong, all her gauges worked, she had estimated those headwinds right *and* done all her math right, *then*, it would be.[391]

It is always better to see where you are going, if you can. But over the Atlantic, the clouds rolled in again, and within minutes after takeoff, she was flying by instrument again. She had only flown 200 miles before the voice from the control tower at Natal began fading in and out, until nothing came from her

---

[389] Mock, *Three-Eight Charlie*, 140; Mock, interview, Mar. 16, 2008.

[390] Brown, *Fate*, 59.

[391] Merriam, "I Flew," 79.

loudspeaker but an occasional crackle, and she couldn't pick up Dakar yet, either. Once again, she was on her own.[392]

She flew by instrument at 5,000 feet for a couple of hours, and the clouds fizzled out. Yet an hour later, she could see lines of huge clouds up ahead.

She got through to Natal long enough to get clearance and climbed to 9,000 feet to clear the tops of the storm clouds without having to worry about hitting another plane. When she reached 9,000, she could see that wasn't enough, so she went up to 13,000 feet. "Still not enough."[393]

Heading back down toward a more normal altitude, at 5,000 feet she ran into torrential rains. Visibility dropped to zero. Beyond the wingtips she could see nothing but water.[394] The rain pounded on the plane, coming down so hard that the windshield began to leak. Water seeped in around the door and across the cabin floor, toward her electric power packs. With her free hand, she reached for her headset and pulled it over her ears, hoping to catch any signal, however faint. Was the windshield going to crack?[395]

She came down to 2,000 feet, then to a mere 500 feet. The undersides of the clouds were ragged, black and boiling. Sea and sky seemed to be all one endless torrent.[396] For the next 150 miles, she flew by instrument, just 400 feet above the ocean.[397]

---

[392] Ibid.

[393] Ibid.; Brown, *Fate*, 60.

[394] Brown, *Fate*, 60.

[395] Ibid.

[396] Ibid., 80.

[397] Ibid., 60.

After two hours of dueling with the elements, the clouds and wind finally dissolved into a gray mist.

Somewhere over the Atlantic, she had flown from the Southern Hemisphere across the equator back into the Northern. She had made it through her first duel with the violent winds converging on the equator, just as Amelia had done, and she was headed northeast toward Dakar.[398]

---

[398] Merriam, "I Flew," 79.

Flying Blind

Friday, April 3, 3:30 p.m. (Eastern European Time)
Over the coastline of AFRICA

Jerrie flew over the "sparkling turquoise" water of the Gulf of Suez, and crossed the "barren" Sinai Peninsula, headed toward the Gulf of Aqaba. She was flying just thirty miles south of Eilat, Israel. If she didn't stay in her lane, she could be intercepted by either the Israelis or one of their Arab neighbors.[399]

Good thing there wasn't a cloud in the sky. One radio station after another along this section was marked "may not be commissioned" and "VOR (VHF Omnidirectional Range) unreliable" on her map. Flying at 7,500 feet, though, she was spared the 140-degree heat on the ground, plus she could see for seventy miles or so. She could pinpoint her location exactly, and admire the shifts and changes of the ocean and the desert below.[400]

Coral reefs turned the water "blue-green." A ridge rose from the gulf to become bleak mountains, peaking at around 2,000 feet above the gulf. Beyond the ridge, the desert began to level out. A "purple-gray" bed of lava broke the monotony of the bone-colored sand. Wrinkles in the ground below must have been dry riverbeds. A sprinkle of dots, evidently black sheep, gathered around a water hole. She angled across Jordan, into

---

[399] Mock, *Three-Eight Charlie*, 141.
[400] Ibid.

Saudi Arabia, and on to Badanah, a small town on the Trans-Arabian pipeline with a radio signal.[401]

From there she turned southeast toward Dhahran. She wanted to shortcut across the Great Nafud Desert to see actual shifting sand dunes, but Air Force pilots had warned her that the Arabian Desert was too hot for a single-engine propeller plane. They told her that if the dry, intense heat was too much for Charlie's engine and she was forced down, she wouldn't survive "eight hours," so, she felt she had to skip the sand dunes and stay within sight of the pipeline.[402]

She still got nice views of little houses made of dried mud along the long, black pipe . . . until that black line began to disappear. Things got blurry, reminding her of "a photograph that has been enlarged so many times the objects lose their clarity." The ground looked like it was moving. She cleaned her sunglasses. Didn't help. She took a shot of oxygen. Didn't help.

Everything inside the cockpit still looked fine. Her problem was not her eyes, or her head, or in the cabin. After avoiding them for days, out here beyond any weather stations to report them, she had flown into a sandstorm.

All she could remember about how to handle sandstorms was to stay away from them. Sometimes engines clogged with sand and quit. If she tried to land, visibility straight ahead could get worse than staying in the air. Just like the smoking cockpit, the best thing to do was simply to keep flying and hope that she would fly out of it. She kept the plane level and prayed for an hour. The clouds of tiny particles eventually swirled and faded

---

[401] Ibid.

[402] Ibid., 142-3.

away, but she had no way of knowing how badly her engine was damaged.[403]

Dah-dit-dit, dit-dit-dit-dit, "Delta Hotel," started coming in from Dhahran. She only had half an hour to get ready to face the next crowd, and the social situation waiting down there might be harder to deal with than a sandstorm.

She had learned during one of her trips to Washington that the Kingdom of Saudi Arabia was a very orthodox Muslim culture. Arabian women were not allowed to see, or be seen by, the outside world, show one's face or even wear bright clothes. If a woman drove a car, both she and her husband could go to jail. European and American women were allowed to go out in public unveiled, but they still couldn't drive.

One of the mini-dramas during the months of preparation came up when the American ambassador in Riyadh received her request to land in Dhahran. He said it would probably be denied. Then clearance actually was granted later, and she figured that it must have required permission from King Ibn Saud himself. Then the king was deposed on March 28, and by that time, she was flying into Casablanca.

Yet Dhahran was also a modern city, built out of one of the most productive petroleum centers in the world, and maybe they didn't get much excitement. All Peter Barker told her was that news of her arrival would probably draw an audience, mostly men, wanting to see their first "Flying Housewife."[404]

From 7,500 feet, Dhahran looked like a tiny village in an endless desert. The low sun burning down onto the mud walls cast "intricate shadows on the brown sand." By contrast, the

---

[403] Ibid., 143.

[404] Ibid., 144.

Dhahran Airport, with its concrete strip and marble columns, looked like "the Taj Mahal." As Jerrie approached, she saw a US Navy Blue Angel jet take off.

"Several hundred white-robed people" had gathered at the terminal. When she landed, an Immigration officer opened her door and spoke in clear English.

"Welcome to Saudi Arabia, Mrs. Mock." He handed her a bouquet of gladioli, "flown in from Cairo" for her. As he helped her down onto the pavement, her new fans shouted and burst into applause.

"They can see by your skirt that you must truly be a woman," her escort explained.

"Handsome" Air Force guards held the crowd back as the Immigration officer walked Jerrie toward the crowd. A man wearing the traditional white kaffiyeh on his head slipped past the guards, ran up to her plane, and before she could stop him, opened the door. He looked inside the cockpit, nodded his head and kaffiyeh with a passion, then turned toward everyone and announced something in Arabic, to which they all cheered again.

Jerrie looked up at the officer.

"He's telling them that it is true, there is *no* man on board," the Immigration officer explained, "and they are all impressed." Over the shouting he went on to explain that the guards, sent by Prince Faisal, would handle her over-enthusiastic fans for her and that he was walking her over to meet the American couple who would take care of everything else.[405]

---

[405] Ibid.; Mock, interview, March 16, 2008.

"Mrs. Mock, allow me to introduce you to Mr. Howard Lynch."

Mr. and Mrs. Lynch stood out from the crowd. "Looks like you're spilling oil," Howard said.

Jerrie turned to notice brown dribbles down the side of Charlie's red-and-white nose. "Oh, those mechanics in Cairo!" she said. "They even spilled gasoline into my *lunchbox.*"

"You can leave the plane to my men," Lynch said. "Grab your bag and we'll walk you to our car. You're staying with us, and you're just in time for happy hour and dinner."

"What about Customs and Immigration?"

Lynch just laughed. "All you have to do is wave to your admirers."

Jerrie followed the Lynches past a Customs man who simply smiled beneath his kaffiyeh and waved them all through.

Before driving away, Lynch took a couple of laps around the airport area so everybody could get one last look at the "lady pilot." Among the crowd, she noticed women "in shapeless black cloaks, and veils with slits for their eyes."

The Lynches drove her to the compound built for TWA and Aramco, the Saudi Arabian Oil Company. The compound included a golf course and swimming pool in the middle of the desert and the Lynches' air-conditioned house. Lynch introduced her to pilots and other people who worked with him at TWA; the American Consul General, John Horner; and the chief of the US Training Mission to Saudi Arabia, Colonel W.W. Wilson, and their wives. They all joined Jerrie for against-the-rules-of-the-Koran toasts to aviation with their "bathtub gin," actually made from some local plant, and a dinner of American steak. Now *"this* was the way to set a world record."[406]

For six months, everyone who knew anything about Dhahran had told Jerrie Mock not to land there. 'So I landed there,' said Jerrie Mock. 'How could I pass up a place that was supposed to be so dangerous?'[407]

Over the Atlantic Ocean, 1:00 p.m. (Fernando de Noronha Time)

After several hours in the air, Joan flew out of short-wave radio range from Natal.[408] She switched to long-range and tried to reach Dakar. No luck. She tried searching for a radio beacon, but her needle bounced around, giving erratic readings, and she couldn't trust that. She should be midway to Africa by now, but she was flying by magnetic compass only. If winds were forcing her off course far enough, she might drift so far south of Dakar she might not even see it in the dark.[409]

She was supposed to report her position every thirty minutes. If her plane went down, a search team would at least know where to begin. Yet for three hours, she could not hear a word, and nobody could hear her. Finally, she picked up a British Overseas Airways Corporation pilot talking to Dakar about her. All he could tell them was that he had heard nothing from her.[410]

---

[406] Ibid., 146.

[407] "Winner Take All," *Flying* Magazine, July 1964.

[408] Merriam, "I Flew," 80; Merriam, "Longest Flight," 47.

[409] Merriam, "I Flew," 80.

[410] Ibid.; Brown, *Fate*, 60.

She tried talking into her microphone to reach that plane, but no luck. She could hear other pilots trying to reach both Dakar and Natal, but they weren't getting through, either. That told her it was probably atmospheric conditions, not just a problem with her radios.[411]

She climbed above the clouds again, trying to get above the storm, and hoping for better radio contact. At 11,000 feet,[412] the bright sunshine began to dry up the moisture around the windshield. She spread rags onto the puddles on the floor, climbed to 13,000 feet,[413] then to 17,000.[414]

After seven hours of fighting storms and anxiety, exhaustion caught up. Her back and head were killing her. She loosened the seat belt and stretched her legs.

She tried to use a sick sack, for its improvised purpose on this trip. But in the tiny, overcrowded cockpit, having to keep one hand on the controls so the plane wouldn't veer suddenly one way or the other made the process too awkward and terrifying. She was forced to hold it. She switched on the cabin light, amused at the "wild" woman looking back at her.[415]

She remembered to try her first food since take-off, a cheese sandwich she had purchased in Brazil. The cheese was so strong and the bread so stale that, after one bite, she put it away, sipped some water, and munched hard candies instead.[416]

---

[411] Merriam, "I Flew," 80; Brown, *Fate*, 60.

[412] Merriam, "I Flew," 80; Merriam, "Longest Flight," 47.

[413] Brown, *Fate*, 60.

[414] Merriam, "Longest Flight," 47.

[415] Merriam, "I Flew," 80, Brown, Fate, 61.

[416] Merriam, "I Flew," 80.

Her plane continued to zip along at 150 miles an hour. Now that she was out of the storm, she looked down at the clear, blue ocean and moved on to the next worry on her list: sharks. She did have a life raft above the gas tank, but how many days could a person could stay alive—and sane—adrift in one of those things?[417] The sun had become almost like an "old friend"[418] to her out there, and now even it was going away.

She switched on the lights across her instrument panel, casting the inside of her cabin with an "eerie" red glow.[419] Through the windshield, the stars had not yet come out, so sea and sky were all one black void.

After the long silences, a voice from the Natal radio tower finally came in. She could hear him asking the man in Dakar if he had heard anything from her. The man in Dakar said they had not.

"She took off at six a.m.!" the man said, his voice rising. "You should be picking her up by now!"

Dakar said, "Roger," signing off with Natal. Then he called Joan. "Apache three two five one Poppa, this is Dakar Oceanic Control. How do you read?"

"Dakar, this is Apache three two five one Poppa. I read you loud and clear." She switched off her mike, switched on her loudspeaker, and waited.

After a long minute, her loudspeaker cracked to life. "Apache three two five one Poppa, this is Dakar Oceanic Control. How do you read?"

---

[417] Ibid.
[418] Ibid.
[419] Ibid.

She could hear them, but they could not hear her, from either side of the Atlantic.

After twenty minutes, the calls stopped coming, as if there were some barrier between her and the people out there trying to help. It felt creepy, like "overhearing my own obituary."[420]

She flew on into the night. By the twelfth hour, she still had no contact. "My destiny was shaping up just short of doubtful."[421]

Without radio navigational aid, all she could do was follow her compass. After fourteen hours, she could hear Dakar calling ships in the area, asking if anyone had reached her. In frustration, she picked up her mike and tried yelling into it. Now she was worried. Her flight-plan time had expired. Unless she had miscalculated, she should be close, but all she could see in the dark was the vaguest hint of shadowy coastline, rising up from the smooth ocean horizon.

After fifteen hours of reading instruments, her eyes could feel the strain. "My concern is growing. Once day turns into night, I'm intrigued to see the sea, sky, and horizon all collapse into a single, starless, black void."[422]

Radio silence, still. She kept transmitting on the emergency frequency, hoping to catch some airliner or ship in the blackness all around her. Her bearing on Cape Verde was off and erratic. She could fly in circles for hours and run out of gas. The thought of a night ditching terrified her.[423]

---

[420] Ibid.

[421] Brown, *Fate*, 61.

[422] Ibid., 60.

[423] Brown, *Fate*, 61.

She didn't know if she were 1,000 feet too high or 1,000 feet too low. "Running out of water. Hungry. No food all day."[424] She kept searching the band on ADF to pick up a signal and look it up to see what station it could be. "In Africa, many stations have the same code letter, AF or AG. Three or four stations would have the same identifications and list the names of the cities on paper."[425]

She switched to her VOR radio beacon. If she should get within 150 miles of Dakar, the needle would move.

Ten more minutes. The needle wiggled. She was only about forty miles off.[426] She corrected course a bit, and there was Dakar, a twinkle of light below.

"Well," she said to her koala bear and her polar bear, "I've lucked out again."[427]

---

[424] Ibid.
[425] Ibid.
[426] Merriam, "Longest Flight," 47.
[427] Merriam, "I Flew," 80.

Two Windows, Two Oceans

Saturday, April 4, 3:15 a.m. (Arabia Time)
DHAHRAN, Saudi Arabia

Next morning, Jerrie gulped down a little coffee and tried to eat one of the nice, hot rolls Mrs. Lynch made for her. But mostly she kept her eye on Mr. Lynch until he got all of her NAA observer forms filled out so they could get to the airport. He kept stopping in the middle of writing to give her flying advice from his years as a pilot for TWA. From what he said, it was evident he was accustomed to the big jets, and her Cessna looked tiny and "fragile" by comparison. He kept talking as she edged toward the door, bag in hand. Finally, he ran out of things to say. His face looked pale.

"Are you worried about something?" Jerrie asked.

"Sandstorms are bad out there."

Jerrie shrugged. "Well, maybe I've already made it through them."

Slowly, he reached for his car keys. Jerrie didn't want to ignore his premonition, but she wouldn't allow him to shake her confidence, either.[428]

At the airport, she found that Lynch and his people had taken care of everything. All she had to do was pick up a weather report ("already prepared"), sign a flight plan ("filled out"), step into the plane, find a spot in the cabin (in between

---

[428] Mock, *Three-Eight Charlie*, 147.

the cans of tomato juice and other goodies given to her along the way) for a bag of hard candies (from Mrs. Lynch), say goodbye, and taxi away. After all the headaches at so many places, this visit had been unbelievably smooth.[429]

Under a clear sky, Jerrie headed out over the Persian Gulf. The stretch of shoreline below her, famous for pearl harvesting, was another place she had read about but wouldn't get to visit. She flew on to Bahrain Island. She had heard a story that a big tree on Bahrain might have been the Tree of Knowledge from which Adam and Eve ate. Another legend says Bahrain is the island where Noah's ark came to rest when the waters of the flood receded. On this day, it appeared to have been taken over almost entirely by an oil refinery.[430]

As she approached the Sarjah Peninsula, she flew into drizzling rain. Clouds clustered around the 8,000-foot mountain peaks. She dropped down out of the clouds, found a low pass through the mountains, and "nervously" wound her way through. She could find nothing to look at below but more sand and sand-colored rocks. After she crossed the main ridge, the slopes on the eastern side were the greenest she had seen for days.[431]

She made it through the peaks okay, and out over the "rich royal blue" water of the Gulf of Oman. A single, white ship steamed north toward the Strait of Hormuz. The rays of the white-hot sun bounced off undersea coral and sent "shimmering gold" streaks across steep cliffs. Folks back home

---

[429] Ibid., 148.

[430] Ibid., 149.

[431] Ibid.

could not imagine that Iran could be this beautiful, and she had no way to capture the image.[432]

She flew on toward Karachi, on the edge of the Arabian Sea, where a new barrage of questions, paperwork, and social expectations would be waiting for her.

An hour out of Karachi, the voice of a captain of a Pakistan International Airline flight came over her radio. "Three-Eight Charlie, PIA Seven-Oh-Five. Karachi requests your occupation."

Occupation? What kind of question was that?

"PIA Seven-Oh-Five, Three-Eight Charlie. Say again please."

"Three-Eight Charlie, PIA Seven-Oh-Five. Karachi requests your occupation."

"PIA Seven-Oh-Five, this is Three-Eight Charlie. If you want my occupation, it's housewife."

There was a "long pause" on the other end, before the other pilot thanked her and signed off. If only she had a way to eavesdrop when the captain called in to Karachi. Pakistan didn't allow anyone except their own people to fly commercial flights in their airspace, so they must have been checking that Jerrie wasn't making money, carrying passengers. Or maybe the boys back at Bône were still talking about that flying madam-of-the-house.[433]

KARACHI, Pakistan, 5:03 p.m. (Pakistan Time)

Jerrie landed without embarrassment at Karachi Airport and made it through the crowd and the first round or two of lines, uniformed officers, and fees. John and Adelaide Tinker from the American Embassy were there to meet her. "I'm a

---

[432] Ibid., 150.

[433] Mock, *Three-Eight Charlie*, 150; Mock, interview, March 16, 2008.

'Flying Housewife,' too," Adelaide said, and invited her to their Aero Club.[434]

Men with the Aero Club put Charlie away for the night. Then she encountered her next new rules. Evidently, flying her own plane meant she was a crew member, and evidently, *that* meant that the Immigration man here must examine every item of jewelry that he could see on her. He listed each item on his form—her Astronaut watch, engagement and wedding rings, her son's class ring, and a $1.98 necklace. He also instructed her to wear all the same items again the next day, when she left Pakistan.[435]

Then he asked her where she was headed next. When she answered, "Calcutta, India," the man froze. He stopped writing and glared at her as if she had pulled a gun on him. Even the Tinkers seemed to stiffen a little. Evidently, in Pakistan, she wasn't even supposed to say the word "India." Still, the Immigration official let her go, and soon Jerrie and her bag were loaded into the car with her new hosts.[436]

The road from the airport into town gradually jammed with people, cars, and camels pulling carts. A contraption that looked like a Chinese rickshaw was weaving in and out between the traffic, pulled by a man on a bicycle.

"What's that thing?" Jerrie asked.

"We call them pedi-shaws," Tinker explained. "Hardly anybody can afford a gasoline engine, so you'll see a lot of them."

"Looks like they can take off and go wherever they want," Jerrie said.

---

[434] Ibid., 151.

[435] Ibid.

[436] Mock, interview, March 16, 2008.

The rest of the ride in their car was hot, bumpy, and hectic, so it was a relief to arrive at their building.[437]

April 4, 1:00 a.m. (Greenwich Mean Time/"Z")
West coast of AFRICA

Dakar radio wanted an explanation of why Joan was late and what happened. She told them she wasn't able to reach them on their published frequencies, and suggested that the erratic reception was probably due to atmospheric conditions. They accepted that and advised her that they had been within one hour of sending out the flying boats.[438]

She felt a "great depth of relief" at the sight of lights indicating she had reached Dakar.[439]

"51-Poppa, you're cleared to land on Runway Two."

Sixteen hours after taking off, Joan touched down in Dakar.[440] Exhausted and starving, she still had to wait for the usual questions and paperwork. People swarmed around the plane, wide-eyed, murmuring in excited French. The crowd included everyone from grandparents to grandchildren, even though it was 1:30 a.m. Joan handed out a few felt-tipped pens that she had brought along and motioned for people to sign *The City of Long Beach*. The grimy red, white, and blue metal fuselage got decorated some more. Even though the words were written by people she might not have time to meet, with names

---

[437] Ibid., 152.

[438] Brown, *Fate*, 62.

[439] Ibid.

[440] Merriam, "I Flew," 80.

she couldn't pronounce, their signatures and messages would add to her own unique souvenir.[441]

Once Customs and Immigration let her through, "an African reporter with UPI and a Piper dealer"[442] walked her in to the terminal for coffee. She checked in to the hotel at the field for pilots, and even that late, she could treat herself to dinner.

She didn't get to have her steak rare, though. It had to be well done. She didn't dare butter anything either, or pour cream into her coffee, or touch even so much as a leaf of lettuce or a slice of tomato, anything that might have been washed locally. She still couldn't eat anything unless it was overcooked, canned, and dull.[443]

Finally, sinking onto a hotel-room bed, she tried to settle down. She was "not quite back to earth, so to speak, after the over-ocean ordeal. How dreadful not to have certainty about where you are."[444] Gradually she fell asleep, recalling what the entire route originally looked like, back when she stretched her charts out on the living room floor at home. It was 3:00 a.m. on April 4, and she had only made it to the east coast of Africa. She was nine days behind schedule, and she still had twelve feet of charts yet to fly.[445]

---

[441] Two photographs: *A World Flight Publicity Photograph* and *Official US Navy Photograph of Joan*, both dated 1964, in *Fate on a Folded Wing*, 98; Swopes, *This Day in Aviation*.

[442] Brown, *Fate*, 62.

[443] Merriam, "I Flew," 80; Merriam, "Longest Flight," 46; Brown, *Fate*, 62.

[444] Brown, *Fate*, 62.

[445] Merriam, "I Flew," 80.

April 4, 7:03 p.m. (Pakistan Time)
KARACHI

The Tinkers' apartment was "airy and modern," yet full of soft chairs, pillows and elaborate wall tapestries. Adelaide led Jerrie upstairs to the guest bedroom, set down Jerrie's bag, and raised one hand. "Out this window, you get a view of the Arabian Sea." Then she raised her other hand. "Out this window, you are looking at the Gulf of Oman."[446]

Jerrie loved watching the sun set, and after she wrote a story to send to Mary McGarey, the reporter assigned to them at the *Dispatch*,[447] Adelaide led Jerrie out onto the rooftop. The clear night sky was filled with more stars than Jerrie had ever seen, even more than over the Atlantic.

"You've added on your own observatory," Jerrie said.

"And music room," Adelaide said. She showed Jerrie four or five stringed instruments, but Jerrie couldn't understand their names, or what they were.

Jerrie looked through the telescope at the lights filling the open desert sky and said, "I can see why ancient people watched the stars."

"Nights usually look like this," Adelaide said. "In Karachi, it almost never rains." Then she led her to the stairs. "Time for dinner. Care for a caviar *hors d'oeuvre?*"

"I don't much like caviar back home," Jerrie said.

"You've never had Iranian." Adelaide handed her a salty dollop on a cracker.

"Now I'll *never* like it back home," Jerrie said. "This is incredible."

---

[446] Mock, *Three-Eight Charlie*, 152.
[447] Ibid., 17.

"Russ sent us word that Joan Merriam Smith left Brazil," Tinker said, "and we've heard that she made it to Dakar okay, but we're not sure if she has left Senegal yet. So, she's in Africa, we just don't know where."

Jerrie almost managed to keep a straight face. Somehow, she had caught up with Joan, *maybe*, but impossible to tell for sure. Plus, they both still had half a planet of weather, mechanical trouble, and paperwork yet to go.

"Joan will be staying with us, too," Adelaide said.[448]

"I'll leave her a map on the pillow," Jerrie said.

Before she could sleep, Jerrie had to choose where to fly the next day. To plan this out right, she had to think two moves ahead. She could spend all day flying to Calcutta or she could fly to Delhi, only four hours away. Russ wanted her to cross the subcontinent as fast as she could, of course, and he had already sent cables to both cities. But Jerrie also had to think about how she would take off from Calcutta with "overflight clearance"[449] granted from the next nation, Burma (Myanmar, today). Back in the United States, they'd had more trouble getting permission from Burma than from any other country.

One of the pilots who had given her some good tips back home, Bob Iba, had warned her that she would have to file her flight plan over Burma the night before. He said it would take at least a day for the Burmese officials to respond, and that the officials in India wouldn't let her leave their country until Burma gave her the okay.

---

[448] Ibid., 153-154.
[449] Ibid., 175.

Jerrie thought about the delays Joan was reported to be experiencing. If Joan had been slowed down that much already, then maybe Jerrie could get away with touring a little more.

So tonight, she made up her mind. Rather than spend all day trying to hurry and worry across the subcontinent of India, just to sit in airport offices all day the *next* day, she would take the short flight to Delhi, file her forms there, and maybe get to sightsee.

Russ wasn't going to like it.[450]

April 4 , 12:00 noon (GMT/Z)
DAKAR, Senegal

Planes landing and taking off awakened Joan to her next new continent. She had been able to sleep until noon, somehow. The manager of Air Senegal called to invite her out for sightseeing.[451]

Her host honked his horn at a man pulling a goat across the street as a Renault sports car zipped past the other way. A woman sat on the side of the road in a full-length dress of bright blues and greens and a big hat made of the same material. Wearing a Timex watch on her wrist, the woman sold oranges and fruits that Joan didn't recognize out of wide, flat, wooden boxes.

Groups of children wandered the streets freely, weaving in and out between women in burkas. A man in a military uniform stood at the corner with a machine gun slung over his shoulder. Among the faces in the crowds, she saw every shade of color

---

[450] Ibid., 155.

[451] Brown, *Fate,* 62; Merriam, "I Flew," 80; Merriam, "Longest Flight,"46.

she had ever seen and many more she had not. She was "intrigued by the natives; tall, dignified, with erect bearing."[452]

Her next flight was too long to begin today, so for a few minutes, there was nothing more important to do but shop. She bought some African trinkets, a 14-karat gold cross for $10, and two figures carved out of mahogany. The figures were saints, and she had something to be thankful for. They would be shipped back to the States so as not to add weight.[453]

She was invited out to dinner that night, but she declined as politely as possible. She felt queasy and went to bed early. A fourteen-hour flight to Fort-Lamy lay ahead. The Air Senegal manager informed her that the weather at the moment was good and she said a silent prayer that it would hold.[454]

---

[452] Brown, *Fate*, 62.
[453] Ibid.
[454] Ibid.

Halfway There

Wall-to-Wall People

Sunday, April 5, 3:30 a.m. (Pakistan Time)
KARACHI, Pakistan

"Allow me to introduce you to Suchria Ali," John Tinker said. The most famous "lady pilot" in the country had come out to the Karachi airport to meet Jerrie.

"I've heard so much about you," Suchria said, and shook Jerrie's hand.

"I love your silks," Jerrie said. The Tinkers had told Jerrie that Suchria Ali was a commercial glider pilot and flight instructor, but Jerrie was even more impressed with her bright pantaloons and embroidered tunic. Her outfit looked more comfortable and stylish than any woman in this or any city that Jerrie had visited in the Islamic side of the world. Jerrie would have loved to trade her own nylon stockings and skirts to adopt this style back home.[455]

Accompanied by Suchria, the Tinkers took Jerrie around to all the necessary offices. Having all these nice people with her didn't make the lines move along or get the forms filled out any faster, but having the company was nice, anyway. She also noticed that today, no official asked to see her wedding ring or checked her bags. She could have loaded all the jewelry she could fit in the plane if she wanted.[456]

---

[455] Mock, *Three-Eight Charlie*, 156; Mock, interview, March 16, 2008.
[456] Ibid., 157.

For her weather briefing, Jerrie had to leave the new and modern main terminal building and walk over to a separate building that looked old and rundown. At her briefing, she was happy to get a forecast of good weather, in English. Then an airport official escorted her out of that meeting and walked her past a big crowd in white robes, all jammed into one room, waiting for their flight.

Jerrie turned to the official. "What are these passengers doing in this building?"

"These people?" He blinked, as if just noticing them. "Well, of course they have to use this building, because, you see, they would get the new terminal dirty."

Throughout the crowd, Jerrie did notice lots of little children, messy lunches, and discarded banana peels. But how did the airport officials draw the line between the messy people and the neat? She had learned in school about the caste system in India, and how some people were considered beneath the dignity of others. But that was only from reading about it in a book. Here, facing the situation in person, Jerrie couldn't tell one group of people from the other, and yet this man acted as if the difference was obvious. She hoped they at least got a cheaper rate.[457]

8:42 a.m.

After six long hours of standing in lines and filling out forms, Jerrie was back up in the air. She could stretch her legs and take in the view on this cloudless day. She was determined to win this race, but this trip was also her only chance to see the

---

[457] Ibid.

world, and she wasn't getting to see much. If she was starting to catch Joan, maybe Joan was having more mechanical troubles than she was. Jerrie was ready to gamble that she might get to see one or two more sights, and still win, if she could just keep that husband of hers off her back, God love him.[458]

She guided Charlie away from Karachi and the western mouth of the Indus River and crossed the river at Hyderabad, looking down onto the famous Indus River Valley. Even though she was passing over one of the cradles of civilization, this was the dry season. From 1,000 feet, there was nothing to look at but endless "brown dust." Her map showed a town to the north called Sukkur, which translated as *hell*. "Hell" was reported to be intolerably hot and dry twelve months a year.[459]

At some invisible point she flew out of Pakistan and into India, because she began to see tiny farms. Low walls divided the land into little, square plots. No green in sight and the fields were bare. It was hard to imagine that anything ever would grow in them. Individuals, small groups and crowds sat, stood, and walked around these small plots, "like one continuous suburb."[460]

This wasn't the kind of sight she had dreamed of seeing on this trip, and it had a powerful impact on her. "Mile after mile of parched farms waiting hopefully for the rain (were) etched upon (her) mind so that the picture (could) never be erased."[461] She would try to recall this image the next time she began to stress over a Customs delay or a gas pump.

---

[458] Ibid., 158; Mock, interview, March 18, 2008.

[459] Ibid., 159.

[460] Ibid.

[461] Ibid., 160.

Now it was time to face her next challenge: How to say local names over the radio. Back in Ohio, she had become concerned that many of the places she was required to report in to bore names that she couldn't pronounce. Now she was approaching some of them: Gharo, Maghulbhim, Chor, Nawabshah, Rahim Yar Khan, and Bhuj. When she had asked an Indian student at Ohio State University if he could help her with the pronunciation and maybe a few Indian phrases, he asked her, "Which one of the forty dialects would you like to study first?" She muddled her way through the names as she reported her position until she was over the Jumna River and descended into Palam Airport, Delhi.[462]

DELHI, India, 2:18 p.m. (India Time)

At Palam Airport, Jerrie was greeted once again by reporters and their questions as soon as she opened her door, and she still didn't have ready answers. Yet she was also welcomed by members of the Aero Club of India. They grabbed her bags, saying they had made all the arrangements for her rides, hotels, everything. This was still new for Jerrie, to be "the toast of the town."[463]

Nobody at Customs and Immigration examined Jerrie's wedding ring, or went through her bags, or came up with any new rules. Still, one man insisted on marking every bag she had pulled out of the plane with chalk. When one of her Aero Club friends picked up her camera, he must have missed it, but when

---

462 Ibid.
463 Ibid., 161.

she picked it up and passed through the door, he ran to swipe chalk on the case.[464]

She was given a ride and was relieved, after what she had just seen from the air, to ride along a wide street lined with flowers and arrive at the comfortable New Delhi YWCA. She checked into her room and came back downstairs to catch her next ride. While she waited, she wrote a quick story for the newspaper, while noticing a sitting room just off the lobby filled with kindly middle-aged English ladies having tea, "pure Agatha Christie." She wasn't invited, but it was too hot for tea anyway.[465]

Her contact in New Delhi was a Colonel G.V. Raja, who picked her up at the YWCA right on time, accompanied by his ten-year-old son. They took her first to the Overseas Communications building, right next door.

She had to recopy her story by hand onto the forms to send it by cable, and then she tried to pay for it. But, the man wouldn't take her credit card without a personal identification card, which she couldn't obtain on Sunday. They wouldn't take her American Express traveler's check, and even though she had accumulated currency from her previous stops, she didn't have any Indian rupees. Colonel Raja offered to pay, but she couldn't figure how she would pay him back. So, Jerrie just wadded up the cable forms, turned to Colonel Raja and said, "Let's go sightseeing!"[466]

They all got back in the car. Here in the city, the women were dressed in bright saris, the men were in either business

---

[464] Ibid.

[465] Ibid., 162.

[466] Ibid.

suits or outfits that looked to Jerrie like "white pajamas," and people looked happy. Colonel Raja took her to see the Iron Pillar, a shaft of solid iron, twenty feet tall, which he said had shown no sign of rust in 1,500 years.

"Teenagers try to encircle it with their arms," the Colonel explained. "If their fingers touch, it brings them good luck. Want to try?"

Jerrie shook her head. "My arms would never reach." She would just have to keep making her own luck.[467]

Next, she was taken to a reception on her behalf at the Aero Club at Safdarjun Airport, where she met people who had known Amelia and had worked on her plane. Yet she also had to speak to the press, of course. One reporter showed her a telegram from his editor, somewhere in Europe, asking her to "please report on the sad progress of Joan Merriam Smith"–as if Jerrie knew.[468]

"Time for dinner," the Colonel said. "We have the perfect restaurant in mind, with an excellent American steak."

"Oh, thank you," Jerrie said, "but I would rather try something more authentically Indian, if possible."

"Then I happen to know the best place in town for that, too," the Colonel said. "Let me make a phone call."

Colonel Raja's mother seemed honored to fix a special dinner, even if it was on short notice. With a roomful watching, Jerrie tasted everything–only a little of the really spicy stuff–and she used the chapatis to scoop up the gravies, like everyone else. She was impressed that several generations all lived together. She met Colonel Raja's mother, father, aunts and

---

[467] Ibid., 163.
[468] Ibid., 164.

uncles, sisters, and cousins, sharing a big house and abundant gardens, they lived "in harmony" as well as any American family Jerrie had ever seen.[469]

Back in Ohio, comments from both pilots ran in the Columbus *Dispatch,* along with a comment that "the two flying housewives . . . exchanged the closest to barbed challenges they have issued since their respective round-the-world tries began."

In the article, Joan blamed Jerrie's lead on various troubles that Joan had to deal with, including "the revolution in Brazil. I had an awful time getting accurate weather forecasts. "

Jerrie was quoted as saying, "I am not in any race with that woman," insisting that her timeline was imposed by rules for recording her flight "with the Federation Aeronautique Internationale."

The paper also quoted Jerrie's view of Joan's stated goal of following Amelia Earhart's route: "She is not going all the way over the challenging route through equatorial forest and rough terrain. She is going just enough of the way to uphold her claim."[470]

DAKAR, Senegal, 4:30 a.m. (Z)

Joan was up and waiting when the Piper dealer from Air Senegal arrived to take her to her plane.[471] Still, the next round of waiting through customs and clearances gave her plenty of time to look around.

---

[469] Ibid.

[470] "Mrs. Smith in Senegal After Bad Weather Hop," *Columbus Dispatch,* April 5, 1964, Geiger and Nesbitt, 50.

[471] Brown, *Fate,* 62.

The jets in Senegal no longer portrayed the familiar logos of Eastern Airlines, Pan Am, or TWA. Instead, she saw Lufthansa, Swissair, Sabena, BOAC, and Aeroflot, further reminders that she had "crossed the pond."

By 9:25 a.m., she was up and away. From the air, Dakar appeared to consist mostly of square, concrete buildings, except for the smooth, golden dome of an Eastern Orthodox Church. A little rectangle of dusty open space was evidently a playing field, except that it didn't have backstops, bleachers, or even green grass, just small soccer goals. One building, taller than the rest, was capped by the dark green turrets of a mosque. Yep, she had left the western hemisphere far behind.

She flew at 5,000 feet, hoping to see "elephants, lions, zebras"[472] that the local folks had promised she might see, but from that altitude, all she could spot were a few scrub bushes, small trees and little else. If she flew lower, she would be fighting the headwinds.[473] The barren landscape reminded her of the American Southwest, with a haze of some sort that she couldn't identify. She didn't think it could be pollution, this far away from any visible areas of development.[474] She only saw one other plane, a DC-3.[475]

The remoteness got her thinking about what would happen if she had to ditch her plane in the middle of the desert. One book she had read on how to survive in these situations advised to stay in the shade of the plane and burn something to make smoke signals. Well, maybe. She had a small pistol, but doubted

---

[472] Brown, *Fate*, 63.

[473] Ibid.

[474] Merriam, "I Flew," 80; Brown, *Fate*, 63.

[475] Ibid.

it would do much good if she were to encounter a lion. She also thought about a World War II bomber that had gone down in the African desert; it wasn't found for almost three decades. One scenario after another circled through her mind. "Thoughts like these come easy when you are alone," she recorded in her journal.[476]

She was getting tired and hungry, and her eyes hurt. Still, the drier air, more like southern California than the Brazilian rain forest, was a welcome relief.[477]

Joan crossed Africa at its widest point. Although Gao, Mali, was on Amelia's route, the region was now under "communist influence," so, to avoid taking any more chances than necessary, she headed due east to Niamey, Niger.[478]

After nine hours and fifteen minutes, she was grateful to be granted permission, in clear English, to land.[479] She began her descent, and saw that the haze below was actually swarms of insects. In the soft light of the sunset, their wings glimmered like golden-orange sparks.

Sunlight faded very gradually, and she was pleasantly surprised by the beautiful lighting and long, modern airstrip greeting her at Niamey. She watched the Shell Oil workers set up for refueling with fascination. Two fifty-five-gallon drums were hooked up to a filtering system in the back of a cart. Three men took turns hand-pumping, and it took them twenty minutes to pump sixty gallons. The local manager of the Aero

---

[476] Merriam, "I Flew," 80-81.
[477] Brown, *Fate*, 63.
[478] Merriam, "Longest Flight," 47; Schubert and Smith, "World Flight."
[479] Brown, *Fate*, 63

Club took her to the airport's new three-story terminal for a bite to eat.[480]

She was handed a bill for 250 francs, or $2, for a landing fee, and 3,000 francs, or $12, for having the landing strip lights turned on for her.[481]

She took off again about 9:41 p.m., which was still twilight, and immediately discovered that her VOR homing device wasn't working. Would she have to turn back, just because of that? But when she called the tower, the operator laughed, explaining that the local omni station had been turned off to save electricity. This practice was unheard of back in the US, but out here, where it took much longer to get dark, it made sense.[482]

Joan treated her dry lips with lip balm and her tired eyes with Murine. She sipped coffee from a Thermos and dealt with the rarified night air at 7,000 feet with a shot from her oxygen mask. Below her, the night was pitch black, except for the occasional fire of a village. She thought at first that a white spot on the horizon off to her right might be a radio beacon, or maybe a town, but it turned out to be the quarter moon, just now rising at 1:00 a.m.[483]

At some point, she entered the air space of the nation of Chad, but, out there, the boundaries of nations and their airspace were just invisible lines in the sand and wind. As the stars came out one by one, she felt as if she were not so much below them, as *among* them.

---

[480] Ibid.

[481] Ibid.

[482] Brown, *Fate*, 64.

[483] Ibid.

After six hours of the anxiety that comes with night flying, she was approaching Lake Chad, "swampy" and "beautiful" in the moonlight, but all she could think about was keeping awake long enough to land in Fort-Lamy.[484]

She touched down at 4:30 a.m., and a representative of the American embassy, Michael B. Smith, was there to greet her. She refueled the plane with another fifty-five gallons in each of the ferry tanks, and refueled herself with enough black coffee to take off again without any sleep at all.[485]

---

[484] Ibid.

[485] Merriam, "I Flew," 81; Brown, *Fate*, 65.

So Many Silks, So Little Time

Monday, April 6, 9:30 a.m. (India Time)
Over INDIA

Jerrie's route followed the Ganges River. For five hours, she flew over villages along the riverbanks and people bathing in the water. Her route drew her close enough to the border with Nepal that she hoped for at least a peek of the Himalayas, but there wasn't enough visibility that day. Meandering off course would be s-o-o tempting, but she dared not have to explain the lost time to Russ. One more sightseeing adventure that would have to wait for that return trip, some day. Calcutta was only six degrees further south than Delhi, but as soon as she touched down at Dum Dum Airport, she felt "engulfed" by the heavy, wet heat.[486]

CHAD, 7:40 a.m. (West Africa Time)

Joan took off, bound for Khartoum.[487]

Her next stop was supposed to be the desert city of El Fasher in Sudan. She hadn't been able to find out much about El Fasher, except that caravans used to stop and trade there in the old days and that Earhart had stopped there on her flight, as well.

The landscape stretched away flat in all directions, with El Fasher laid out on a grid. The buildings and trees were arranged

---

[486] Mock, *Three-Eight Charlie*, 166-167; Mock, interview, March 16, 2008.
[487] Merriam, "I Flew," 81; Brown, *Fate*, 65.

within patterned squares and rectangles. The only airstrip down there looked tiny, rough, and made of sand. The wreckage of a plane angled off the runway. It looked as if the crash had just happened, but in this dry climate, the plane could have been sitting there for years. It would have been a nice break, but she couldn't trust the landing strip, so she kept on flying.[488]

The desert terrain of the southern Sahara continued to shift, subtly and slowly, for mile after mile. All hints of green faded until it was "just blowing sand."[489] She had been struggling against headwinds since Natal, and they just kept getting worse.[490]

By high noon, the thermal columns became "almost unbearable, even at 10,000 feet."[491] Three hours after takeoff, she lost all radio contact, and she didn't see any planes, either. She couldn't use her autopilot or even take her hand off the wheel.[492]

The coffee had worn off, and she had been in the air twenty-six hours without sleep. With each passing hour, she slipped closer and closer toward falling asleep at the controls. She tried splashing water on her face, but to handle the water bottle she had to take one or both hands off the wheel. At the slightest loss of touch, her plane would veer off course until she could squeeze her knee up under the wheel, get a hand free, and regain control. Her plane's refusal to help her out and coast straight irritated her more each time, but it also jolted her

---

[488] Merriam, "Longest Flight," 47; Brown, *Fate*, 65.

[489] Brown, *Fate*, 65.

[490] Merriam, "Longest Flight," 47; Brown, *Fate*, 65.

[491] Merriam, "I Flew," 81.

[492] Brown, *Fate*, 65.

awake.[493] She had to be certain she was staying on course, which was difficult without any contact. This was just as bad as over the Atlantic. "No contact then. No contact now."[494]

CALCUTTA, India, 3:07 P.M. (India Time)

Officials in turbans, the local Cessna dealer, the press, and representatives from the American Embassy waited to take Jerrie upstairs for tea. Hot tea? In 100-degree heat? At least the Aero Club gathering was held in an air-conditioned room, and she got her tea over ice.

"Could you give us any idea where we might find Joan Merriam?" This question came from one of the gentlemen from the American Embassy, and when he asked, the rest of the room grew quiet.

"The American Embassy in Rangoon is still trying to find Mrs. Merriam Smith," a second official explained, "so they can tell her that she doesn't have permission to fly over Burma. Our embassy in Burma was able to obtain overflight permission for you. It took us six weeks, but we got it." The man shrugged, directing his statements toward Jerrie. "They feel sure they can do the same for Joan, but first, she has to apply for it. Personally. And the last anyone heard, she didn't know that she had to apply."

Jerrie had heard about this situation with Joan when she had visited the Burmese Embassy in Washington. When Jerrie went to their office to ask for her visa, she had "seen a letter" advising Burma that Joan would be making the flight as well. But the ambassador told Jerrie that Joan had not asked them for a visa.

---

[493] Merriam, "I Flew," 81.

[494] Brown, *Fate*, 65.

The Burmese gentleman went on to tell Jerrie that if Joan ever did get around to asking for her visa, he would turn her down, but until then, he would not advise her.

So today, the American Embassy representative was anxiously explaining to Jerrie that he could not help her competitor until he found her. Everybody had lost track of her, and he clearly hoped Jerrie would help him, somehow.[495]

Jerrie could only shrug. Maybe Joan was somewhere over Africa where they had all lost track of Jerrie for a while, too. Jerrie was relieved when a man from the US Consulate, a contact Russ had made named Mr. Kyler, offered to give Jerrie a ride to her hotel, and then out to a bazaar where she could go shopping.

They were met by a Mrs. Roy, the American mother of one of the Cessna representatives, and her Indian daughter-in-law and grandchildren. The Roys led Jerrie on a walk through a series of stalls in a giant building. They had an especially wide assortment of saris for sale, the one item Jerrie wanted to bring home. Her hostesses walked her past row after row of brilliant silks, no two with the same pattern.

"Indian women want to be different, like women back home," Jerrie said. "And they must like to shop. It would take days to look over everything here."

"Let me help you." Mrs. Roy's daughter-in-law had grown up learning how to bargain. Plus, she could take Jerrie around to the shopkeepers that she personally knew. When the price was too high, she said so. Jerrie kept finding saris she liked, but Mrs. Roy kept turning them down, until they found one that

---

[495] Mock, *Three-Eight Charlie*, 167-168; Mock, interview, March 16, 2008.

passed both of their tests. Jerrie found a couple more things, but they would have to be shipped home. There was no room in the plane for souvenirs. Soon, the heat was nearly making her sick. Lucky for her husband, the big store wasn't air-conditioned or she could have shopped much longer.[496]

Dinner was served at the Kylers' apartment, where Jerrie was grateful for ice in her drink. They sat on a big porch under a high ceiling, cooling off under a large fan. The porch overlooked an overcrowded street. These were not the nicely dressed people of New Delhi, but an endless stream of men, with only white cloths draped around their waists and legs.

On the drive to her hotel, she passed more people walking, standing, lying down on the streets, with no escape from the brutal heat. Thankfully, the Great Eastern Hotel was air-conditioned.[497]

KHARTOUM, Sudan, 4:55 p.m. (Central Africa Time)

At dusk, Joan got her next first-in-a-lifetime-view. In her descent over the flat desert, she zipped over the White Nile River, headed toward the twinkling lights of Khartoum and the airport. After thirty-six hours of flying without sleep, including almost eleven straight hours of bucking headwinds, she was finally bringing the plane down.[498]

Nobody was there to meet her.

She tried calling the American Embassy, but she was told that the office had closed at 2:30 that afternoon. She was greeted

---

[496] Mock, *Three-Eight Charlie*, 168-169; Mock, interview, March 16, 2008.

[497] Mock, *Three-Eight Charlie*, 169-171; Mock, interview, March 16, 2008.

[498] Merriam, "I Flew," 81; Brown, Fate, 66.

by Shell and Esso, and they argued briefly over whose gas she should buy.[499]

After the plane was gassed up and stowed, Joan went inside the airport, searching for assistance. As she looked around at the people in the airport, she was "intrigued" by the different styles of dress and ornamentation. Some of the local people bore the distinct marks of ritual scarification on their cheeks, while a different group wore beads embedded in their foreheads in a continuous line from eyebrow to eyebrow. The "natives" of Khartoum, in turn, looked at her skirt and blouse with curiosity; their expressions turned to astonishment when she pulled out twenty dollars' worth of francs for trinkets.[500]

For accommodations, the airport manager offered her an adobe hut. It didn't have restrooms, privacy, or air conditioning; just nine beds in one big room, with openings for windows, without glass or screens. The manager said it was used by the local men who worked at the airfield.[501]

Joan couldn't see how she would get much rest in 110-degree heat, hanging on to her purse all night, and eventually having to use her sick sacks to relieve herself. She heard there was a place in town operated by Americans with an "air cooling device" of some sort, but it wasn't quite getting communicated to her where that might be.[502]

---

[499] Merriam, "I Flew," 81; Brown, *Fate*, 66.

[500] Brown, *Fate*, 66-67.

[501] Ibid., 67.

[502] Schubert and Smith, "World Flight;" Brown, *Fate*, 67.

Will I Make It to the Golden Dome?

Tuesday, April 7, 3:30 a.m. (India Time)
CALCUTTA

BAM, BAM, BAM!

Hotel fire? Jerrie found the lamp, her bathrobe, and the doorknob. A teenaged boy walked into her room, turned on all her lights, smiled at her, and headed toward her bathtub. She handed him the first bill she could find and got him out of there.[503]

Mr. Kyler waited in the lobby to drive her to the airport. As they left the hotel, dawn was breaking, and people were still asleep by the "hundreds," everywhere. "Whole families were stretched out side-by-side, for block after block."[504] On her ride out of town, Jerrie watched people "get up, wash at public faucets, and pull their clothes on, their personal lives an open book." She was relieved to return to the airport, where she no longer felt quite so distant from the people around her. Yet the sadness stayed on her shoulders like a heavy blanket for days, and it made her miss her own dear family and comfortable home that much more.[505]

---

[503] Mock, *Three-Eight Charlie*, 172; Mock, interview, April 11, 2008.

[504] Mock, *Three-Eight Charlie*, 173.

[505] Mock, *Three-Eight Charlie*, 174; Mock, interview, April 11, 2008.

7:15 a.m.

After more delays, Jerrie escaped into the air once again. Even though many people were working the rice paddies that she flew over, the flight still felt "lonely."[506]

As soon as she reached cruising altitude, acres of rice paddies gave way to swampy jungle. Sadly, she was leaving India and crossing into East Pakistan. The green canopy was too dense to see any tigers or elephants down there. As she angled the plane over the Bay of Bengal and away from the shore, she felt as if she were leaving all signs of civilization behind.

She knew that typhoons often hit the coast of East Pakistan and Burma, but today, the water was "sapphire blue, with white caps sparkling like diamonds in the sun." When the green coastline of Burma appeared, it looked like "a spray of emeralds."[507]

Trying to verify her position, she picked up a strong signal from the next station, probably coming from a town named Vishakhapatnam, even though she couldn't be sure where the signal originated. She maintained her course, flying over more swamp, canopy, rice paddies, and mountains, and then over the Irrawaddy River, the Rangoon River, and other rivers that ran through the dark green landscape. She was relieved to hear a controller with an American-sounding voice give her clearance through this next region. There was no hint today that she had crossed an invisible line into territory controlled by a government that had refused to grant her a visa to land and had nearly refused to allow her to fly over it at all.[508]

---

[506] Ibid.

[507] Ibid., 175.

[508] Mock, *Three-Eight Charlie*, 174; Mock, interview, April 11, 2008.

She flew over the Andaman Sea to the Malay Peninsula and over the Bilauk Taung mountains into Thailand, switched to Bangkok radio and reported in. Right away, she heard "November Three-Eight Charlie" being granted clearance to descend to 4,000 feet. She headed down, but her chart showed peaks at around 6,000, so she climbed back up and passed over the last ridge before starting her descent.

She never did figure out why Burma would not allow her to land. Communicating with air traffic control operators around the world, she continued to run into obstacles. Despite all her homework, manuals, maps, and charts, she could not get caught up on *all* the rules. For instance, nobody told her that she was supposed to write to the International Civil Aviation Organization in Montreal, Canada to find out rules for flying in Africa and Asia. Blissful in her ignorance, she ended up flying US-style VFR all around the world. In the United States, pilots flew visual above cloud layers. In some other regions, it was required to keep in sight of the ground or water. So, she was perpetually obeying, then disobeying their direction, trusting her intuition to know when to keep in sight of mountains or anything else she might hit.[509]

Her first sight of Bangkok was a "golden dome above the treetops," but she knew not to come any closer to the temple. Overflying the city was not allowed.[510]

KHARTOUM, Sudan 8:00 a.m. (Central Africa Time)

The extreme heat presented a problem for Joan. The hotter

---

[509] Mock, *Three-Eight Charlie*, 175-177.
[510] Mock, *Three-Eight Charlie*, 178; Merriam, "I Flew," 81.

the air, the thinner it was, making her plane heavier. Yet she also needed her gas tanks full for the *next* long flight. That meant that her plane would be too heavy to clear the runway, until the temperature dropped. She would have to wait, so she would be spending the day in Khartoum.

Some American pilots got in touch with the Embassy for her.[511] William Rountree, US Ambassador to Sudan, came out to meet Joan and invited her to his air-conditioned home later that evening; she was happy to accept.[512]

Time to find a bite to eat. She found a restaurant, and she knew to ask for bottled water only. Then she watched as the staff turned on the tap, filled a bottle with tap water, and served that to her. Next, she tried asking for a Coke. This request was fulfilled by a bottle of bright red liquid, which, she was told, was "ginger beer," but to her, one sip was like "eating red hot pepper."[513] Still, the Sudanese spoke English, and were friendly to Americans. An Arab woman wearing a purple lace gown asked if Joan would like to take her photo.[514]

The day took a turn for the better when Mr. Rountree brought her over to his office, then off to shop with some of his aides, followed by lunch with his wife. Mrs. Rountree was also a gracious hostess that night. Joan liked getting to visit the social scene of an American Embassy, and yet she also liked not having to be in it for much more than a visit.[515]

---

[511] Brown, Fate, 68.

[512] Brown, *Fate,* 68.

[513] Ibid., 68.

[514] Ibid,68-9.

[515] Brown, Fate, 68.

She "longed to linger" in Khartoum, and ride the Nile in a river boat with a single sail.[516] But by midnight, she was back at the airfield, trying to get everything set up for an early morning takeoff to beat the heat. The controller in the tower was sound asleep, his radio "blaring in all directions."[517] It took her an hour and a half to refuel and another half an hour to send telegrams to Jack and to her publicist, John Sarver.[518] The airfield crew had dripped gas again, and she had to stop a man from trying to wipe sand off her windshield with a dry rag before he had scratched up her plexiglass.[519]

BANGKOK, Thailand, 3:53 p.m. (Hovd Time/HOVT)

Jerrie landed without too many bounces, only to discover that her next few miles closer to the equator brought her into a few more degrees up the thermometer and a bit more moisture in the air, yet again. The hope that a hotel with a cool bath might be waiting at the end of the day kept her from giving in to a headache from the heat.

The plane needed a refill on gas, and the pilot needed a refill of her water bottle. Opening her door, she spotted Shell and Esso gasoline trucks hustling toward her. By now she had learned to get gas quickly, before the trucks drove off again. So, with both drivers watching, she said, "I'll flip a coin: Shell, you won." But the Shell driver opened his hand to the Esso man, and let him have it. Apparently, people on this side of the

---

[516] Brown, Fate, 70.

[517] Brown, Fate, 68.

[518] Ibid.

[519] Ibid., 69.

world went out of their way to be courteous, even to their competition.[520]

A couple of US Air Force pilots walked past in their orange flying suits without taking any notice of the only single-engine civilian plane on the airfield. Had she disappeared from American view again, just when she needed a local guide?[521]

"Mrs. Mock?" A man and a woman approached her. They introduced themselves as Mr. and Mrs. Bundit Watanasupt.

The Watanasupts were friends of Dr. Keith Tyler, who had been one of Russ and Jerrie's professors back at Ohio State. Mr. Watanasupt introduced his wife to Jerrie as the public-relations director of Radio Thailand. Their English was clear and she hoped they could help with translating. As it turned out, they did—some.[522]

With the plane fueled, it was off to face the dreaded *offices*. She followed the Watanasupts through the Bangkok terminal for hours, sometimes understanding what was going on at each office, most times, not. At the telegraph office, she was told she had a telegram from Manila and was then given a bill for it.

"He wants *how much*?" Jerrie said.

"Yes, Mrs. Mock," Mr. Watanasupt said. "That would be $56."

"You tell that man I don't want a collect telegram."

This discussion went around and around until everybody was upset. Eventually, she was handed a document with "propeller aircraft" written on it and "$56," written opposite that. Then she understood that this bill was also for an airport

---

[520] Mock, *Three-Eight Charlie*, 178-179.

[521] Ibid., 179.

[522] Ibid.

fee, which, even though Charlie was being charged at the same rate as an airliner, she still had to pay.

Then she got her telegram, too, which told her that United States Industries would take care of Charlie when she made it to the Philippines. Russ had set that one up for her. Maybe she would get those badly needed brakes after all.[523]

That turned out to be her last stop. "All things finally wear out, including government officials,"[524] and she was free to explore anything that might still be open, so the Watanasupts drove her into the city.

They stopped first at a large, modern downtown park and drank "cool coconut milk" from an ice-cream chest on a vendor's bicycle. With skyscrapers in the background and people walking around in Western-style clothes, it almost looked as if they were touring San Francisco. But by the time they made it to a gigantic pagoda, the big iron gates were closed. All she got to see was its "golden-spired dome, gleaming aloft in the rays of the setting sun."[525]

For dinner, the Watanasupts took her to a restaurant overlooking a canal. The menu included shark's fin soup, abalone stew, and, naturally, rice. After flying over rice paddies for hours, it was "good to see some of it in a bowl," and Jerrie was relieved that she could manage chopsticks.[526]

But before she could eat, she carefully studied the view. All she could see were large, dark leaves and bamboo in a garden across the canal, and small merchant boats passing below.

---

[523] Ibid., 179-180.
[524] Ibid., 180.
[525] Ibid., 181.
[526] Ibid, 182.

"What are you looking for?" Mr. Watanasupt asked.

"I don't know. I guess I'm looking around for the people who can't afford this meal," Jerrie said.

"Oh, not to worry," Mrs. Watanasupt said. "Here in Thailand, there is plenty of food for everybody."

Hearing that helped her eat dinner in peace, hoping that she wasn't surrounded by starving people on the streets this time.[527]

After dinner, they looked for a hotel for Jerrie. By sightseeing first, they had gotten a late start on finding her a room, and the first-rate hotels were all full. The Watanasupts had said their goodbyes before she discovered the catch at the place they did find: no running water.

"No cool bath?" she blurted.

"No problem, ma'am," the manager said. "The boys will bring buckets."

While she sat in the tub in her birthday suit? "Oh, no thank you," she stammered. In her room, she tried to fiddle with the knob on the air conditioner in the window, but she could tell there was way too much water in the air for one little window unit. Exhausted or not, she kept waking up in the brutal heat throughout the night.[528]

---

[527] Ibid.

[528] Ibid.; Mock, interview, April 11, 2008.

Trouble Over the Ocean

Wednesday, April 8, 5:00 a.m. (Central Africa Time)
KHARTOUM, Sudan

Joan got off the ground early enough to get ahead of what was forecast to be a 130-degree day. She passed the dry, jagged peaks of the Asmara mountain range of Ethiopia, rising to 11,000 feet, from her clearance at 13,500 feet.[529]

At Massawa, she changed course toward Assab. Earhart had landed at Assab, but today, Joan would not be taking any chances with the sand and or the short runways there.[530]

She had hoped to see more of this part of the world that she had heard stories about since childhood. Instead, she was just flying over more flat, dry, barren plains, forced to stick to her schedule for fear of having to ask for additional clearances and flyover approval. She passed Massawa on the west coast of the Red Sea at 7:55 a.m. local time. Then down the Ethiopian peninsula past rugged coastlines and swamps, through some fog, and along a stretch of coastline with a bit more color. The low brush of the desert gave it a little brown, the lava flow was black, and salt beds white, sometimes rising high enough to resemble dunes.[531]

---

[529] Merriam, "I Flew," 81; Brown, *Fate*, 69.

[530] Brown, *Fate*, 70.

[531] Ibid., 70-71.

BANGKOK, Thailand, 3:30 a.m. (Hovd Time/HOVT)

The air conditioner "sputtered and moaned" all night, invading Jerrie's dreams. She rode with the Watanasupts in the dark, trying to wake up, appreciating all the people around the world who got up early for her. The air was already heavy and humid, maybe worse than the dry heat of the desert.[532]

At the airport, she tried to telegram a story to the *Dispatch*. The man behind the desk was sound asleep and wearing only a pair of pants, but at least he was on duty at 4:00 a.m. He woke up and tried to help her, but he wouldn't take her traveler's check and he didn't know what her credit card was. The Watanasupts paid her bill, and Jerrie promised to pay them back when she got home, but they didn't look happy about it. Then she had to work her way through the usual obstacles of getting a weather report, paying fees, filing a flight plan, and filling out forms she didn't understand or trust, such as signing a blank piece of paper without understanding why. She kept that smile on her face anyway, and dumped a stack of papers that she had accumulated around the world so far into the airport ladies' room trash can.[533]

By 7:40 a.m., she was ready to take off, with one catch. Today's flight plan required a slight change. Back in Washington, the State Department had "advised against" flying over Cambodia. No reason for this decree had been offered. So she had planned another stop. Yet once here, she found out that she could skip that stop by flying around Cambodia. However, the new route would add distance. If she had known all that the day before, she would have asked for another twenty gallons

---

[532] Mock, *Three-Eight Charlie*, 183.
[533] Ibid., 184 -186.

while she had the gas truck. Now, rather than lose an hour looking for another truck, she decided to gamble that she *probably* had enough gas to make it across the ocean to the Philippines.[534]

She said her goodbyes, put on her trusty Mae West life preserver, and took off. Once in the air, out over the Gulf of Siam, she refigured her mileage. She had not added it up correctly. Plus, she had a headwind that was slowing her down. Between the miscalculation, the change in route, and the wind, she could come up short by as much as 170 nautical miles, and three hours. If she were going to stop for emergency fuel, she would have to attempt a landing in Saigon–in the middle of the Vietnam War.[535]

As she approached the coast of Vietnam, all she could see were "trees, swamps and rice paddies." Beneath which of those clumps of green leaves was the next salvo of rockets about to be launched by the Viet Cong, or the next American helicopter about to take off? No way to tell. She didn't want to land there unless she had no other choice. As she flew past the Saigon airport, she reported her position.

The Saigon approach controller called her back. "November Three-Eight Charlie, do you have a man on board?"

"Negative," Jerrie answered. "No man on board."

"Well, good luck," came the answer from Saigon.

Well, boys, good luck with your war, Jerrie thought.[536]

North of Phan Thiet, she flew parallel to the coast until the coastline began to swing away from her. Out her left window

---

[534] Ibid., 186.

[535] Ibid., 187-188.

[536] Ibid., 189.

stretched "mile after mile of gray-green water and dark-green jungle." Ahead and to her right was only the endless expanse of the Pacific Ocean, but that was where she had to go. This jungle was her last glimpse of Asia. It was frustrating to leave the East already after seeing hardly any of it. Her flight path gradually angled Charlie away from shore and off toward the next 900 miles over the South China Sea, trying not to think about running out of gas.[537]

An hour after leaving land behind, she tried to get a radio signal from Manila. Forgetting to turn off the motor to the radio antenna back in Africa meant that she didn't have the trailing antenna now when she needed it. The man at Pantronics had tried to talk her into a hand-crank, but that had sounded like too much trouble. She "wondered what kind of antenna Joan was using."[538] Without the long antenna, she was learning to use her "woman's intuition" to guess at how close she was approaching a station by the strength of the signal. Eventually, she picked up a faint *dit-dah-dit, dit-dit-dit* ("Romeo Sierra"), maybe 600-700 miles out from a radio tower named Rosario, the first strong signal from the Philippines. She flew in peace and solitude for another hour, watching cloud formations, writing for the *Dispatch,* and listening for any voice she could talk to over the radio. Once, she thought she heard someone say, "November Three-Eight Charlie." She answered, but heard no more.[539]

The radio was silent, but she thought she detected some slight shift in the sounds of the airplane. She turned off all her radios and listened, straining to pick up the difference.

---

[537] Ibid, 189-190.

[538] Ibid., 191.

[539] Ibid., 190.

The steady drone from the nose of the plane stumbled. The engine sounded "rough."

She pulled out the carburetor heat knob. The engine "smoothed out." She let it go a few minutes, then tried pushing the knob back in. The engine turned rough. Her instruments showed Charlie was losing power. She pulled the heat back on, and the engine calmed down again, but if she left the carburetor heat on indefinitely, she would run out of gas even faster. Once again, she had to make herself sit still and try to figure out what was wrong. Out over the ocean, with no land in sight, wasn't the most convenient spot for an emergency landing.

She was stuck having to sweat it out, once again.[540]

According to the temperature gauge, it couldn't be carburetor ice, and outside the plane it was in the high eighties. She checked everything again. If it was too warm to be ice, then what was clogging the carburetor? *Sand.* Had to be. That sandstorm back in the Arabian Desert had not forced her down then, but it had left fine particles that were giving her trouble now.

She slowly thought through every step of the problem. Running the carburetor heat would help the engine get better air, but keeping the heat on indefinitely would give her even fewer miles to the gallon. What if the headwinds turned out to be stronger than the weathermen predicted? She got out her cardboard Jeppesen "computer" and turned the wheel, looking at the numbers and making calculated guesses. When the sun went down behind her, it grew dark over the water, and "Manila seemed far away."[541]

---

[540] Ibid., 191-192.
[541] Ibid., 192.

The engine was going to need all the gas she could give it, so she was going to have to transfer gas from one tank to the other in mid-air. She would have to "pump every drop of gas out of the cabin tanks and into the right wing tank." In order to do that, as Dave Blanton had coached her, she would have to switch on the transfer pumps and let them run . . . "*until the engine stopped*." That meant they would pump nothing but air for a few seconds, which would disrupt the steady flow of gas into the engine. Then the second she switched off the pumps, the engine could start back up.

So Dave Blanton said. And so she had done. Once. This was why Blanton had made her fly with him and show him she had the guts to kill the engine.

Yes, it was objectively true that she had been able to do that. Her brain had stored the memory of hearing the engine come to a stop, and then start back up, and of watching the propeller come back to life. All of that had been over flat, familiar Kansas and Blanton right there with her. Not all alone over an ocean, with hungry sharks waiting below. She had to make herself do it. Then, if it worked, do it again for the second tank.

She pumped gas from the first tank. She watched the gauge inch, inch, inch down to near empty, keeping her finger on the switch, ready to flip off the pump the instant the engine stalled. The whole thing would only take a minute or two. But sitting and waiting with her finger on the switch, each minute seemed to take "an awful lot of slow seconds."

The engine "shuddered as the flow of gas was interrupted by the first bubble of air." She turned off the pump. Silence. Then the propeller began spinning again.

She allowed herself to breathe. Then she drained the second tank. She watched the needle on the cabin-tank slowly slide all the way over to empty as the needle on the wing-tank inched toward full. "Then came the cough . . . Charlie hesitated." The propeller stopped turning and the nose "dipped," as if the plane were startled. Jerrie felt as if she stood still in mid-air. She turned off the pump. The engine sputtered, and then went back to its "rhythmic throbbing."[542]

Jerrie sank back against her seat cushions. The wing-tank may be full now, but the pilot was completely drained. She couldn't be sure the gauges were perfectly accurate, so she *still* didn't know if she really had enough gas. She eased back on the throttle. Going slower would give her more miles to the gallon. Without the long-range radio making contact yet, she couldn't tell Manila why she would be late.

There were no stars and no moon, only a "soft red glow" from her instrument panel, creating the only pool of light in the black night.

Even over the desert, she had picked up an occasional voice of a pilot talking to other pilots. Out here, her radios faded into silence one by one, as if everybody in this half of the world had "gone to bed." There was only the one *dit-dah-dit, dit-dit-dit* left, the signal she had been picking up from that first tower for the past couple of hours.

She felt nervous and isolated. She kept the carburetor heat on, the only adjustment she could make. She was desperately thirsty, but she never did get that water refill in Bangkok, and she wouldn't dare drink the last drops, in case she needed it,

---

[542] Ibid., 192-193.

sitting in a life raft down there in the middle of the ocean. She remembered stuffing that life raft back into the plane, and she had moved it around since then, but she didn't actually know how to inflate it.

She looked at Gary's class ring and prayed. Then she prayed again. Then again. She wished more than anything she could talk to her family just in case, but maybe it was better they didn't have to worry.

She heard a faint signal and tried the radio. "Manila, this is Three-Eight Charlie."

"Three-Eight Charlie, this is Manila."

She was "back in the land of the living."

As she flew within sight of Lubang Island, she spotted the lights of another plane coming in, followed it to the airport, and touched down on solid ground.[543]

RED SEA, 10:30 a.m. (East Africa Time)

Now that Joan was traveling east from the Prime Meridian, she would have to start subtracting from local time instead of adding, in order to arrive at the correct Greenwich Mean Time.[544] Her flight path took her out over the Red Sea just as it became the Bab-el-Mandeb strait.

According to her charts, the name "Bab-el-Mandeb" meant "Gate of Tears." For centuries, as ships tried to sail through the strait, they sometimes struggled between the Gulf Stream flowing south along the African coast, and north along the Arabian coast, where pirate ships could launch from a cove. Yet on this day, these were merely entertaining stories for a pilot

---

[543] Ibid., 193-194.

[544] Brown, *Fate*, 70.

flying over the water, as the coastline of Africa disappeared behind her.[545]

MANILA, Philippines, 11:04 p.m. (Philippine Time)

Even though Jerrie was hours late, a crowd still waited. After twelve hours and nineteen minutes of silence over the water, she couldn't even step down from the plane without having to respond to direction from a photographer and field reporter's questions.

"Mrs. Mock, do you think you will disappear like Amelia Earhart?"[546]

After her long night out there, having to face people was hard to adjust to, even though they all acted happy to see her. After what she had just been through out there, this wasn't the best time to have a chat about her chances of surviving. From all that she had seen and endured and learned since she left America, it seemed trivial to face reporters asking the same old questions about a story that happened twenty-seven years before.

They sat her down on a bench, with microphones in her face. A bottle of Coke was put in her hand, but she didn't get to drink more than a sip. The reporters all talked over each other, and nobody waited to hear any answers.

"You're not worried? Why not?"

"But Mrs. Mock, your plane is so small. Smaller than Miss Earhart's."[547]

Whatever she did say went into all the microphones, and sometimes it sounded as if she were answering "yes" to

---

545 "Bab-el-Mandeb," *Wikipedia*, 1.
546 Mock, *Three-Eight Charlie*, 195.
547 Ibid.

something that was supposed to be "no." On top of that, some reporters tried using interpreters, which only added to the streams of words flowing and echoing around the room.

"But no woman has ever done it before! Do you know why?"

"Sometimes small planes are safer than big ones," she said, and sneaked in another sip of Coke. "Practically everything has improved since Amelia Earhart. But as to why women have fallen so far behind men, I really can't say."[548]

It seemed they had all decided, before she got there, that she was so late because she had wandered off course. She just had to let them think that. She didn't say a word about the rough engine.[549]

"Mrs. Mock? John Murray." Mr. Murray was the Cessna dealer who had cabled her in Bangkok, and he couldn't have shown up at a better time. "We'll begin the 100-hour inspection first thing in the morning."[550]

Those words sounded like magic. Some friends of Jerrie's sister, Barbara Sarr from Ohio State, Terry Bernadino and her father, Dr. Emiliano Ramirez, met her, too. She was able to escape the interrogation and go out to eat Philippine *adobo*.[551]

The *Honolulu Star-Bulletin* ran an article on April 8, reporting that Jerrie had "landed in Manila . . . looking cheerful but 'feeling very tired.'"[552]

---

[548] Ibid.

[549] Ibid.

[550] Ibid., 196.

[551] Ibid., 197.

[552] *Honolulu Star-Bulletin*, April 8, 1964, 3.

When she lay down in the bed in the hotel room that night, it felt good to know she would not have to wake up at 3:30 a.m.

PORT ADEN, Yemen, Noon (Arabia Time)

Flying across Yemen was prohibited, so Joan stayed south of Perim Island. The desert eventually became Saudi Arabia over there somewhere, stretching endlessly off to her left, "more desolate than anything yet,"[553] until she spotted a rocky promontory jutting into the Arabian Sea. Several small peaks protected a cluster of buildings against the squalls coming off the sea on one side. On the other side, a larger mountain range protected them against the desert sandstorms. That would be the Port of Aden.[554]

The port looked almost crowded with ships. As she descended along the coast, she passed so close to the sunbathers that she could see some of them cup their hands over their eyes to watch her plane, impressed. One even waved. As she came down to Khormaksar Airport,[555] she noticed two jets on the ground with a red ball inside a blue circle on the tail, the emblem of the British Royal Air Force.

Waiting to get through Customs, she recalled that the ambassador at Khartoum had given her the tip that Port Aden, like Hong Kong, was duty free, described in a tour guide as a "shopper's paradise."[556] She was met by Mr. Griffin with the American Embassy, and some British RAF personnel, who

---

[553] Brown, *Fate,* 72.

[554] Brown, *Fate,* 72; Saunders, "How an Ohio Housewife Flew Around the World."

[555] Brown, *Fate,* 71.

[556] Ibid.

began refueling as soon as she was out of the plane. Here there were good mechanics who knew something about light aircraft, so she would also get an oil change, and stay overnight.[557]

Yet her allies seemed to be confined to the airfield and the Embassy. In this international port, she was "mildly amazed"[558] to see so few Americans. From the field she made an appointment in the city at a beauty parlor for a shampoo, looking forward to getting the sand and grime out of her hair. But by the time she got checked in to a hotel and out to the hairdresser, she was late and they wouldn't take her. Okay, so she tried to shop around for a souvenir. Nobody would take a traveler's check; they all wanted cash, and she didn't want to be stuck with change from one country that she might not be able to exchange in the next.[559]

After a few of these go-rounds, a British tourist explained to her that the local people just didn't like Americans that much because they didn't spend enough money.[560] On top of that, Joan knew to ask the going rates. So, when her cab driver tried to charge her double for a ride back to the airport, and she refused to be gouged, she got chewed out in a language she didn't understand.[561]

She got back to the hotel and turned in at 10:00 p.m., leaving a call for 2:00 a.m.[562]

---

[557] Ibid., 72.

[558] Schubert and Smith, "World Flight."

[559] Brown, *Fate*, 73.

[560] Ibid.

[561] Ibid.

[562] Ibid.

Take Me to See the Bamboo Organ

Thursday, April 9, 9:00 a.m. (Philippine Time)
MANILA, Philippines

Terry and her chauffeur didn't come for Jerrie until the leisurely hour of 9:00 a.m. "You picked a good time to visit the Philippines," Terry said. "This is Bataan Day. Let us show you some of the country on the holiday."[563]

"Sounds like fun, if we could make a quick stop at the airport first."

At the airport, she was relieved to see that Mr. Murray was on the job and getting things started. Some of the parts she needed had been passed from one commercial airline pilot to another, tag-team style, halfway around the world: another maneuver Jerrie learned from her airport manager days, and that Russ and their Bendix sponsors had set up. But the holiday meant some of her parts were locked up in Customs–marked for a "disabled Cessna N1538C"–until the next day. Still, Murray's crew could start trying to take those tanks out.[564]

Didn't sound as if there was anything she could do to speed things up. But as Mr. Murray spoke, Jerrie could see local men starting their work on the plane.

She walked toward the group of Filipino workers. "But they're trying to take the tanks out the wrong way," she said.

---

[563] Mock, *Three-Eight Charlie*, 198.
[564] Ibid., 199.

When they saw her coming, they stopped. She turned back to Mr. Murray.

"I'll talk to them," he assured her, but he didn't say anything to them right away. Nobody moved, as if waiting for the woman to get out of their shop.

Used to that by now, she just said, "Thanks for everything," and walked back to the car.[565]

Terry's chauffeur took them to pick up Terry's father, Dr. Ramirez and then headed out into the countryside, passing palm trees and fields of pineapples and sugar cane. The driver turned off the highway into a little town and stopped at a church.

"This is the town of Las Piñas, 'The Pineapples'," Dr. Ramirez explained as they walked Jerrie into the sanctuary.

"Notice anything different?" Terry said.

"The organ pipes," Jerrie said. "What are they made of?"

"Bamboo," Dr. Ramirez said. "The entire organ. It's 150 years old."

They drove on, up the slope of a volcano, then down into its crater, to Lake Taal in the crater, and a lodge on the shore of the lake. On the wooden deck of the lodge, with a cool breeze, lunch, her hope that the plane was actually getting taken care of, and the company of people treating her as if she had already won this race, Jerrie tried to allow herself to relax.[566]

After lunch, they looked for a cable office that would send her next story home. They drove around to four communication offices before they found one that would take her credit card,

---

[565] Ibid.
[566] Ibid., 199-200.

but at least she found one. The editors at the *Dispatch* had told her it would be *"so easy."*[567]

Back at her hotel room after the outing, the ring of the phone made her nervous again.

"I see you found Rosario okay." The voice sounded male, American, and calm.

"Rosario? Oh, the radio beacon. Who is this?"

"Just the pilot who told you how to find Manila. Congratulations."

Then she remembered a ferry pilot she had met once in Florida.

"Bob Iba! Where are you?"

"In the same hotel you are."

"But what are you doing here?"

"Oh, I flew a plane over, just like you did. Only, I came the easy way, across the Pacific. Let me take you out to dinner."

"Wonderful!"

"Stop for you at seven?"

"Can you make it seven-thirty? I'm getting my hair done."

"Women. Okay, seven-thirty."

Dinner with an experienced overseas pilot gave Jerrie a chance to vent her frustrations with all the rules and delays getting in the way of trying to fly across these longitudes. Bob listened until she ran out of breath.

"Remember, I told you it would be like this," he said.

"You didn't say how bad it really is. You didn't tell me that almost nobody flies over here, or that some countries won't let people fly at all, or all these ridiculous fees and forms, or having

---

[567] Ibid., 200.

to wait for them to hand-draw a weather folder, or having to take questions from reporters who don't know anything, and then read how they got it wrong!" She had been carrying all this inside her for so long, it was hard to keep the emotion from pouring out.

"Well, the officials have to have something to do," Bob said. "And you can ignore the newspapers. Anyway, the worst is behind you. When you get to Guam, you'll be back on American territory."

She propped her elbows on the dinner table. "You have to help me fight the red tape."

They clinked glasses. "Here's to keeping our freedom of the skies."[568]

PORT ADEN, Yemen, 2:00 a.m. (Arabia Time)

Joan had to get up in the "dead of night"[569] again. When the room phone woke her up, she was startled from a deep sleep and then worried that she had her time zones mixed up. But it turned out that her wristwatch agreed with the desk clerk's watch, so she was on track after all. In the lobby, she met a BOAC crew also wanting to get away before the heat, and they all waited out at the airport, drinking coffee together, black, as always.[570]

Two and a half hours after her wake-up call, Joan was taxiing for takeoff when she noticed that the fuel pressure was fluctuating. She had to return to the tarmac, stuck until 8:30 a.m. when the mechanics would arrive and be able to check out the

---

[568] Ibid, 200-202.

[569] Brown, *Fate*, 75.

[570]Ibid.

problem. One filter had collected grit over the desert, and by the time they had cleaned it, she couldn't get away until afternoon.[571]

With full tanks, her maximum altitude for the first fifteen minutes was 800 feet. The desert coastline began to warm up, and she watched as the inevitable cumulus clouds formed, exactly what she had been trying to beat. The plane wouldn't respond to the autopilot, so she had to hand-fly along the coast of Saudi Arabia.

Eventually, she managed to take the plane on up to 3,000 feet. She watched the waves roll up against the sand, rocks, and cliffs for a while, then put on the Mae West life preserver and headed out over the water. Out there, the turbulence began to fade away, but her fuel pressure began to fluctuate again. The sun disappeared behind her, and the world grew dark. An hour out of Karachi, she was able to make radio contact, and landed at 9:23 local time.[572]

She was greeted at the airport by Adelaide Tinker, her next contact in the Ninety-Nines network, and Adelaide's husband John, the American Ambassador to Pakistan, along with plenty of photographers and reporters. The Tinkers also invited Suchria Ali out to meet Joan,[573] as, they told her, they had just done with Jerrie.

The Tinkers invited Joan to their home, but the BOAC hotel house was right there at the field, so she asked if she could just stay there. BOAC also sheltered 51-Poppa in their hanger for the night.[574]

---

[571] Ibid.

[572] Ibid., 75-76.

[573] Brown, *Fate*, 76.

[574] Ibid.

Sitting on her bed reviewing her charts and clearances, Joan decided to try one minor deviation from her original plan. She had originally obtained clearance to fly to Delhi, but if she flew to Ahmedabad instead, she could save 150 miles. Like Delhi, Ahmedabad was an airport of entry, as well, so the authorities *should* have no reason to object.[575]

Friday, April 10
MANILA, Philippines

Next morning, Jerrie got back to the airport to see what was going on. John Murray's men had replaced the tail-wheel bracket, so the tail would quit bouncing around, and they were working on the new motor for the antenna. They had taken the tanks out so Murray could check the battery and add water. So far, so good.

A couple of men approached, carrying the big tank over to the plane. "Can I show them how to put it back in?" Jerrie asked.

"Thanks anyway," Mr. Murray said, "but the boys might get along better on their own."

"Oh, okay," she said. "I can tell they don't want me around, but would you please be sure they get the hoses hooked up correctly, with the arrows pointed up?"

"No need to worry," Mr. Murray said. "How about a tour of the Cessna dealership and lunch?"

Once seated in their air-conditioned country club, Jerrie tried again to relax. After dessert, Murray excused himself and went

---

[575] Ibid.

back to work, so when Jerrie was driven back to the hangar to look over the repairs, she was on her own again.

The gas tanks were reinstalled and the mechanics were picking up all their tools. She ran over to those tanks and peeled away strips of black electrician's tape covering up the arrows. Just as she had feared, the arrows were pointed the wrong way.

"Hey!" She ran after the men leaving the hangar. "Come here. Look. These arrows are going down. They're supposed to go up." She pointed at the rubber hoses. "You're going to have to redo them, because the gas won't flow into the tank with them this way."

One of them just mumbled, "Mr. Murray," and they all walked away. She could hardly take off, knowing she would run out of gas over the Pacific.

She paced, fighting to stay calm. She left the hangar and asked Terry's chauffeur to give her a ride. May as well go pick up a flight-plan form and tend to other errands. When she returned and checked the hoses, they had been switched out and lined up correctly.[576]

Someone handed her a telegram from Russ. "ATMOSPHERICS NO GOOD VOICE CONTACT IMPOSSIBLE PRINTED WORD LAST RESORT." Reading it, she had her hopes up for a break.[577]

She only had to get all her stuff and load it back on the plane. Only now, she was also supposed to take all the broken parts back to the States with her, so the pile had grown. Loading up shouldn't be too hard, if she weren't exhausted, and if she could get to it. It had all been stored in a loft over her head,

[576] Mock, *Three-Eight Charlie*, 203-204.
[577] Russ Mock to Jerrie Mock, telegram, April 8, 1964, photocopy given to author by Jerrie.

unreachable except by ladder. At the moment, there was not a person or ladder in sight.

Jerrie sat down, struggling to keep back tears. Since nobody was around to help, she got up and went looking. She rounded up several men and a ladder and they began taking all of her stuff down from the loft, broken part by broken part. She got as far as transferring her things from the loft, down the ladder, and onto a heap beside her plane when a phone rang. A man waved for her to come take it.[578]

She walked away from her pile to get to the phone.

"Hey, you're still in Manila! Why didn't you leave today?"

Russ. The last person she needed to talk to. The connection was really bad, but she took a deep breath and gave her best shot at explaining the holiday and everything else that had slowed her down this time.

"Speak slowly." That was the operator, cutting in.

"Yeah, speak slooow-ly, like the operator says," Russ said. "I can't hear you. Now, look, what time is it over there?"

"About six," Jerrie said. "What time is it over there?"

"Five a.m. If you take off now, you can be in Guam in the morning."

"I can't leave now," she said. "I'm exhausted, and the plane isn't packed."

"Speak slooow-ly," the operator said.

"Jerrie, talk slowly," Russ said. "Sounds like you're saying, 'Oo-a-oo-a-oo.'"

"Russ, I am talking slowly. I can't leave tonight. I'm worn out."

---

[578] Mock, *Three-Eight Charlie*, 205-206.

"Ma'am, please, you're talking so fast that the party can't hear you," the operator said.

"Jerrie, you've had a long rest there in Manila," Russ insisted. You're ahead so far, but the weather might change. Joan might catch you. Leave tonight."

"I can't leave tonight. If you could see what I've been through getting the plane ready, you–"

"Please, try to speak more slowly," the operator repeated.

"Still sounds like you're in a reverberation chamber," Russ said. "I can't hear what you're saying."

Too bad she could hear him. Even if he could hear her, he wouldn't listen. Russ and the operator were still talking when Jerrie hung up. She was not about to fly tonight.

Sometimes Russ wanted this first-in-history accomplishment more than she did. Right then, Jerrie wasn't sure she cared. If she did end up being an "also ran," maybe she would just "head the plane out over the water where there wasn't any land to find," and no one would ever have to see her again.

When she returned to the plane, the crew she had assembled to help her pack were all gone. She asked Terry's chauffeur to hand her items until she got the plane packed. The sun had gone down and the airport lights had come on by the time she locked up the plane. She was exhausted, irritated, and dripping in sweat. No matter what Russ said, 3:30 a.m. would come soon enough.[579]

---

[579] Ibid., 206-207.

April 10, 7:00 a.m. (Pakistan Time)
KARACHI, Pakistan

As Joan walked through the Karachi airport, surrounded by the announcements and chatter of one foreign language after another that she couldn't even name, it was a great relief to be welcomed by another group of Ninety-Nines. She couldn't talk long, once again, since the Customs officials needed to complete their inspection, and they had waited until morning out of courtesy for her. As soon as she made it through that process, she was happy to be introduced to the only other people in the building who spoke English without any accent.

The two men in Pan Am uniforms and caps were just as happy to see her. "Mrs. Merriam? Fred Paris. This is Pete Fernandez."[580]

"I remember you both from flight school," she said.

"Thank you, but you're the famous one now," Pete said.

"You should be, after all the MIGs you shot down in Korea," she said.[581] "Anyway, getting my name in the paper doesn't get me through Customs any faster," she said. "Where are you boys headed?"

"We may not be going quite as far as you. We're just ferrying a DC-3 over from Miami. From here, we'll get her to Calcutta, and then on to Bangkok."

From Karachi, Fred and Pete were bound for Ahmedabad, India, same as Joan. She was able to take off by 9:12 local time, and they were only ten minutes behind her. It was a short flight, and both planes landed without difficulty. Then all three pilots

---

[580] Merriam, "Longest Flight," 47; Brown, 76.
[581] Brown, *Fate*, 76.

got to enjoy the 100-degree heat together as they waited their turns in line.[582]

Joan got the usual greeting from the Customs official, "come with me." In the Customs office, she was questioned as to why she had flown to Ahmedabad, since her original clearance had been written "Calcutta via Delhi." She tried to explain that she wanted to avoid night flying, and showed documentation that she had filled out all her forms and paid all her fees before she left the United States. Yet nothing she said sped it up, and she was stuck there for three hours. Pete and Fred got a similar interrogation and had to sit there even longer.[583]

They finally let her take off from Ahmedabad at 2:30 in the afternoon, and she flew into the afternoon thunderstorms almost immediately–exactly what she had been trying to avoid. The landscape below only offered a few small mountain ranges, 2,000 feet at the highest, followed by many of the small farming patches characteristic of India, still dry this time of year, before the monsoons. She flew over the city of Nagpur, and the name made her wistful about the Taj Mahal to the north, one more sight she would have to miss on this trip.[584]

The noise filter in the left magneto went out, creating static in her radios, but she had been promised there was a chance of getting a few things fixed in Calcutta.[585]

By 6:30 p.m. local time, lightning was crackling off to her left. The air direction finder needle tended to point toward the electrical discharges. She spotted a tiny light out there and she

---

[582] Merriam, "Longest Flight," 47; Brown, *Fate,* 76.

[583] Merriam, "Longest Flight," 47; Brown, *Fate,* 76.

[584] Brown, *Fate,* 77.

[585] Ibid.

thought it might be an approaching plane, but it turned out to be the first star of the evening again. Then the Big Dipper began to emerge from the gaps in the clouds as well. By 9:30 p.m. she asked to climb to 9,000 feet to get above the thunderstorms. Then the tower operator in Calcutta called her on her approach control frequency, asking if by chance, she had come across any DC-3 pilots.[586]

"Affirmative," she replied. "They're probably still being held by the Customs officials in Ahmedabad."[587]

She landed at Dum Dum Airport to be greeted by Jim Kiley with the US Consulate; T.J. Malik, the airport manager; and G.B. Singh, the controller of thirty-five airports in India. Mr. Singh had also been in Karachi when Amelia Earhart landed there in 1937, and Joan looked forward to talking with him.[588]

But first, she was escorted into a V.I.P. room to meet the waiting press. At least it was air-conditioned. She also liked the bright colors of the saris worn by the women in the group.[589]

One reporter asked, "What is your impression of India?"

"I had hoped to see a camel."

"At the airport?" he responded.

Everyone broke into laughter, and Joan laughed along with them. They didn't keep her too long, and she was driven to the Great Eastern Hotel. After the cramped cockpit and the heat and humidity out there, the hotel also offered the magic words "air conditioning."[590]

---

[586] Ibid., 78.

[587] Merriam, "Longest Flight," 47; Brown, *Fate*, 78.

[588] Brown, *Fate*, 78.

[589] Ibid.

[590] Ibid., 79.

Still, the crowds in the streets were a bit of a shock. She recorded, "the people huddle, anonymous as ants, by the thousands . . . [and] just bunk out wherever they happen to be when night falls." The local people mostly wore white, and she saw rickshaws everywhere, sometimes pulled by children.[591]

---

[591] Ibid.

Thanks for the Party, But I've Been Sent to My Room

Saturday, April 11, 4:15 a.m. (Philippine Time)
MANILA, Philippines

From the back seat of Terry's car, Jerrie couldn't see any moonlight, and the airport kept the streets dark to help pilots. The corners of buildings showed up in the car's headlights as they turned, as if the power was out.

She was able to pick up her hand-drawn weather folder. Then she found out that in this country, she had to go to not one, but two different Flight Service Stations and turn in two different flight plans. Okay, okay, done with all that. What would be the next delay?

Turned out, Murray's plan was to get up early enough to be waiting for the officials to come in to work, but he didn't seem to know exactly when that might be, and another large commercial jet had to be inspected ahead of Jerrie's little propeller plane. At the terminal, Jerrie sipped coffee and tried to eat a doughnut, watching Murray have a big breakfast. Then she waited by the plane for so long that she had to step into the shop to clench her fists in rage where nobody could see. Finally, the Customs and Immigration men showed up, looked inside the plane briefly, filled out her forms and let her go, simple and fast.[592]

---

[592] Mock, *Three-Eight Charlie*, 208-210.

Jerrie said her goodbyes, photographers got in a few more snaps, and Terry handed her some going-away gifts and snacks.

Jerrie pushed her starter button, listened to the engine come alive, taxied Charlie out to the "lonely end" of the runway, and headed out over the Pacific. With all the repairs and a good weather report for the day, she ran out of things to worry about. She was bound for home.

She got away just in time to watch the sun inch over the horizon. A few clouds scattered below the plane glowed orange and gold, and the big red ball peeked from behind puffs of clouds ahead. The white caps on the waves below, usually warnings of rough water, only passed beneath Charlie's propeller faster and grew smaller as she took her plane on a steady, easy ascent.

Today's flight would take eleven hours, at least. With weather reports over the radio in flight for the first time on her trip and nothing but ocean to fly over, there wasn't much left for this lone traveler to do but daydream about Magellan and the other explorers who had gone before her, and watch the day's weather patterns unfold.[593]

As the sun continued to climb, its warm rays turned the moisture in the air into enormous cloud formations. As she flew all day, the sun inched on up above the windshield, then down behind the plane. The cloud towers gradually dissolved into thin streaks that melted away by twilight and the sun found the horizon again directly behind her. The stars came back out again, Charlie chugged steadily along, and Jerrie sat tight in the

---

[593] Ibid., 211.

red light of her cockpit, enjoying a couple of the chocolate cookies that Terry had baked for her.[594]

With her antenna repaired, the voice from Guam boomed in over the speaker, and all she had to do was follow the directions. She touched down at 8:05 p.m., Guam time.

The second she switched off the engine and the propeller slowed down, a crowd swarmed the plane. Her door was pulled open. Trumpets, tubas, and drums hit their first note of a Sousa march. Welcoming hands reached in to help her step out. As her sandal touched the ground, someone shouted, "Welcome back to the United States," and a cheer went up. She was still 6,000 miles from the California coast, yet a Navy brass band had come to play for her, way out here.

Yet even in the middle of all that, with the cameras going off all around her besides, she still had to sign a stack of papers to make sure she had "permission to land."[595]

Next, she had many hands to shake. Photographers' flashbulbs kept blinding her through the blur of introductions:

She was introduced to the Honorable Manuel F. Guerrero, Governor of Guam, and his wife. She shook their hands.

"Mrs. Mock? I'm Admiral Thomas Christopher, and this is Captain Barlow." She shook their hands.

"I'm Homer Willies, with the FAA." She shook his hand.

She must have looked uncertain about what she had to do next, because these nice people quickly took charge.

"We'll take care of the plane for you," Captain Barlow said. "You just ride with the Governor." He gestured toward the open door of the waiting limousine.[596]

---

[594] Ibid., 212-214.
[595] Ibid., 214-215.

Jerrie obediently got in. "Are you taking me to the hotel?"

Mrs. Guerrero laughed. "We'd like to have you stay with us tonight, if that's all right with you." They drove her to the Governor's mansion, on a hillside overlooking the city of Agana. As they led her through the front door, a crowd burst into applause. People stepped back, allowing her to make her way toward an appetizer table in the living room. She reached for a cracker and almost got it to her mouth before she had to answer somebody's question. She reached for another cracker, but had to say something else, and on it went.

"Mrs. Mock, excuse me, but we need you to take time out from the party just now." The Governor's assistant escorted her out the front door toward the limousine again.

At least she got to eat that one cracker. "Where do you want me now?"

"We're going to take you down to the television station for an interview." When they brought her in to the island's TV station, she could see on the monitors that tonight's feature was a cowboy movie. As soon as Jerrie walked into the studio, they stopped the movie reels so they could interview her.

They asked the usual questions. "Mrs. Mock, what can you tell us about the secrets to your success?"

She gave the usual answer. "Well, I suppose I don't take any chances that I don't have to take." She waited out the usual discomfort about being the center of attention.

When it was over, she couldn't tell if the television station ever went back to the movie. She hoped the children of Guam found out what happened to the good guys and the bad guys.[597]

[596] Mock, *Three-Eight Charlie*, 215-216; Mock, interview, April 11, 2008.
[597] Mock, *Three-Eight Charlie*, 216.

She was escorted back to the limo for a quick ride up the hill to the Governor's mansion and the food table. She reached for her second cracker.

"Mrs. Mock?" The Governor's assistant waved her away from the table again. This time, it was to pick up the phone in the Governor's study.

"Congratulations!" It was Russ. "How was the flight?"

"Once I got off the ground, nothing to it."

"Good. UPI just called. They say Joan's just now on her way to Calcutta. Looks like you're in the lead, and everyone here's excited."

"Then I can get a little rest. Governor Guerrero and his wife have asked me to be their guest for a few days, and go for a swim. Isn't that wonderful?"

"No, you *can't*. You leave in the morning, early! Joan has a lot more experience than you, and she only has to get to Oakland."

"But, dear, don't be a meanie. Let me have a *little* fun." All these people around here being so nice was making it hard to worry about Joan.

The Governor's assistant saw the look on her face and reached for the phone. "Hello, Mr. Mock," he said evenly. "We've all been telling your wife that she needs a rest, and Guam is the place to get it."

Jerrie could hear Russ yelling from across the Governor's enormous desk. "What's this business about swimming in the morning? That woman's in a race with a clock. A race with the history books!"

"But, my dear fellow. She's flown over 1,500 miles today, and she's tired. And from here–"

"She flew 1,500 miles the day before and the day before and probably the day before. And she's got seven or eight thousand miles ahead of her. If you want to help, why don't you send home those people who are making that racket I hear and let her go to bed. Then get her up and keep her moving!"

Jerrie felt like "sinking through the floor." Her kind host tried one more time. "Well, she's doing just fine, and a day's–"

"Hey, man! We've been working on this for two years, and I'll be damned if a day's relaxation is going to cost her a place in history. Put her to bed and let her get some rest *now*! Then get out of the way." Russ hung up.

At least she didn't have to be the one to hang up on her husband this time. He had been talking about her as if she were the plane. She didn't want to go to her room. She wanted to swim and hang around, if even just for a day.

"I apologize for Russ," Jerrie said to this man who had turned red in the face. When he didn't answer, she realized that the "racket" Russ had heard wasn't so loud any more either. She walked back out to face a kitchen and living room full of people who had just run out of things to say. They began heading for the door in twos and threes almost immediately.

So that was it. Nobody seemed to care what the pilot wanted. On the other hand, she *still* couldn't be sure of where Joan was, no matter what they were being told, so she really couldn't afford to take any chances.

After a quiet dinner and a few minutes on the terrace overlooking the lights of Agana with the Guerrero family, she asked them for a wake-up call at 3:30 a.m. Traveling the world this way was not much better than flipping through *National*

Geographic back home. She went to bed, missing the days "before telephones had been invented."[598]

Saturday, April 11, before sunrise (India Time)
CALCUTTA, India

In the morning, Joan was driven back to the airport, past more disturbing scenery.

"Mile after mile of open-air shacks, with a bed and a cook stove in each, lined the road; dogs, cows and kids running wild." Her driver zigzagged around bumps and holes in the dirt road, honking at anyone or anything in the way. She was relieved when the ride was over in thirty minutes.[599]

At the airfield, Joan had her spark plugs checked while Mr. Singh brought photos she had asked for, of him with Amelia Earhart. Talking with someone who actually knew her heroine reminded Joan that she was approaching Lae, the last place Amelia was ever seen.

Joan recorded her thoughts: "I feel a cold chill which I don't manage to shake despite the day's heat. At this point in her route, A.E. and Fred Noonan had nothing but confidence and assurance of success in their flight. So must I."[600]

Mr. Singh said, "We were very, very sorry they weren't found. We were hoping against hope. Now it seems like history is repeating itself in another great lady, you. You have much courage to complete the Earhart-Noonan flight."[601]

---

[598] Ibid., 216-217.

[599] Brown, *Fate*, 79.

[600] Brown, *Fate*, 79-80.

[601] Ibid., 80.

Sunday, April 12

Joan would have liked to visit more with Mr. Singh, and hear more about his own accomplishments as a pilot, and his recollections of what India was like in Earhart's day, before the nation was partitioned. But the plane was ready and the sun was rising, so it was time to go.[602]

She climbed into 51-Poppa, and was cleared for take-off. She was giving it full throttle and lifting off the runway by 7:00 a.m., with Singh and her other new friends waving goodbye, which made her sad. Then she flew right into a flock of birds, which made her nervous.[603]

She was back in the heat and humidity, which were rough enough on the pilot, but she also knew these conditions were "murder" on her plane. The heavy humidity reminded her of the Okeefenokee Swamp back in Georgia.[604]

She climbed slowly up to 6,000 feet, and even up there it was hotter than when she took off. She had been warned it might get even hotter.[605]

She spotted a few tiny villages below, and the inevitable clouds were forming up ahead.

After only thirty minutes out, she noticed oil dripping out of the left engine. The oil pressure was still reading normal, but, facing a six-hour flight, she couldn't chance it. Aggravated, she had to turn back, so she radioed Dum Dum. "One reaches a point in bad luck when it's either quit or plod on without

---

[602] Ibid.

[603] Ibid., 81.

[604] Ibid.

[605] Ibid.

dwelling on the cost. Time is money, and I was forced to spend time as if I had a monopoly on it."[606]

Several trucks were lined up awaiting her landing. She had them wash down the engine first and then check it. She had lost two quarts of oil. There appeared to be a leak at the oil sump bolts. They tightened up the bolts, hand-wiped it all down, and it seemed to be all right again. After an hour on the ground, she took off again, just before 10:00 a.m.[607]

Back in the air, she spotted more oil on the left engine covering. She hoped they had just missed it when they wiped the plane down.[608]

The coast of Burma was just a stretch of marsh, followed by a mountain range, then marsh again; not very exciting. Four hours out of Calcutta, she heard a plane calling in, somewhere above her and perhaps half an hour ahead. She was careful to fly around Rangoon, tracking in to the airport north of the city. It was a restricted area, with many temples, including one that was covered in gold. "What a spectacle!"[609]

She wished she could stop. But her "clearance to land there had expired,"[610] and they might send an interceptor plane after her instead.

The city of Mandalay would be just up the road, north of Rangoon. Amelia got to visit there, by road, and one of her favorite songs was "On the Road to Mandalay." Joan had a record of Frank Sinatra singing it, and back home she played

---

[606] Ibid., 81-82.
[607] Ibid., 82.
[608] Ibid.
[609] Ibid., 83.
[610] Ibid., 82.

that record often. She tried singing it now, but decided that "Frankie did it better," and quit.[611]

Thinking of music brought back memories of her father, who also loved music, especially the Italian opera star Caruso, and this remote part of the world made her miss her dad that much more.[612]

Cruising along now at 9,500 feet, she turned inland over the Burma coast, then a 100-mile hop over the Gulf of Martaban, then seventy miles or so over land again to the border of Thailand. She was using the turbochargers and making 145 knots (168 miles per hour). "Whee!! Tail winds for a change."[613]

The haze was thick over the Burma mountains, making navigation difficult. She requested clearance to fly at 7,500 feet, which enabled her to fly below whatever weather she was about to encounter. The cloud tops were 16,000 feet high.[614]

Driving rain cut her visibility. She heard her VOR beep for the first time, so she was getting close to Bangkok, and she needed to remain vigilant of her position. Boxed notices on the charts for this area advised fliers: "WARNING. Flying is prohibited over the city of Bangkok," and, "Low flying is prohibited over the Royal Palace Huahin."[615] She told herself, "Watch out for royal palaces!"[616]

On her charts, much of this area was marked "terrain uncharted," and "relief data incomplete," along with descriptions

---

[611] Ibid., 83.

[612] Ibid., 82-83.

[613] Ibid.

[614] Ibid.

[615] Ibid.

[616] Ibid., 83.

such as "Numerous buildings that do not cluster into villages are prevalent along the coast and major river valleys of Burma and Thailand."[617]

She landed at Bangkok about 5:00 p.m., and there, grinning, stood Fred Paris.

"I see they finally let you boys go from Ahmedabad," she said.

"Just in time for the holiday!' he said, knowing how another delay would irritate her. The nation of Thailand celebrated their New Year on April 13. Joan would record, "I was great at hitting religious or national holidays everywhere I went,"[618] but that wasn't Fred's fault.

"We're checked in," Fred said. "Here's the hotel, and they have a room for you. When you get through Customs, take a cab and meet us at the front desk, so we can all go out to dinner."

"I'd be honored."[619]

---

[617] Ibid.
[618] Ibid., 84.
[619] Ibid.

Are Those Rockets Going to Hit Me?

AGANA, Guam, 5:30 a.m. (Chamarro Time)

Jerrie got to stay on Guam for nine hours and twenty-five minutes. All of the great help from the Governor, the Navy, and Pan American Airways got her off the ground faster than most places, which, of course, just made her want to stay longer.[620]

She studied their hand-drawn weather folder and her charts. Russ thought that her flight from Guam to Wake would be the riskiest leg of the entire trip. Out there in the endless Pacific, 2,000 miles from anything, Wake Island (technically three "islets"[621]) is only two and a half square miles in total land area.[622] If she couldn't find it, well . . .

No need to worry about that today, she told herself. The big compass was never repaired, but she was still relying on the back-up compass, plus all the other instruments, then trusting her intuition as to which ones were not working right at the moment. She was still averaging it all out and making calculated guesses to stay on course, and she had been right enough, so far. Also, the radio signals from both Guam and Wake were good and strong. As if to confirm her hunch, at 9:11 a.m., she spotted, several thousand feet down and directly

---

[620] "Mock in Guam," *Sunday Star-Bulletin* (Honolulu), April 12, 1964, A-2.

[621] "Wake Island," *Wikipedia,* last modified Jan. 17, 2023, https://en.wikipedia.org/wiki/Wake_Island.

[622] Editors of Encyclopedia Britannica, "Wake Island," last modified Oct. 14, 2022, https://www.britannica.com/place/Wake-Island-Pacific-Ocean.

beneath her, a twin-engine plane, also headed in to Guam, so she had to be right in the center of the airway. The other pilot had probably been in the air all night.[623]

Throughout the day, the ocean got some showers, but at 11,000 feet, she flew above them, watching cloud formations and an occasional rainbow.

Night crept up on her. Only that soft red glow of her instruments and the steady *dit-dah, dit-dah-dah, dah-dit-dah* ("Alpha Whiskey Kilo") coming in from Wake Island's radio beacon kept her company.[624]

The air traffic controller came through her microphone, and she followed instructions, descending from 11,000 feet to 4,000 to 3,000, watching her needles all the way. Shreds of clouds below her showed up in the moonlight as "milky patches against the black of the water," until she saw lights.

She put on her headset and switched on her mike to ask permission to come in to Wake Island by visual approach.

The controller's voice came in, but his words clicked in and out: "Nov– three . . . –roach . . . nine–"

The next cloud passed beneath the plane, and she lost sight of the island. She wouldn't be able to see her way in, so she had to switch to instruments, but what was the man in the tower trying to tell her? Hoping he could hear her, she told him that she couldn't understand him. She circled out to come back in for an instrument approach toward what she hoped was the right runway.

---

[623] Mock, *Three-Eight Charlie*, 218-220.
[624] Ibid., 221-222.

As she banked around and headed in, "white fire"[625] exploded all around her. She jumped in her seat. Piercing white lights shot toward the stars, then sputtered and fell. Had she flown into a war nobody told her about? Was the military practicing out here? Or were they aiming at her? She hadn't been in the neighborhood long enough to make anybody mad at her *already*, had she?

Surrounded in all directions by 2,000 miles of water, she had little choice but to continue her descent through the cloud layer and point the propeller toward the spot where the runway was supposed to be.[626]

The air traffic man kept talking, but she missed most of his words. Then the lines of runway lights came into view and she angled the plane toward the earth. Her landing lights reflected off the waves, then the coral, on either side of the runway. When the wheels touched down, she was jolted a bit, but, boy, was it a relief to make it out of "all that firing going on up in the sky!"[627]

After the jolt, the controller's voice came through her radio just fine.

She rolled the plane to a stop. Several hundred people stood waiting at the airport. She didn't know the island had that many people on it.

"ALOHA!" As soon as she opened the door, a lei of shells was draped around her neck, and people crowded around her. Children wanted autographs, and of course, more cameras.

---

[625] Ibid., 223.
[626] Ibid., 222-223.
[627] Ibid.

"Mrs. Mock, welcome to Wake Island!" Two men, one with a Pan Am logo on his shirt and another in an FAA uniform, offered her their hands to help her step down from the cockpit.

"Which way to Customs?" she asked.

Both men laughed. "You don't have to go to Customs. You just flew from one US protectorate to another."

"I knew that." No Customs meant no Immigration, either. No jewelry inspections or mystery fees, no debates about what to call her occupation, no belongings getting marked in chalk. "Then could you tell me why they were shooting when I was trying to land?"

"They sent flares up to help guide you down. Now, how about dinner? Our airport restaurant is staying open late tonight for our special guest."[628]

The man from Pan Am grabbed her bag and, as they walked to the terminal, the man from the FAA introduced himself as Hal Sellers. "I'm the airport manager, which, in effect, makes me the manager of the rest of the island, too."

"Then, will you be the one to take me to the hotel?"

Hal Sellers cleared his throat. "Ah, about that hotel . . . Well, let's order dinner, first."

A plateful of hot American meatloaf and green beans tasted great. Listening to Sellers talk about the history of Wake Island was fun, and it also sounded encouraging when he said, "You'll not only have a room to yourself for the evening, you'll have an entire hotel."

Wait a minute. "Okay. Why?"

---

[628] Ibid., 223-224.

"The hotel was built back in the days when planes couldn't make it across the Pacific nonstop, so they had to stop here and spend the night." He paid the bill, took her bag, and led her out the door. "Then, when the Japanese bombed Pearl Harbor, they hit Wake, too. The hotel was destroyed, along with most of the other buildings here."[629]

"Where will I sleep?"

By this point in the conversation, they were in the car. Sellers slowed down to turn onto an unpaved road. "After the war, Pan Am rebuilt a smaller facility, just for flight attendants and crew. Then later, when the new jets came along, flights didn't have to stop here, and there's been no need even for crew to spend the night at Wake Island." He stopped at a dark building and got out of the car. Jerrie followed. Sellers set down her bag, fumbled around for a key, and unlocked the door. "But the facility is still maintained."

He opened the door and switched on the light. Rows of empty beds backed up to the walls of a deserted dormitory that needed dusting. One bare light bulb dangled from the ceiling. Populated with flight attendants, this room might not have been so bad, but at the moment it looked as if "it should be inspected for crawling animals."[630]

Sellers looked around the room, then at Jerrie's face. "Look, Jerrie, this is the first time I've seen this place. I don't think you'll be very comfortable here."

"Oh, don't worry about me," she said, trying to smile. She was reluctant to seem ungrateful. "After all, I'm out for adventure."

---

[629] Mock, *Three-Eight Charlie*, 223-224; Mock, interview, April 11, 2008.
[630] Mock, *Three-Eight Charlie*, 225.

"Well, look," he said. "The FAA has some houses on the island, and some of them are empty right now. Let's go see what we can find."

Jerrie didn't argue. Hal switched off the light, locked the door, and picked up her bag. He drove her to a row of small houses, "huddled bravely" at the water's edge, and pulled up to an empty one.

Exhausted, Jerrie wasted no time settling in and turning off the light. Hearing the surf helped her relax until she was dreaming of the waves out there.[631]

The *Honolulu Star-Advertiser* covered her arrival on Wake Island in an article on April 13: "Wearing a white blouse, blue skirt and carrying a matching handbag, Mrs. Mock was greeted by a crowd of about 600 persons on Wake Island. A yellow Mae West lifejacket she wore over her trim outfit looked strangely out of place."[632]

BANGKOK, Thailand

The Thai people were friendly enough, but at the flight office, Joan's bills started coming. She was politely asked for $5 for a plane parking fee, $5 for her ride to the terminal, $12 for Customs–even though she hadn't seen anyone from Customs, $5 Immigration fee, $8 for a ride into town, $100 for handling radio fees and flight plans–even though she flew visual and only needed to speak to the tower maybe six times, at the most– plus $161 for a landing fee.[633]

---

[631] Mock, *Three-Eight Charlie*, 224-225.
[632] "Honolulu Next," *Honolulu Star-Advertiser*, April 13, 1964, A-2.
[633] Brown, *Fate*, 84.

She appealed to the airport manager. He was sympathetic, but she still had to pay. During all these months of planning, she had never been told about any of these fees. The only explanation she received was that a private Thai firm owned the rights to the radio frequencies. Everyone who used their radio in Thailand's air space had to pay them for the privilege.[634]

This was another moment that made a pilot appreciate the good ol' "U-S-of-A," free of all these shakedowns. She was determined to alert the pilots association when she got back, so they could spread the word about the plethora of hidden fees.[635]

She wanted to get out of Bangkok right away, but she decided to sit down for her first chicken dinner in a long time. She checked in early at the hotel for a little sleep before checking out again at 3:00 a.m.[636]

From Thailand, Joan was bound for Singapore, Malaysia, and then Surabaya, Indonesia. Thunderstorms were reported over Singapore, but that was typical for this time of year, so there was no point in waiting around for better weather.[637]

Indonesia's leader, Sukarno, was riling up trouble at the moment, and Malaysia didn't have much use for the political problems of their neighbor to the south. Consequently, unfriendly countries wouldn't be sharing much weather data, so she may as well go with what little information she had.[638]

---

[634] Ibid.

[635] Ibid.

[636] Ibid.

[637] Ibid.

[638] Ibid., 84-85.

Fun with Clothespins

Monday, April 13, time: Didn't matter!
WAKE ISLAND

No phone rang on this morning. Jerrie was awakened only by the sun coming in between the curtains, and the surf crashing on the shore. She didn't have to bother with lipstick or a skirt for the cameras or even look at her watch, just pull on comfortable slacks for a walk outside.

Looking inland and across a white shell-and-sand road, she faced an emerald lagoon. To the other side, she faced the waves that beat relentlessly onto the coral reef and kicked white foam high into the air. Beyond the spray, there was nothing but water. This tiny bit of rock and sand seemed "insignificant" by comparison, except maybe to offer her a spot to stand still, take it all in, and try to remember it forever. After a long while, she crossed the road, sat down on a rock, and let the gentle waves of the lagoon bathe her toes.[639]

She could have stayed on that rock all the way to sunset. But just like every other day, there was work to do, starting with laundry.

Hal Sellers had told her the night before that the FAA had shipped in nice new washers and dryers for every house, but the wiring was inadequate. Jerrie didn't care. She washed her drip-dries by hand, then took them to hang outside to dry. With

---

[639] Mock, *Three-Eight Charlie*, 226-227; Mock, interview, April 11, 2008.

the Pacific in her backyard, even pinning her underwear onto a clothesline was fun.

Sellers drove up. "Good morning! Time for a tour."

"Thanks, but please give me a ride to check on everything first."

Pan Am was fueling the plane as a personal favor to her. Excellent.

At the weather room, the weatherman recommended she wait for a squall to pass through the area and not take off until 10:30 that night. Even better.

Hal took her to see the communications office, which wasn't working. Best of all!

That explained why she hadn't heard from Russ.

"We're sorry, Mrs. Mock," said the man behind the desk. "Our new phone system is just getting installed. I can put one test call through to Columbus for you and tell everyone you're okay, but I'm not authorized to allow you to talk, I'm afraid."

"Wonderful!" Jerrie said. No orders from Ohio today. She took a minute to write a story for the *Dispatch* and handed it over, and then she was free to leave.[640]

"Just in time for lunch," Hal said. "Wake Island Bowling Center has a nice party waiting for you." The bowling alley was run by a kind Asian man. She didn't catch his name, but he had set up a long table with snow-white linen, sparkling glassware and china, for fifteen people. The menu: "chilled Ayala champagne, cream of crabmeat soup, shrimp salad, chicken a la king, rolls, ice cream, coffee, and wine, cognac, or

---

[640] Ibid., 227-228; Mock, interview, April 11, 2008.

brandy." Good thing she had the afternoon to get in a nap before take-off.

After lunch, Sellers drove her around. They passed by rusting equipment left over from World War II, even abandoned Japanese pillboxes from the period when Wake was occupied. Seeing the rest of the island didn't take long.

"Oh, would you stop here?" Jerrie asked. She spotted what must have been the radio antenna that had guided her landing, surrounded by a flock of birds. "What species are they?"

"Gooney birds," Sellers said. "They winter here, summer in the Aleutians."

"Looks like thousands of them," Jerrie said. "Let me get a picture."

"Keep your windows closed," Sellers said.

"Will they fly into Charlie's propeller?" An engine full of birds might shut down.

"By the time you take off, they'll probably be down for the night. Otherwise, there isn't much we can do about it. Wake is a bird sanctuary."

"They're fun to watch." On the ground, the gooney birds waddled and flopped around, and their wobbly take-offs and crash-landings were more awkward than Jerrie's worst, but in the air, they swooped and dove with ease.

Later, a group of officer's wives took her for the swim she wanted, despite the chilly breeze and even colder water of the lagoon. Back in the house, she tried taking that nap, but she couldn't sleep. After a hamburger with Sellers at the bowling alley, her first burger in three weeks, plus a to-go box from the manager, this "delightful" day was already over, and it was time to tie on her Mae West and say goodbye. She started her engine, listened with renewed confidence as the propeller "snarled to a deafening whine," taxied her plane between the runway lights and took Charlie up into the dark night. When she reached 1,000 feet, she settled in and began listening for what she might pick up on one of her radio sets. Maybe she could find someone out there to talk to during her next fifteen hours over the Pacific.[641]

BANGKOK, Thailand, 7:45 a.m. (Hovd Time/HOVT)

Joan was happy to get off the ground and away from Bangkok with all their little surprise charges. Once in the air, she changed her course from the east coast of the Malay Peninsula to the west, where there were more airports. She could see kampongs, or settlements, tucked away in the indentations of the shoreline.[642]

"Towering cumulus clouds like foreboding sentinels"[643] loomed ahead of her. Three hours out of Bangkok, she approached Songkhla. The weather grew worse as she flew farther south, approaching the equator. She crossed Kuala Lumpur through rough air and under the real handicap: heavy rain. The autopilot wouldn't work at all. She really needed that autopilot to help control for the weight shifts and "wing heaviness" caused when fuel dissipates.[644]

Joan had to hand-fly the plane, following her charts and instrument navigation. Hand-flying for thirty or forty hours over the Pacific was going to be hard on her hands–and her

---

[641] Mock, *Three-Eight Charlie*, 224-236; Mock, interview, April 11, 2008.

[642] Brown, *Fate*, 85.

[643] Ibid.

[644] Ibid., 87.

nerves.[645] "It's like a juggler who suddenly finds one hand gone numb."[646] Plus, she spotted oil dripping again.[647]

Joan flew over terrain that "was a lush green, indicating plentiful rainfall."[648] She was fascinated with the "tongue-twister"[649] names of the towns: Kampong Telek Kerbau, Kampong Siliau, Kampong Telak Marlimau, Bandar Kaharini, Batu Pahet. Occasionally, places with names that were easier to pronounce for a westerner–Fort Sweetenham, Fort Dickson–were thrown in the mix.[650] At one point, when she called in with a position report, the radio operator responded with the correct pronunciation, and it sounded so different from how she had thought it was pronounced that she had to "double check"[651] that they were referring to the same place.

The control tower required her to stay on visual flight for twenty minutes in what was obviously instrument-flying weather, which was "aggravating."[652]

Just as she flew into Singapore omni range, Joan could see that the runways were wet. So many larger, faster planes were coming into the field that traffic control asked her to hold her position, circling, for thirty minutes until they could obtain an instrument landing clearance for her.[653]

---

[645] Ibid., 85.

[646] Ibid.

[647] Ibid.

[648] Ibid.

[649] Ibid.

[650] Ibid.

[651] Ibid.

[652] Ibid.

[653] Ibid., 86.

Air traffic was heavy, and Joan had to keep an eye out to avoid a collision. She had been holding for twenty minutes, circling, wondering what the fees would be this time, when she noticed that one of her cylinder temperature gauges had gone out. She finally got permission to land. Singapore International Airport was a lovely, modern airport, yet with all the air traffic, it still only had only one runway.[654]

Joan was greeted by the local Piper dealer, who helped get her through Customs quickly and then escorted her to the Singapore Flying Club.[655]

Chief mechanic Reudi Frey, who was sixteen years old when Amelia Earhart came through Singapore in 1937,[656] scheduled his crew to work on Joan's plane in the morning. The buffeting and hard flying that 51-Poppa had been subjected to had caused several problems to build up, which the crew would tackle. They might even be able to fix that autopilot.[657]

William J. Houston from the US Consulate drove her to the hotel, where Joan made a long-overdue phone call to catch up with her publicist, John Sarver.

Sarver shared upsetting news that someone back in the States had contacted various sponsors and the bank that financed Joan's plane, accusing Joan of being "incompetent" and only having "500 hours of flying time," among other fabrications. Sarver didn't want the news to come as a shock if she heard it from someone else, and advised that she ignore it.[658]

---

[654] Ibid.

[655] Ibid.

[656] Ibid., 87.

[657] Ibid.

[658] Ibid., 114.

Joan asked Sarver, "Have you done nothing to check out the source of these libelous and malicious calls?"[659]

He informed her that they were "the work of the president of a small manufacturer of fuel tanks in the Midwest who had been a partial sponsor of the woman who was flying around the northern hemisphere at the same time I was flying the Earhart equator global route."[660]

Well, there wasn't much she could do about any of that. The US Consul General in Singapore, Sam Gilstrap,[661] and his wife Mary took her to dinner. Joan ordered her usual, well-done steak and bottled water. She was too worried about being stuck in an airplane, alone, with food poisoning to enjoy other foods such as fresh salads, raw vegetables, fish, and dairy products. Her gracious hosts let their guest get to bed at 9:00 for a "long, late sleep."[662]

---

[659] Ibid.

[660] Ibid., 115.

[661] Brown, *Fate*, 87. Joan referred to Gilstrap as "our ambassador to Singapore."

[662] Brown, *Fate*, 87.

Queen of the Ocean Skies Dines Alone

WAKE ISLAND, 10:25 p.m. (Wake Island Time)

Flying across the Pacific all night turned out to be smooth and quiet. That gave Jerrie time to try and catch up with time, again.

At her last several stops, people had confused her about dates and timetables. Her NAA form from Guam said she had landed there at 10:05 a.m. Greenwich Mean Time, April 11, and then took off at 7:30 p.m. GMT on April 12. According to that, her stay at the Governor's mansion would have lasted thirty-three hours, not nine–time enough for that swim. She figured out that the snag had to do with GMT versus local time. When she left Guam, it was already April 12 there, but it was still April 11 in Greenwich, England. In fact, for three days, until she passed the 180th meridian (International Date Line), the NAA observers recorded her as landing at the end of a flight before she had taken off to begin it.

No wonder she felt as if she had lost a day. When she described her fatigue at Wake, they said that when she crossed the International Date Line, she would "catch up" on the hours she had missed. Nice theory, but most of that missing time was lost sleep. As she flew into yesterday, she couldn't figure out how she would get any sleep in the cockpit.

Somewhere in the dark, around 4:30 a.m., she crossed the line, but there was nothing out there in the ocean or the sky to mark the spot.[663]

Tuesday, April 14, 8:00 a.m. (Singapore Time)
SINGAPORE, Malaysia

Joan got to "sleep in" for one morning, but then it was back out to the airfield to make sure things were happening as promised. This time, they actually were. She was relieved to see that experienced mechanics were changing the oil and the fuel filters and they were inspecting for anything else that might need attention.[664]

She relaxed over breakfast and coffee and visited with Mr. Frey. Although just sixteen when he met Amelia Earhart, Frey remembered the moment well, and took lots of pictures during the aviatrix's 1937 visit. A big part of Joan's mission on this world flight was to learn all she could to "add to the aviation lore" about the famous pilot who had gone before her.[665]

Monday, April 13 (after crossing the International Date Line and "gaining" a day)
Somewhere over the PACIFIC

The dawn unfolding through the windshield helped Jerrie quit worrying about missing a few winks. From 13,000 feet, daybreak was worth it. Thin scattered clouds below the plane became light patches against the dark water. Miles ahead, a sliver of faint light appeared across the curve between the water

---

[663] Mock, *Three-Eight Charlie*, 237-238; Mock, interview, April 20, 2008.

[664] Brown, *Fate*, 87.

[665] Merriam, "Longest Flight," 47; Brown, *Fate*, 87.

and the light blue sky. Then out of that long sliver of light, the first edge of the familiar red-orange curve inched slowly up. At 150 miles an hour, Charlie and Jerrie "raced to greet the morning."[666]

Back at Wake, the weatherman had suggested waiting until nighttime to take off, so that she wouldn't face thunderheads coming into the area until daylight. But when she found those clouds, they weren't scary, just fun. Puffy cumuli towered above her on all sides of the plane, soft and white. She flew straight into a tall, opaque cloud that looked just like a snow-covered mountain slope. It was like "driving the family station wagon through a tunnel on vacation, not knowing what view is waiting on the other side."[667]

Through one stretch, the dark blue water looked like "a lake surrounded by snow-dusted mountainsides." A minute later, it looked as if she were angling her way "through a narrow fjord, with cloud icicles nearly brushing the tips of Charlie's wings." These cloud formations looked like "rivers, valleys, and prairies covered in snow." She felt as if she were queen of it all. Her subjects, "the foamy clouds and glowing rainbows," put on this performance just for her. Playtime up here was one of the rewards for all of Jerrie's "hard work, worry, and sleepless nights" leading up to this moment. Happily exploring, she felt she had become, for at least a while, "Queen of the Ocean Skies."[668]

Soon the past thirty hours without sleep began to catch up with her, anyway. Still hampered by that one errant compass,

---

[666] Mock, *Three-Eight Charlie*, 238-239; Mock, interview, April 20, 2008.

[667] Mock, *Three-Eight Charlie*, 239.

[668] Ibid., 239-240.

she couldn't be sure she was on track. But by the time she made it to a reporting point on the airway named Swordfish, she could radio in. Coming in to Honolulu, she struggled to stay alert after the long night behind her, and pick up the faint radio signal. At least this time they probably had her on radar, so nobody had to guess just how close she might be coming to a mountain.

She broke through the cloud layer to discover a crowd waiting below at Honolulu International Airport. She came in for the landing with brakes that worked, and it was a lot easier to touch down without bumps.[669]

"ALOHA!" Most of the people were contained behind a chain-link fence, but when she got out of the plane, reporters, photographers, and officials all surged toward her. People reached forward to drape leis of red and white flowers and white seashells onto her shoulders.

"Excuse me, Mrs. Mock!" A man in some sort of uniform stepped forward, disrupting the celebration. "I need to see your International Certificates of Vaccination."

Jerrie had to duck back into the cabin, find those papers where she had put them on top of everything else, let him okay them, and get them back into the cabin, before the leis could begin dropping onto her shoulders again.

"Mrs. Mock, throw your arms up in the air in victory celebration for me!" (Snap!)

"Mrs. Mock, put your hands on your hips. There, that's good!" (Snap!)

---

[669] Mock, *Three-Eight Charlie*, 241-242; Mock, interview, April 20, 2008.

These photographers never tired of asking her to pose and look triumphant.[670]

"Mrs. Mock, it's Columbus." The phone was on her side of the fence. She managed to force a smile as she thanked the man, put the receiver to her ear, and listen to Russ talk about all those luaus that the Hawaiians had arranged for her, but not to worry; he had cancelled them so she could sleep.

"But, now that I'm on the ground, I'm not tired at all. How could you ruin things before I even got here?" Surrounded by so many people, there wasn't much else she could say, and they also gave her the excuse to hang up quickly.

"Mrs. Mock? Gib McCoy, with the FAA. We'll take care of the plane. If you'll just grab your bag out of the cabin, let me escort you to the terminal. We've cancelled the parties, as your husband asked. Everyone here will respect your wishes and leave you alone."

"But I don't want to be left alone. I want to see Hawaii."

Nobody was listening. Instead, a gathering of important people was herding her toward their big terminal–but, not so fast. Next, she had to deal with a Customs official who wanted to search her suitcase for souvenirs because he said she was a "crew" of her plane, and not allowed to bring in anything. Jerrie countered, "When you fly your plane home from Mexico or the Bahamas, you're not a crew!" After her long flight, she figured she probably looked "almost hysterical," and he finally just shrugged and gave up.[671]

Then it was time for more introductions, which quickly evolved into a polite disagreement among them over where

---

[670] Mock, *Three-Eight Charlie*, 242.
[671] Ibid., 242-243.

their guest should spend the night. Finally, Mrs. McCoy said, "Jerrie, let me give you a ride to a quiet hotel."

Jerrie ducked out of the argument and followed her. In the car, she asked Mrs. McCoy, "What does 'aloha' mean?"

"It means, 'hello,' 'goodbye,' and 'we know you'll be back,' all at once."

They pulled up to the hotel where more photographers waited. She paused to pay her dues to fame, posing for still *more* snapshots.

Once inside, the hotel desk clerk handed her a key. "I can assure you, Mrs. Mock, that nobody will be allowed to bother you. No phone calls will be put through, and you can have a good sleep."

"Oh, no, I can't sleep in the daytime. It's 1:30 in the afternoon! Put the calls through, please."[672]

Her room turned out to be several floors up. She came out onto a balcony overlooking a garden of exotic tropical blossoms she had never seen before. A couple of Hawaiian women wearing long wrap-around skirts strolled into the garden. One played a guitar, as they sang island songs.

Jerrie was "enchanted."[673] When the women left, she decided it was time to go downstairs and explore. As she opened the door, she nearly knocked over a bellboy trying to slide notes under her door. Turned out, plenty of people had called to invite her out. Despite her having specifically asked the desk clerk to put her calls through, her room phone had not rung one time. They had left their names and numbers, but there were no times on the notes, so she couldn't tell who had called first. She

---

[672] Ibid., 243.
[673] Ibid.

didn't want to offend anyone, so she didn't know whose call to return first. Maybe somebody else would call. She ran downstairs to the front desk. "*Please* let my calls through!"

But the calls had stopped. She went outside to look for the beach, but never found it. By 8:00, she gave up hope of any more offers, and walked in to the hotel dining room. It was full of guests, but nobody spoke to her.

The head waiter led her to a table. She enjoyed a couple of local drinks with their fruity flavors and paper umbrellas, and had chicken baked in a coconut. It was all wonderful, but Jerrie was more lonesome than she had been weaving through the clouds in her tiny cockpit. Out there, she was "supposed to be a solo adventurer."[674] Here, she was surrounded by couples in love, a guitarist, hula dancers, colored lanterns casting rainbow patterns across the palm trees, waitresses wrapped in sarongs. The waves beat a soft rhythm for the "laughter and gentle conversation" between people who cared for each other. All of that swirled around her, going on whether she sat there or not.

The only one who noticed Jerrie was the head waiter. From the looks he gave her, she got the impression that he thought this woman dining alone in his hotel could be trouble. So, she gave up. She paid her bill, stopped at the front desk and said, "Now, please *hold* my calls. I'm going to sleep." She went up to her room and listened to the guitarist from her balcony a little longer.

When she turned off her light at eleven, the love songs still floated up on the breeze, coaxing her into "dreams of romantic scenes on South Sea islands."[675]

---

[674] Ibid., 244.
[675] Ibid., 243-244.

The Honolulu papers dutifully reported the important details of Jerrie's arrival. "Mrs. Jerrie Mock, a green-eyed Ohio housewife in open-toed shoes, landed here at 4:11 p.m. yesterday, three stops and 6,000 miles away from two round-the-world records for light planes," the *Honolulu Advertiser* noted on April 14.[676]

The *Honolulu Star-Bulletin* ran a story the same day. "On yesterday's 2,000-mile Wake-Honolulu lap, her total provisions consisted of one roast beef sandwich and one orange. . . . Photographers had her stroke her airplane, wave her arms, and clutch her lei."[677]

Wednesday, April 15, 7:45 a.m. (Singapore Time) (before crossing the International Date Line)
SINGAPORE, Malaysia

As much as Joan would have preferred to hang around with pilots and mechanics, look at pictures of Amelia and drink more coffee, she had to admit that, as the saying went, "*tempus* is *fugiting*."[678] She was off the ground again and headed toward the island of Java.[679]

The next set of challenges started with the place names in this part of the world. They all sounded alike to her, and it was hard to tell one from another. She also had to fly within a tight military corridor to Djakarta, Indonesia, which meant she had to follow the "straight and narrow," literally. As she approached

---

[676] *Honolulu Advertiser*, April 14.

[677] Paul W. Lovinger, "Aviatrix: the Flying's Easy," *Honolulu Star-Bulletin*, April 14, 1964, 1.

[678] Brown, *Fate*, 88.

[679] Ibid.

the equator for her third crossing, she ran into unusually heavy storm activity for this time of year. Along the equator, storms could extend for hundreds of miles.[680]

Singkap radio beacon station was trying to reach her. Joan relayed a message to another plane, who passed the message along to Singapore. One hundred miles out, her high frequency (HF) reception began to click in and out, and it should do better. And whatever Frey's expert mechanics thought they did to fix the autopilot, it still wasn't working. Having to hand-fly "hour after hour" was exhausting.[681]

Approximately 130 miles north of Djakarta, she flew into the next equatorial front. At 7,000 feet, lightning "slice[d] through the sky,"[682] but she had to fly straight into it. She wasn't getting much information from Djakarta on her HF band, and she was still too far out to reach them on VHF. The static and turbulence were so bad that she lost all radio communications; nothing but "loud screeching noises"[683] emanated from the speakers.

The weather forced her to fly at 1,500 feet, but even that low, there was still no visibility. Flying on instruments with no radio contact was terrifying. Then she saw a thin line of light up ahead, offering a glimmer of hope. Finally, she able to descend out of it all, only to be told that she had to follow a tight military corridor again.[684]

---

[680] Ibid.

[681] Ibid.

[682] Ibid.

[683] Brown, *Fate*, 88-89.

[684] Merriam, "Longest Flight," 47; Brown, *Fate*, 88-89.

Lagoon and Husband

Tuesday, April 14, 5:53 a.m. (Hawaii-Aleutian Time)
(after crossing the International Date Line)
HONOLULU, Hawaii

Chirp-chirp.

Jerrie's dream of a hula dancer and a warrior king paddling his canoe across a lagoon to meet her was interrupted by an annoying little bird chirping its way into the scene.

"Stupid bird. Go. Fly away."

Chirp-chirp.

She woke up enough to realize that the sound didn't come from her dream. It was the phone.[685]

"Hello."

"Good morning, Mrs. Mock! I'm calling from the *Honolulu Advertiser*. So that you won't be bothered too often, I'm representing all of the news people. We'd all like to know what time you plan to depart."[686]

Furious at getting pulled out of a deep sleep, the first response that came to mind was one that "no lady would say."[687]

"Huh? When am I going to leave? How should I know? It's the middle of the night. I'm trying to sleep! The hotel was told to keep calls away!" She wanted to slam the phone onto the

---

[685] Mock, *Three-Eight Charlie*, 245; Mock, interview, April 20, 2008.
[686] Mock, *Three-Eight Charlie*, 245.
[687] Ibid., 246.

receiver, but this phone didn't have one. She slammed that annoying bird-phone onto the table as hard as she could.

Her head pounded. Sleep deprivation pulled on her like a giant weight, but the headache kept her awake. She managed to get a couple more hours' sleep, but her "whole morning was shot." Sight-seeing in Honolulu would be limited to the view from a "high, rotating dining room" that looked out over the harbor.[688]

After a bite, it was back to business. She called Gib McCoy, and he picked her up.

"You know, you gave us a scare when you wandered off course out there," he said.

Jerrie had to think about this comment before responding.

"But your air speed didn't vary much," McCoy went on, "so we figured you must be okay."

"How far out were you able to track me?" she asked.

McCoy just smiled. "I'll show you in a minute." He gave her a ride over to the FAA Air Traffic Center complex, built inside the crater of the extinct Diamond Head volcano. He led her past row after row of men monitoring radar images on their console screens. Their scope extended back to Wake and then some. Every blip was identifiable as a particular type of aircraft, and Jerrie could see each plane's speed and direction. The new jets were so much faster than the small propeller planes. For better or worse, she had made it back to the part of the world where people would know exactly where she was and what she was doing at every moment, maybe even better than she knew herself.[689]

---

688 Mock, *Three-Eight Charlie*, 246; Mock, interview, April 20, 2008.
689 Mock, *Three-Eight Charlie*, 246-247.

Weather to Oakland looked fine, and she asked Gib to drive her back to the hotel. It was time to pack, and she owed the *Dispatch* her next update. Before giving her husband the story for the newspaper, Jerrie needed to clear something up with him.

"Russ, you know I love you, but you completely spoiled my fun here in Hawaii. I never even got to see the beach. And badgering me about not phoning and cabling all those times you wanted me to hurry home didn't help. You have no idea what it's like on the far side of the world. You can't just pick up the phone and call Columbus. Half the time, the place is closed, or the phone doesn't work."[690]

"But when you did send a cable," he said, "why was it so short? You never put take-off times in it."

"How could I know when I was going to take off before I went to the airport? It isn't like home. Some places wouldn't take the credit card."

"Yeah! The Watanasupts said you didn't want to spend your traveler's check."

"The man in Bangkok wouldn't take it! And at a dollar a word, if I'd sent a 150-word story every day, I'd have run out of money at some airport in Asia. Some places, if I'd tried to call or cable just before take-off, I'd have wasted half a day."

"I'm sorry," Russ said, "but we didn't know. We thought you were just having fun."

"Fun! You sure did a good job of ruining my fun. All that telling people I wanted to go to bed. What I could have done to you!"

---

[690] Ibid., 247.

"Yeah, I have to get you home *first.*"

"I know, for the sponsors. They're more important than wives. But the quickest way from one place to another isn't necessarily to take off in a hurry. When I agreed to make this flight, I knew that I'd have to put aside personal pleasures, if necessary. I have a conscience. And keeping true to a sponsor also means being true to my conscience, my husband, and God. Everybody wants me to be first, so I haven't taken time out for fun if it would slow me down. But to take off into bad weather, or when I was tired, or needed work done on the plane, or when I could tell that the officials and all their rules would slow me down if I took a certain course? No. That wouldn't have helped anyone. And I was the only one right there to decide. When I'm pilot-in-command of a ship, nobody gets me off the ground until I'm ready."

"Yeah, but for a few days it looked like Joan might still catch up with you."

"Russ," Jerrie said in exasperation. "Remember back in January, when we first heard about Joan from some of our suppliers, and we found out she was still looking for equipment that we had lined up months before? She took off in a rush while we paid attention to the details. And it sounds as if she's had a lot of mechanical trouble."

"Yeah, I know," Russ said, "and I take credit for getting her off in a rush by announcing to the press that you were leaving any day. I didn't think she was ready, either. But now it looks like you're in the lead. Now give me the scoop so I can call in a good story."

The two of them went back to working together. She dictated, and he wrote. At one point, he asked about a distance that she didn't have in her head. She set the phone down on the table, gently, and looked it up in her charts. When she came back to the table and picked up the phone again, all she heard was the dial tone. She had done that, but accidentally, this time. While she waited for Russ to call back, she decided that her husband "must have some sort of record for having been hung up on from the most faraway, crazy places."[691]

Then the phone rang, and they finished up.

"Great," Russ said. "Now I'm trying out to fly to Oakland to meet you."

"I can't wait to see you," she said.

"I'm still not sure yet. But if I can make it, Mary McGarey from the *Dispatch* might be flying over with me."

"Then you can take us all out to dinner," Jerrie said.[692]

Wednesday, April 15, mid-day (Indonesia Time)
DJAKARTA, Indonesia

"How blessed"[693] Joan felt to finally land at Djakarta and to be greeted by Air Force officers Colonel W.A. Slade and Major T.H. Canady. They helped her file a flight plan and get weather reports and clearances.[694]

Yet once on the ground, she could see and feel almost immediately that Djakarta was in the middle of political turmoil. At least fifty Russian MIGs were parked at the airport, along with many more Russian-supplied jeeps. She took a cab to a hotel for a bite to eat, and on the short ride she spotted a

---

691 Mock, *Three-Eight Charlie*, 247-249.
692 Mock, interview, April 20, 2008.
693 Brown, *Fate*, 89.
694 Ibid.

billboard depicting "American planes being shot out of the sky."[695]

The hotel was right across the street from the British Embassy which had been burned barely six months earlier; some large boards partially camouflaged the damage. "Leftist slogans and pro-Communist insignia"[696] were everywhere.

There were more reminders of Third World poverty. Joan passed a canal where naked people were bathing. A few blocks further, she saw the same canal being used as a toilet.[697]

She realized she was missing her sunglasses, and hurried back to Customs, where she remembered putting them down. There were only two men in Customs and she had only been gone five minutes, but they denied seeing any glasses. She didn't dare push it. Djakarta was "no place to linger," and she wanted to fly out of there as soon as she could.[698]

Tuesday, April 14, 5:26 p.m. (Hawaii-Aleutian Time)
HONOLULU, Hawaii

Jerrie finished packing, and Gib McCoy drove her to the airport. Her plane got an oil change and 171 gallons of gas, and seemed ready to make its longest nonstop flight yet.

American officials moved all the flight planning along so much faster than the indifferent bureaucrats at most of the stops around the world. Yet by now, she was also getting slowed by

---

[695] Ibid.

[696] Ibid.

[697] Brown, *Fate*, 89, 92.

[698] Ibid., 89.

the growing crowd and all the people wanting pictures with her. She "couldn't understand what all of the fuss was about."[699]

McCoy handed her a roast beef sandwich and an orange, but when she tried to put her snack-sack on board, the Immigration man grabbed the bag, and inspected it. "Sorry, but the orange can't go," he said.

"I don't want to bring it all the way. I want to eat it. I like to eat oranges over the ocean. Then I feel like Amelia Earhart."

"I'm sorry, but no fruit can go into California."

"But I'm going to eat it before I get there!"

Still, the answer was no, and he wasn't taking his eye off her. A minute later, McCoy slipped the orange into his coat pocket and walked with another FAA man back over to the plane. While the other man stood in the doorway, McCoy stashed the orange in her map pocket.

"I promise I'll throw out the peelings before I get to California," she whispered.[700]

She started up the plane, climbed to 9,000 feet, waved goodbye to her fans, along with the "emerald palms and white foam-edged beach," and headed east, over her next 2,400 miles of ocean.

Alone in the darkening sky again, Jerrie entertained herself with the exotic-sounding place-names of the points to which she would be reporting her position. She was headed over Koko Head, Papaya, Crab. Here was Sunrise, and later she would pass over Sunset. Other names in this neighborhood included

---

[699] Mock, *Three-Eight Charlie*, 249.

[700] Mock, *Three-Eight Charlie*, 249-250.

Magnolia, Bamboo, Hula Girl, Orchid, Seaweed, Porpoise, and Tuna.[701]

Once she crossed over Koko Head, she left behind all sight of land. She wanted to believe what they said about the word "aloha," because she hoped to return some day and see the rest of Hawaii. About the time that she felt confident she was on course, the sun slipped below the ocean behind her. She switched on her lights and tried to tidy up the cabin, one more time.[702]

Wednesday, April 15, mid-afternoon (Western Indonesia Time) DJAKARTA

Joan was relieved to get away from Djakarta. As she flew along the northern coast of the island of Java, the weather deteriorated. It would get even worse within the next day over the mountainous terrain of this string of small Indonesian islands. When she landed at Surabaya, a small city on the far eastern edge of the island of Java, the weather was "definitely marginal."[703]

As she descended over rice paddies that checkered the land, the airport tower instructed her to circle around again, a full 360 degrees; she flew low over the red tile roofs of the city and fishing boats in the harbor until cleared to land.

The runway came at her too fast to be able to tell how rough it was going to be, and she worried about the gas tanks getting jostled. One hard bump would be enough to knock one of the

---

[701] Ibid., 250.

[702] Ibid., 250-251.

[703] Brown, *Fate*, 89-90.

tanks loose, and she'd have another gas spill on her hands. But the landing was fine.[704]

She was greeted by a welcoming committee including the director of the Indonesian-American Friendship Association James McHale; an official with the United States Information Agency (USIA), Fred Coffey, Jr.; American Ambassador Alan McLean; and several dozen Indonesian citizens. She hoped they would put a guard by the plane all night. She'd had enough things stolen already. Instead, she had to settle for having 51-Poppa locked up in their hangar, and did her best to smile and say "thank you" for that.[705]

Surabaya didn't have a hotel or even a sandwich bar, but McLean took her to his home for dinner with his wife and family, which was a lovely oasis of normal. Then it was back to the airport to sleep in one of those tiny rooms in the officer's quarters, driving through dark streets because that night they were "saving electricity" again. "It's just as well," she was told. "Lights attract mosquitoes." In the room, her bed was canopied with a mosquito net that didn't smell *too* musty, after she learned not to roll over into it.[706]

---

[704] Ibid., 90.

[705] Ibid.

[706] Ibid., 91, 92.

The X Factor

Wednesday, April 15, 12:35 a.m. (Zulu Time)
Over the PACIFIC

Nine hours after leaving Honolulu, Jerrie flew over the US Coast Guard ship *Ocean Station November*. She was late by forty-five minutes. Slowed by unexpected headwinds, such a delay wasn't her fault. Still, by now she knew she was being tracked. Those forty-five minutes would be reported around the world as if the delay had been dangerous, or she had gotten lost, or maybe even that she had gone playing in the clouds again, and she would be facing silly questions about it later.[707]

Clouds beneath the plane kept her from seeing the weather ship below her. Despite the delay and the clouds, it still felt good to fly straight over and hear an American voice over the loudspeaker, reporting her position on radar.

The only thing she had to worry about for the next eight hours was staying awake. Every hour, she used her oxygen mask. She tried to use it when she wasn't expecting a radio transmission, but, of course, that was exactly when a ground controller would call in. She couldn't take off the mask, reach the oxygen bottle, switch off the valves on the bottle, turn on the microphone, and adjust all the radio settings in time to answer, before the man in the tower went into a panic thinking she must be lost at sea.

---

[707] Mock, *Three-Eight Charlie*, 251; Geraldine L. Mock, "Summary of Arrival and Departure Times," filed with the NAA.

Yet she discovered that adrenalin or some other internal factor helped her do things she couldn't ordinarily do. She ate and drank very little on board, only ate small meals on the ground, never ate breakfast, only drank a cup or two of coffee, never really caught up on her sleep, and still made flights of ten, fifteen–tonight would be eighteen–hours, many times with only five hours of sleep. There was no way to simulate or practice for this "X Factor."

She ate her sandwich and orange, then she cracked a window and let the orange peels fall free, eliminating all evidence of smuggling.[708]

With *dit*s and *dah*s streaming in steadily from the San Francisco Consolan, it was easy to keep flying in a straight line. The sun inched up over water and sky, making the whitecaps sparkle below. Sadly, it was already time to give up her throne as Queen of the Clouds. At the same time, she hoped Russ had made it to Oakland ahead of her, and she couldn't wait to see her children just a few days later, in Columbus. Yes, she had gotten homesick.

Out in the ocean stood a rocky little hill, all by itself, covered with trees. It was one of the Farallon Islands, and it meant she was only thirty-eight nautical miles to Oakland. After three weeks away from the United States, the last eighteen hours over endless water, the California shoreline was suddenly coming up *fast*. San Francisco's distinctive skyline appeared on the horizon, and then the bay. Haze blocked out her view of the Golden Gate Bridge, a bit north of her. Another sight she had to miss, this time.[709]

---

[708] Mock, *Three-Eight Charlie*, 252; Mock, interview, April 29, 2008.
[709] Ibid., 254

As she flew across the bay, heading for Oakland International Airport, she heard the tower operator talking with someone in a camera plane. She heard her name. Someone was already up there with her, snapping photos of Charlie. She still hadn't gotten used to reporters and photographers.

She slowed and dropped down, watching the pavement rise toward her windshield. She tried to get the two front wheels and the tail wheel even, aiming for a three-point landing.

Touching down. Bouncing once. Bouncing again. The *third* bounce was embarrassing, in front of so many people.

She slowed to taxiing speed, followed the ground controller's directions and turned, but she never made it to the hangar. Hundreds of people were out there, waving, shouting, breaking past the police barrier, and running at the plane. She tried to get the engine turned off quickly, before anybody got too close to the propeller.[710]

A reporter for an Oakland newspaper described Jerrie as "an Ohio housewife who travels a lot."[711]

---

[710] Ibid., 255

[711] "Mrs. Mock Sets Down," Oakand (UPI), *Honolulu Advertiser*, April 16, 1964.

Home and Away

I Can Navigate the World,
But I'm Lost in Oakland

Wednesday, April 15, 1:04 p.m. (Pacific Time)
OAKLAND, California

The first man to reach Jerrie's plane flung the door open, and crowd noise flooded her cockpit. Every mouth out there seemed to shout; every arm waved.

Then there was Russ, pushing through them all, climbing on the step, and giving her a big kiss. He turned his head and kissed her again from a different angle. A million cameras clicked and snapped behind him.

Somebody said, "Hold it," and Russ held his kiss longer.

Then, "Turn this way." Russ tried to turn her head toward the voice. Not quite the way his lady might have wanted to be greeted, but she didn't get a chance to object.

She was pulled out of the plane, squinting in the hot sun. She held her skirt down with one hand and plucked her nylon hose off the doorframe with the other, which left no hands free for the straps of the life jacket. "Russ, wait! Let me comb my hair. Can you find my purse? My high heels?" Russ pulled a comb out of his own pocket and jumped back into the cockpit for her shoes. She got one shoe on before she was surrounded by microphones and men– "tall men, short men and fat men. All the men's mouths seemed to be working."[712]

---

[712] Mock, *Three-Eight Charlie*, 256.

"Why did you choose a single-engine airplane for such a hazardous flight?"

Okay, time for answers they might like. "Well, you see, we just happened to have one . . ."

"Now that you're sure to be the first woman to fly around the world, what's it like?"

She was not sure at all, yet. Nobody told her exactly where Joan was, and the finish line of this race was still half a continent away. Someone handed her a big stack of telegrams and flowers. One floral arrangement was sent by Jo Eddleman on behalf of the Santa Clara chapter of the Ninety-Nines.[713]

"Mr. Mock, put your arm around Jerrie. That's right."

"Jerrie, how old are your children? Do they miss you?"

"Don't you feel safer back on the ground?"

"I bet your husband's glad to have you back. How are you going to celebrate tonight?"

That wouldn't be anyone else's business, now would it?

Behind the reporters, someone else was shouting. Jerrie stood on tiptoe to watch a photographer arguing with a police officer. "I'll report you to your superiors."

"Mister, you quiet down before I book you."

"You've no right—"

"What's going on back there?" Jerrie asked.

Russ laughed. "As you came in for your landing, that guy broke through the police barrier, running right at the plane, trying to get a picture. Your propeller would have taken his head off, but the cop tackled him."[714]

---

[713] Ibid., 257.
[714] Ibid.

Then the crowd was back on her again. "Jerrie, can I have an autograph?"

But Jerrie was done with questions. She needed to get out of the sun, and find the first office she had to report to, but she didn't know which building. She stepped back from the microphones and tried to walk away.

"What's wrong?" Russ looked down, startled. He took her arm and somebody else Jerrie recognized took her other arm: Mary McGarey, the reporter from the *Dispatch* who had flown in from Columbus with Russ.

Jerrie looked up. "Hi, Mary. Can–can we sit down?"

Russ said, "Let's see if we can make it to that lounge over there."

Inside a building with a working air conditioner, Jerrie gratefully sat on a couch. The reporters and photographers followed them in. She pulled out the sari Mrs. Roy had picked out for her, slung it over her shoulder, and posed for yet another photo or two.[715]

When Russ thanked everyone and finally sent them on their way, she hoped to be done. Then he escorted in a girl who looked maybe twenty. "Jerrie, this is Darlene Ceremello. She's been waiting patiently."

"I am thrilled to meet you," Darlene said, reaching behind her head. "I am about to enter a convent, and I must give away all my worldly possessions." She brought her hands in front of her. "One of my most precious is this St. Christopher's medal. I want you to have it, so you will be protected from harm."

---

[715] Ibid.

"I promise to wear it constantly," Jerrie said. "Without God protecting me, I could not have made it this far." Russ said goodbye to the young woman, and went on to tell Jerrie about ministers and others praying for her, too, for which Jerrie was grateful.[716]

Finally, everyone was gone, and Jerrie could get back to taking care of business. "Russ, that compass has been ten degrees off this whole time," she said, going down her checklist. "On the phone, you said Randleman wants me to go all the way to El Paso to get in enough miles for the record. In that case, I'll need more charts for the rest of the way." She tried to think of everything she needed from him in order to finish this thing.

"I haven't found any more charts yet, but I'll keep looking," Russ said. "Now why don't we all get in the rental car and escape to the hotel?"

"Sounds good to me," she said, but when they made it to the car, Mary got in the driver's seat.

Jerrie looked at Russ, but he just shrugged. "She says I'm having a little trouble with the power brakes," he said, opening the passenger door for Jerrie.

"Trouble?" Jerrie said, getting in.

"His trouble is that the brakes on this car work too well," Mary laughed, as Russ got in the back seat. "Now Jerrie, maybe you can tell me which road to take out of the airport."

"Try this one." In the big plan of the trip, with all those maps at her command, Jerrie hadn't thought about getting hung up on this one small part of it, but an hour later, they were still driving around. Jerrie heard a giggle from the back seat.

---

[716] Ibid., 258.

"My wife can find Oakland from Honolulu, but not from the airport."

Mary pulled up beside a police car and rolled down her window. "Sir, could you help us?"

The officer took his time getting out of his car and walking over to the driver's side. He leaned in the window and took a long, hard look at everybody until he got to Jerrie. Finally, he said, "You're the one I've been reading about. You just follow me."

He wheeled his squad car in front of theirs, turned on his lights and siren, and escorted them directly to their hotel. He stopped his car in the street, walked back to theirs, and leaned in the window. "This little service is going to cost you," he said. They were stuck out there in the street, completely at his mercy, and nobody knew what to say. Then he smiled. "How about your autograph for my little girl?"[717]

Russ led Jerrie to a hotel room filled with flower arrangements, fruit baskets, a pile of telegrams, and champagne. She was exhausted, but it was still daylight. "Russ, I'm so glad you could make it out here to meet me. Yesterday, you had me worried when you said you might not."

"I was ready to give up," he said. "I just didn't have the money. But Jim and Happy Hubble insisted that I take their vacation money. Jim said he remembered a time during the Depression when he was to have been a guest of honor at a banquet, but he didn't have the money to go. Not too many people understand things like that."

---

[717] Ibid., 259.

"That was wonderful of them," Jerrie said. "Now call Mary over from her room," she said. "Let's all toast together." As Mary came in, Jerrie asked Russ, "How is everything at home?"

"It's been a wild ride," he said. "The phone rings all night, and people show up at all hours. I work the phone, and just go in to the office whenever I can. Look! I've lost eighteen pounds worrying about you."

Jerrie gave him the look. "You needed to lose eighteen pounds."

"Yeah, so I *did*. And I've worn a path through the living-room carpet, pacing the floor all night."

"That we didn't need."

Mary didn't say or drink anything; she just kept her pen and pad ready.

"My mother is all confused," Russ went on. "She cleans the house, cooks the food, feeds the kids, and answers the door. When the phone rings, Mom gets up, pads around in her slippers, says, 'Thank goodness,' and goes back to bed. With two different generals calling the house, she seems to think every officer is a general. You should see Art Weiner's face when she calls him General Weiner."

Jerrie giggled into her champagne. "I'm sure the captain appreciates the promotion. But who is calling our house in the middle of the night?"

"The Pentagon, dear! Every time you make a position report, it's relayed to Dick Lassiter at the Pentagon, then he relays it to Lockbourne, then the guy on duty calls Bob Strauss. Then Bob calls the house, but usually a captain or somebody from Washington will call us at the same time he calls Lockbourne. He always says, 'This is Captain So-and-So, from the Pentagon.

You'll be hearing from General Strauss in a few minutes, and don't tell him you've talked to me.' Then he tells me you're over *November,* or wherever you are, and sure enough, in about ten minutes, the phone rings again, and this time I hear, 'Russ, this is Bob Strauss. We've just received a report that Jerrie's over *November.*' Then, an hour and a half later, when they get your next position report, the whole thing's repeated, sometimes with a third guy, too. Each time, I call the *Dispatch.*"

"Oh, dear," Jerrie said. "They actually wake up our house and the Strausses every night. I'm sorry. I didn't know."

"Betty Strauss was afraid you might say that," Russ said, "Seems that her husband came home one evening saying 'General Lassiter has decided the Air Force should help some crazy woman and I've inherited her!' She's having fun with it, and she wants to catch up with you when you get back."

Jerrie fell silent. She had been concentrating on her flight so hard that she hadn't had the time or energy left to remember all the many people who had been working for her, too.

"The boys are excited to see you," Russ said. "Val said, 'Tell Mommy I love her whole lots, as much as the whole world, the ocean, and the sky.'"

"I miss them all, too," Jerrie said. "Now, I've had to make a sandwich and an orange last me for thirty hours. You think we can find good seafood?"

Russ put down his glass of champagne. "Mary, you're still driving."

The search for a restaurant sent them back out into this city, now darker, trying to find their way around streets they didn't know, and up and down inclines that they couldn't see well. At the bottom of a steep hill, a car pulled out. Mary tapped those power brakes, and Jerrie tried to crack the windshield with the top of her head. To think, one of those reporters had wanted to know if she was happy to be "safe on the ground."[718]

Thursday, April 16, 6:00 a.m. (Western Indonesia Time) SURABAYA, Indonesia

It seemed that all of Joan's energy had to be concentrated on "wakefulness" in the air and sleep on the ground. At 6:00 in the morning, she found captains and stewardesses enjoying a breakfast of "rice, sweet and sour pork, fried eggs, tea and coffee."[719] Still having to take every caution about her diet, she settled for hot boiled tea. Maybe she would prefer rice with chicken or mushroom gravy for breakfast? "No thank you. I seldom eat much breakfast."[720]

Back in the cockpit an hour later, she had to deal with the telegram from John Sarver that she had received the night before. The message let her know that yes, Jerrie Mock had made it back to Oakland, and what that probably meant.

Joan had answered Sarver, "I have my heart set on flying the Earhart trail." She hoped her publicist could get reporters to print that, and that everyone would believe it. Sarver's press release on April 17 stated:

> [T]he happenings to this girl are unbelievable. . . . It almost seems as though Amelia Earhart was resenting anyone

---

[718] Ibid., 259-261; Mock, interview, May 5, 2008.

[719] Brown, *Fate*, 91.

[720] Ibid.

following her path and is throwing the book at Joan to delay and harass.[721]

Anyway, it was time to put those thoughts out of mind, because below her sprawled the fabled island of Bali. She could see the volcanoes on this little seventy-by-forty-mile island. The view brought to mind the haunting melody of the song, "Bali Hi," sung by Mary Martin and Ezio Pinza in the musical *South Pacific*. She would have loved to drop in, but Bali would have to be one more stop that she would miss this time.[722]

Each island along the Lesser Sunda chain seemed to have one prominent peak, which helped with navigation. She could enjoy a sandwich and Mrs. Mclean's homemade cookies, but this wouldn't be a good time to visit the ladies' room. Using a sick sack would require an uncomfortable degree of "acrobatics."[723] Without an autopilot, she would have to keep one hand on the controls, for fear of the plane suddenly veering off one way or another. She decided the call of nature wasn't urgent, and she would have to wait.[724]

She had to follow her flight plan, forcing her to miss Flores Island in the Indonesian chain just to the north. It had three lakes all close together, one red, one blue and one green. "What a color slide that would have made!" Yet to save time and fuel, her "wandering thoughts had to be caged and disciplined."[725]

---

[721] Sarver, press release, April 17, 1964.

[722] Brown, *Fate*, 91.

[723] Ibid., 92.

[724] Ibid., 91-92.

[725] Ibid., 92.

She crossed the Savu Sea for 250 miles over open water. The weather was good for bit, and she was "truing out" at 171 miles per hour. True airspeed was almost always higher than indicated on the airspeed instrument in the cockpit, even into headwinds.[726]

She passed over the island of Timor, glimpsing a few boats and huts dotting the shoreline, and the Kupang airway, painted at both ends. She tried calling their tower, but no answer. Either it was another part-time operation, or she had caught another tower at siesta time.[727]

Then it was on out over the Timor Sea for another 450 miles. She had to keep her seat all the way back to operate the turbochargers, cramping her back and legs.[728]

She maintained radio contact to avoid restricted areas, spotting the deep blue of the Timor Trough and the softer blues and greens of the Sahul Shelf, until finally she spotted land.[729]

It had to be Australia, and that was great news. She'd never relished over-water flying, and she would never own a pontoon-equipped plane. She picked up the Norelco tape recorder and began talking into it again.[730] Recalling the different planes she had bought, and all the different things she had considered doing with them, one memory in particular came to mind. She went to an air show in Sarasota, Florida, and watched a stunt flier named Bevo Howard. She got to meet him after the show, and he let her look over his plane. From that

---

[726] Ibid.

[727] Ibid., 93.

[728] Ibid.

[729] Ibid., 92.

[730] Ibid.

event, she developed a "sudden infatuation" with acrobatic flying, and bought a clip-wing Piper Cub for acrobatics.[731] Acrobatic flying still impressed her now, but it would have to wait. At this moment, she said, "My gross-loaded Apache has the aptitude for acrobatics that an elephant has for ballet."[732] Still, she thought she might go back to acrobatic flying someday, with a different plane, "once I finish what Amelia Earhart started, this equator flight."[733] As always, completing the Earhart route was her primary objective.

Darwin Airport was just ahead. She put her koala bear in the cockpit window so the Australian people could see him; they consider the koala bear to be good luck. She just had to hope that nobody gave her a real one. Coming in to Australia brought the memory of Dianna Bixby, from back in Long Beach, to Joan's mind and heart. She recalled that Dianna had "named her plane the Southern Cross, in deference to her Australian mother."[734]

She ran the turbochargers until the last second, then brought the plane down, relieved that the quick descent didn't hurt her ears. She was in the air for two hours, but she crossed two time zones and "gained" time, so she was on the ground at only 6:29 a.m. Darwin time. The tower operator told her not to open the door; that the authorities would be coming to her. Even though

---

[731] Ibid., 93.

[732] Ibid.

[733] Brown, *Fate*, 93.

[734] Ibid., 94. The Southern Cross is a constellation only visible in the Southern Hemisphere.

he didn't say why, she remembered that Amelia Earhart had her plane fumigated for Indonesian mosquitoes and bugs.[735]

Sure enough, they spray-bombed the outside of the plane, the cockpit, and the pilot. Once thoroughly fumigated, Joan was welcomed by Captain Slade and manager Ken Davidson of the "Red Flying Kangaroo," Trans Australia Airlines. These men were helpful with mailing her stamped flight covers, and some of her recorded tapes, and they got her plane safely tucked away in their hangar, locked and guarded. Then they gave her a ride to the Hotel Darwin.[736]

---

[735] Brown, *Fate*, 94.
[736] Ibid., 102.

So Long, Reporters! Can't Quiz Me Up Here!

Thursday, April 16, 3:12 p.m. (Pacific Time)
OAKLAND, California

Jerrie's day began with way-too-early phone calls, an interview in front of a television camera, and a disappointing update.

"Are you getting excited about all this?"

She was getting "bored with all this."

"The man who looked at the compass says he can't fix it."

She had made it this far without it, anyway.

Still, she didn't get away until mid-afternoon. Once Russ was with her, he hadn't been in such a hurry for his wife to beat the sun into the sky. She promised herself that "if I ever get to go on that long sightseeing trip, I'll bring him along."[737]

Finally, she was back in the air, up and away from reporters, cameras and flashbulbs for a little longer. Russ hadn't found any charts for her next leg, after all. But that meant she was taking off without yet knowing whether she was bound next for Phoenix or Tucson. *That* meant she had managed to take off without saying where she was going, either.

The hills of central California showed up soft green against a brown mountain ridge beyond them. She flew parallel to the ridge, past Bakersfield and Palmdale, then angled east around a restricted area. Green valleys faded into brown desert. Then the

---

[737] Mock, *Three-Eight Charlie*, 262; Mock, interview, May 5, 2008.

sun dropped behind the ridge over her shoulder and she was left "suspended in a black night," punctured here and there by faint lights of a small town. She was approaching Tucson, so she picked out a field where she felt like landing.[738]

7:48 p.m. (Mountain Time)
TUCSON, Arizona

Jerrie called in to the Tucson tower, fifteen miles ahead. There was the beacon, blinking green, white, green, white. She brought Charlie down without too many bounces and taxied in. A gas truck pulled up. She spotted a man right behind the truck, walking toward her with a camera. How could he have known she would be there when she had just decided fifteen minutes before, and hadn't told anyone except the tower? Still, one reporter was easier to talk to than twenty, and this interview went better than usual.

There was a hotel right on the airfield, called the "Airport Rontel." The name came from aviator lingo, a combination of "RON," which was short for "remain overnight," and "hotel." The manager of the Airport Rontel would not take her money for the room, dinner, or even the plane's gas. Then he left her alone to enjoy "flaming shrimp with brandy sauce" without having to talk to any more reporters or strangers. Yet even after this nearly perfect day of flying, when she made it to the room and got in the bed, she had to call the front desk and ask for another wake-up call for 4-ouch-30 a.m.[739]

---

[738] Mock, *Three-Eight Charlie*, 263-264.
[739] Ibid., 264.

Friday, April 17
DARWIN, Australia

Joan got up at 4:30 a.m. and called the airport, only to find out that a low loft over the Owen-Stanley mountain range in New Guinea, wide and severe for 200 miles, would keep her on the ground for another day.[740]

Her hosts wanted to show her some places of interest, anyway. They took her to a memorial stone plaque and pillar at Port Darwin, recognizing the first aerial flight from England to Australia, on December 10, 1919. "The pilot's name was Sir Charles Kingford-Smith," one of her hosts noted with pride. "Another Smith, like yourself."[741]

Also in Darwin, an air ambulance service offered to buy 51-Poppa. Joan could sell it at a $10,000 profit–if she were willing to abandon her flight at this point and return home on a commercial airliner. Joan declined politely, and excused herself from that conversation quickly. "I've set out to fly the Earhart equator route and no shortcuts or half measures will suffice. What is $10,000 against ten years of dreaming and planning?"[742]

Each time someone offered to buy the plane, or talk her into cutting the length of the trip "just to beat the other girl," she would think it through and return to the same conclusion: "I wouldn't be able to live with myself if I had."[743]

Sarver's telegrams kept her up-to-date about Jerrie's relentless advance toward Ohio. In a press release on April 17,

---

[740] Brown, *Fate*, 102.

[741] Ibid.

[742] Ibid., 102-103.

[743] "Two women Fliers Killed," *Los Angeles Times*, Feb. 18, 1965.

Sarver noted Joan's pluck in the face of multiple adversities and stated that, "the so-called race is far from over."[744]

Joan expressed her feelings later in an interview with James Gilbert with *Flying* magazine. "How can you make a race out of two flights that are almost 7,000 miles different in length?" Gilbert wrote that this distinction "was lost on the world's press."[745]

Joan told Gilbert, "The thought went through my mind for about a half a day of skipping the Earhart route and just making a route of about 20,000 miles. But I felt that this would only be cheating myself."[746]

Okay, so she couldn't do anything about the narrative or the record books until she got back home to Long Beach. From Darwin, she just had to make it back home. At the hotel, she read a newspaper article referring to her as "California's Flying Housewife."[747] The press had taken to calling Jerrie "the Flying Housewife," which was appropriate since Jerrie was, indeed, a housewife. And yes, Joan was Jack's wife, and proud of it, but "housewife" wasn't exactly the image she was going for. She was a professional pilot, not a housewife who took up flying as a hobby.

Friday, April 17, 6:07 a.m. (Mountain Time)
TUCSON, Arizona

Back in small American airports accustomed to small planes, and with no Customs or Immigration or crowds, Jerrie was on

---

[744] Sarver, press release, undated.

[745] Gilbert, "The Loser," 80.

[746] Ibid.

[747] Between April 18 and April 20, more than seventy newspapers picked up a news story that called Joan "California's Flying Housewife."

schedule again and in the air before daybreak. From Tucson, she had to fly only 267 miles to El Paso.

An hour and a half after take-off, she approached the town. On this clear morning, she could see for miles, beyond El Paso and across the border into Mexico.

The airport was "shimmering white in the early-morning sun."[748] Once again, she hadn't told anyone where she was going, and she had gotten away quickly, so only her NAA observer should be there to meet her.

But, no. As she taxied toward the Cessna hangar, another crowd came running.[749]

EL PASO, Texas, 7:45 a.m. (Mountain Time)

As Jerrie climbed out of the plane, people surrounded her and escorted her into a large room with banners on the wall saying, "Congratulations, Jerrie!" and "Welcome to Texas!" She was led toward the seat of honor, past nicely set tables, and large, fresh flower arrangements.

"Jerrie? I'm Ruth Deerman. Pleased to meet you."

"Ruth Deerman?" Jerrie recognized her name right away. "Aren't you one of the Ninety-Nines?"

Deerman had flown in the first Transcontinental Women's Air Race back in 1929. After that race, ninety-nine women who were licensed pilots formed an organization to promote aviation. Their first president was Amelia Earhart.

"Yes," Ruth said. "Actually, I'm International President now."

"How do you put all this together on such short notice?" Jerrie asked.

---

748 Mock, *Three-Eight Charlie*, 265.
749 Ibid.

"We've been following you all the way. Have a seat!"

The room was filled with the sounds of talking and laughter, chair legs scraping against the floor as people took their seats at the tables.

"Do I smell breakfast?" Jerrie asked.

"Oh, yes," Ruth said. "The mayor is on his way. Do, please sit down."

Breakfast? Mayor? The word "speech" would be coming next. Jerrie stood back up. "Ah, yes, well, this all really sounds like fun." She cleared her throat. "But … I still have to fly 1,500 more miles today. And a storm's coming in."

The microphone picked up her voice and the chatter of the crowd faded. Jerrie spoke into the mike. "I'm very sorry," she said to a now-silent room. "You have all done a lot of work on what must have been very short notice, and I wish I could stay. But this race isn't over yet."

Nobody said a word. Among a crowd of three or four hundred, the only sound was the clink of a glass in the kitchen. Finally, Ruth stood up, smiling politely. "Can we at least get some pictures?"

Jerrie smiled for the camera. She gulped a little coffee, answered some questions, and became an honorary citizen of El Paso. She got a brief weather report, plus those last charts. She answered questions from Russ, who called her from a pay phone at Chicago's O'Hare Airport. Then she waved goodbye to her disappointed fans, and within sixty-five minutes after touching down, she was airborne again.[750]

---

[750] Mock, *Three-Eight Charlie*, 265-266; Mock, interview, May 5, 2008.

In the air, she couldn't forget that roomful of sad, maybe even insulted, faces. This trip was changing her life. She "couldn't understand" why her flight brought out such a huge reaction. Hadn't male pilots circled the globe many times already? When she had first flown out over the Atlantic and left the continental United States behind, she had had to worry about the Air Force not recognizing her. Now, back in America, the crowds kept building up until they were actually getting in her way.

Flying had been the easy part. All the work on the ground had been tougher, and the hardest part had been changing people's minds. She had flown her way through indifference, into disbelief, hostility, respect, and finally to admiration. Navigating the barrier of public opinion seemed as difficult to her as it must be for another pilot to break the sound barrier, and the sonic booms were being heard all over the world.

She had never asked for any of it.

Now she was supposed to act like a celebrity, but she didn't know how. She "felt much more at home talking aerodynamics with an aircraft engineer than being welcomed by mayors, committees, and mobs of photographers."[751] Well, at least she had escaped them all for another hour or two.[752]

For the first few hundred miles, she flew with a tailwind, between cloud layers above and below her. Then the clouds above her began to drop, little by little, until she either had to get on the radio to ask for clearance to fly by instrument or descend to where she could see. Searching the clouds, she spotted a hole and spiraled through it. Below the cloud, it was

---

[751] Mock, *Three-Eight Charlie*, 267.
[752] Mock, *Three-Eight Charlie*, 266-267; Mock, interview, May 5, 2008.

rainy and uninviting, but she could see just far enough ahead to tell where she was going.

Here in America, the radio gave her weather broadcasts every half hour. This storm was heading for Memphis, right along with her.

Lightning crackled across the "purple-black" sky. The heavy mist forced her to keep descending. She wound her way through every light spot she could find, and prayed. Again and again, she found just enough of a break in the clouds to make it through, as if perhaps she wasn't alone up there after all.

She called into Memphis to request clearance and this time the tower answered right away. "November Three-Eight Charlie, Memphis. Request your route to Columbus."

She looked at her charts and picked out a town on her airway that she had visited before. "I'm going by way of Bowling Green."

After Memphis, she left her radio on, and it came to life. Some people called in to congratulate her, others just to chat. Eventually, she had to turn the volume down again and concentrate.

Dang it! The needle on that gas gauge was bouncing around on top of the E. Having to set the plane down in some cornfield just a mile or two short of Columbus would be annoying on multiple levels. Ten minutes out, she got back on the radio, called Bowling Green, and got clearance for a quick stop.[753]

A reporter in El Paso wrote, "Dressed in a powder blue skirt and sweater, Mrs. Mock, 38, powdered her nose."[754]

---

[753] Mock, *Three-Eight Charlie*, 267-268.

[754] "Aviatrix on Flight's Finale," *Honolulu Star-Bulletin*, April 17, 3.

BOWLING GREEN, Kentucky, 3:08 p.m. (Central Time)

Five minutes later, Jerrie was on the ground and taxiing past the office of the fixed-base operator, at the direction of a line boy. Beside the line boy walked a man with a camera. Now, how did he know to be here on five minutes' notice?

"Fill up just one of the wing tanks, would you, please?" Hopping out of the plane, trying to dodge the inevitable flash-and-snap, she walked quickly over to the office. She hoped to find one last mirror and freshen up to face the photographers and crowds in Columbus. But the second she walked into the office, she heard, "Telephone for you, ma'am."

"Telephone for me?"

"Yes, ma'am. You *are* Jerrie Mock, aren't you?"

She picked up the phone.

"Hi, honey!" It was Russ.

"How did you find me here? I didn't tell anybody."

"You sure didn't! The whole FAA, from Najeeb Halaby on down, has been trying to find you, and the Air Force, too! They've been calling every station anywhere near your route!"

Najeeb Halaby? "You mean the head of the FAA? Did I do something wrong?"

"Oh, for God's sake, woman! He wants to fly to Columbus to meet you when you land, and he wants to know what time you're getting in. Plus, the *Dispatch* and just about everybody else in Columbus all want to know, too. Now, give me an estimate."

"I don't know how far it is to Columbus. My chart's in the plane."

"Three hundred miles," volunteered the man behind the desk.

"Okay, so maybe two more hours, after I get gas."

"You'll be on the roll in ten minutes?"

"Twenty."

"Make it fifteen!"

Jerrie headed down the hall to the mirror.

The phone rang again. "It's for you, ma'am."

"Congratulations, Jerrie. This is Norm Crabtree," the caller said. Crabtree was the director of the Ohio Board of Aviation. "Jerrie, let me know when you're getting in. The governor wants to meet you. He's in a meeting in Springfield and doesn't want to leave until the last minute. But he wants to be there in time to see you land."

"Oh, gee, Norm. I told Russ two and a half hours if the phone doesn't ring again."

"All right, gal. We'll be waiting for you."[755]

Saturday, April 18, 7:00 a.m. (Australian Central Time) DARWIN, Australia

Trans Australia Airlines served Joan breakfast, fixed a lunch with hot coffee to take with her, and they had even made a tow bar for 51-Poppa.[756] She thanked everyone, said goodbye and took off, bound for Thursday Island. She climbed to 6,000 feet, then dropped back down to 1,000 feet, flying above and below the rain, and in and out of it, too, sometimes visual, sometimes by instrument, and finally settled on 3,000 feet.[757] That was still only a guestimate; since she had yet another complicating factor. The next stretch across east Australia still had plenty of

---

[755] Mock, *Three-Eight Charlie*, 269-270.

[756] Brown, *Fate*, 103.

[757] Ibid.

unexplored terrain, and her chart merely said, "relief data incomplete," That was as low as she dared go to avoid an "uncharted" mountain.[758]

---

[758] Merriam, "Longest Flight," 47; Brown, *Fate*, 103.

Can the Autopilot Give the Speech?

Friday, April 17, 5:30 p.m. (Central Time)
BOWLING GREEN, Kentucky

Jerrie escaped into the air once again and, once again, tried to get ready for the next and final landing. Lots of important people would be waiting for her. It was enough to make her want to skip the landing, and just keep flying on out over the Atlantic.

Her little adventure had started out as a sightseeing tour. Then it became a race, a race she had to worry about winning. From the start, she had had to be persistent about details nobody else cared about, details that could have gotten her killed if they were overlooked.

All the way, she had encountered men who were sure they knew her job better than she did. The more important they were, the harder they were to deal with, and the people she was supposed to talk to seemed to become increasingly more important as this race progressed. If she ended up having to make speeches and shake hands all the way up to the president of the country, it could get harder still. She had heard that President Johnson could be especially touchy, if you didn't do things his way.

Anyway, she had run out of time for any more analysis. Now, as this journey of a month and a lifetime was coming to an end, suddenly, she only had a minute or two of private time left with her plane. After sitting in this cockpit for so many days and nights, she thought of *The Spirit of Columbus* as "something more than an arrangement of nuts and bolts." Charlie had become "her second home, a friend." The plane "seemed to have as much fun with the oceans and deserts as she did." She gently patted the instrument panel. "Thank you, Charlie, for taking such good care of me," she whispered. "Sorry about the sand in the carburetor." Then she prayed, thanking God for watching over both pilot and plane.[759]

She returned her attention to finding Columbus. The clouds faded and out came the stars.

"Three-Eight Charlie, this is Columbus Radio. Do you read?"

She turned the volume back up. "Columbus, this is Three-Eight Charlie."

"Congratulations, Mrs. Mock. You're almost home. Contact Approach Control and give them your position. They'll pick you up on their radar and bring you in from here." Then: "Jerrie, we've got a cold one on the rocks waiting for you."[760]

Over the radio, Jerrie couldn't tell if this was the same man who, back when she had taken off at the beginning of her quest, had told the local crowd that they might never see her again. She wondered how many of the people who heard him say that had come back tonight. She wondered why, after she had found her way around the globe alone, they had all decided she needed their help finding her way back to the same airport they had watched her leave. But she didn't say any of that. Let them have their fun. "Roger, calling Approach Control."[761]

---

[759] Mock, *Three-Eight Charlie*, 270-271; Mock, interview, May 5, 2008.
[760] Vail and Edwards, "Winner Take All," 66.
[761] Mock, *Three-Eight Charlie*, 271; Mock, interview, May 5, 2008.

The controller gave her magnetic headings leading her toward Columbus, then across town to Port Columbus Airport on the other side. The city lights passed under Charlie in a blink. Russ, Roger, Gary, and Valerie would all be with her once again, in just a few more minutes.

A "strange, prickly sensation" rippled through her as she picked out the "green-and-white flashing airport beacon, then the long line of yellow-white runway lights, flanked by the lines of blue lights," on either side of her runway. Any airport can be a spectacular sight at night, but she had been working her way back to this particular one for four weeks.

"Three-Eight Charlie, we need you to make a low pass down runway nine, then set up for an approach for runway two-three. Your NAA observer wants to clock you past the field."

Oh, yeah! Thinking of her family, Jerrie had momentarily forgotten about the record. She was about to make history. The NAA men waited down there to complete the forms they would mail to the FAI in Paris. Once her flight was recorded in their official book, she would officially be the first woman to fly around the world on her own, and she would be that woman for all time.

She closed in on runway nine, switching on Charlie's taillight so that it flashed at the official observers below. Were they using stop watches to get it down to the second?[762]

---

[762] Mock, *Three-Eight Charlie*, 271-272; Mock, interview, May 5, 2008.

Saturday, April 18, 7:30 a.m. (Australian Central Time)
Somewhere over Australia

Joan "disregarded the warnings of Australian weathermen" and took off, "heading for either Port Moresby or Lae, New Guinea, depending on the flying conditions she would run into."[763]

Darwin radio called to warn Joan that the weather ahead was only getting worse. She thought about turning back, but the weather was bad back there, too. Evidently, she was fighting an almost direct crosswind. At Cook Island she broke out of the overcast and homed in on the Thursday Island navigational sea beacon. With the rain, Thursday Island was down to one-mile visibility.[764]

She picked up a Cessna 205 on the pilot intercom frequency and talked to him. He had turned back from Moresby and recommended that she land at Horn Island, or fly down the Cape York Peninsula.[765]

As the clouds grew thicker and darker, the plane got knocked around more and more. Up in the air, then down, then off to the right. She held on to the wheel and fought the winds. Lightning flashed through the dark gray like a giant strobe light.

She started talking to the tower at Horn Island, and anyone else she could find, until she also picked up Starlight One, an Air Force jet taking reconnaissance pictures of weather patterns. By then she was back on instruments. She circled the area that should be twenty-five miles south of an airport, but she couldn't

---

[763] "Woman Flier Defies Weather, *San Antonio Light*, April 18, 1964.
[764] Brown, *Fate*, 103.
[765] Ibid.

see any islands where the flight chart indicated they should be. She flew low in circles through the haze and fog until she spotted two islands, but no landing strip. She finally executed a missed approach procedure and started climbing, to head back to Darwin. At 1,000 feet, she glanced out the window, and there, directly below her, was Horn Island. She made her approach and, with a sigh of relief, landed.

What was estimated to be an eight-hour flight had taken ten. The wind had been so severe that it had taken decals and paint off the sides of the plane.[766] Weather, she recorded in her journal, "is an obsession with every pilot."[767] But she was determined not to let the weather keep her from Earhart's route. For now, she was safely on the ground.[768]

PORT COLUMBUS, Ohio, 9:32 p.m. (Eastern Time)

Jerrie brought the plane down to just 100 feet, then shoved in the throttle, holding the plane level while the engine roared for the crowd. She headed back up, climbing and turning to approach runway two-three. Then she brought it down for a gentle, no-bounce stop.

"Three-Eight Charlie," the controller spoke again, over the loudspeaker this time. "You are cleared to taxi and cross into the ramp area. As you come toward the crowd, they will signal you when to cut your engine and they'll push you into the parking area for Gate C-4."

Why would they do all that? Seemed like the long way around their airport. Well, it didn't matter. She just had to

---

766 Ibid., 105.

767 Ibid., 104.

768 Ibid.

follow directions, wondering what was waiting for her this time.

Her lights picked up a couple of men motioning for her to stop. She had just gotten off the runway, and stopping here didn't seem right. Were these guys sure they had the right plane?

Then her lights picked up the crowd beyond them. "Crowd" was an understatement. *Thousands* of people were out there, "jumping up and down and waving banners."[769] No wonder they had to push the plane the rest of the way for her.

Startled, she shut down the engine. Police tried to hold everybody back from the spinning propeller. The second the engine quit and the propeller slowed, people broke through the barrier tape and took off running across the concrete.

Someone opened the cockpit door. The shouting sounded like fans at a football game, a really *big* game. Jerrie couldn't move, staring at the mob. Russ, Roger, and Gary appeared at her door. Everybody hugged, kissed, talked, and congratulated all at once.

"Where's Valerie?"

Someone handed their three-year-old to Russ and he passed her, looking lost, to Jerrie. She held her daughter tight.[770]

Governor Rhodes took Jerrie's hand. The police pushed people back from the plane so she could step down, and the governor's daughter draped a lei of white orchids onto Jerrie's shoulders.[771]

---

[769] Mock, *Three-Eight Charlie*, 273.
[770] Mock, *Three-Eight Charlie*, 272-273; Mock, interview, May 5, 2008.
[771] "Global Flight," *Honolulu Advertiser*, April 18, 1964.

Two policemen took Jerrie by the arms, while other officers encircled her family, ushering them forward and pushing back the crowd.

"Where are we going?" Jerrie asked.

"To the platform where everyone is."

Everyone? There were plenty of people around her already.

Somebody's foot came down on her shoe. The foot didn't move, but the policemen kept walking, so Jerrie did, too.

"Hold on! I lost my shoe back there!"

An officer retrieved the shoe and they kept moving. Once on the platform, Jerrie was surrounded by her parents, Russ's mom, her two sisters, their husbands and her grandfather. Many of the friends who had helped raise money, buy the plane, and teach her how to land were there; men from Champion Spark Plugs, Continental Motors, and Cessna, Al Baumeister, and Dave Blanton. It was impossible to speak to everyone. She would have to go to the microphone and say something to this crowd, to the throng that filled the tarmac as far back as the airport floodlights could reveal.

Melvin Tharp, the *Dispatch* advertising director, spoke into the microphone first. Jerrie could hardly hear him over the shouting, but by the time he had introduced a long list of people, the crowd had settled down. Tharp must have been a bit flustered himself; he called Governor Rhodes the "mayor of the great state of Ohio."[772]

Governor Rhodes, Congressman Sam Devine, then Mayor Maynard Sensenbrenner, all said kind things about Jerrie. The Governor said Jerrie should receive the "reverent homage we

---

[772] Mock, *Three-Eight Charlie*, 274; Mock, interview, May 5, 2008.

bestow only upon the brave." The mayor proclaimed Jerrie Mock Day. Bill Shulte, Assistant Administrator for General Aviation Affairs at the Federal Aviation Agency, read a telegram offering congratulations from FAA Administrator Najeeb Halaby: "Magellan, Francis Drake, Wiley Post, Nellie Bly, and now Jerrie Mock. You are in fast company." The FAA was going to strike a special medal just for her.

Shulte then read a telegram from President Johnson: "Your tremendous solo exploit in circumnavigating the globe in a light plane adds another notation to the record book of American triumphs, one already replete with the aeronautical exploits of American women."

A telegram from Amelia Earhart's sister, Muriel Earhart Morrissey, read, "I rejoice with you as you complete your successful flight. I am sure Amelia's courageous spirit rode with you all the way."[773]

Jerrie had never imagined she would be up here listening to all these people saying such wonderful things about her. She had just wanted to have fun flying a plane. But it wasn't over yet.

Captain Weiner, Brigadier General Strauss from Lockbourne, and Brigadier General Lassiter all spoke. Dick Lassiter admitted into the microphone how he had been "skeptical" of her idea for this flight.

"I know," Jerrie cracked back, and thousands of people burst out laughing.

---

[773] Vail and Edwards, "Winner Take All," 66.

Tharp slipped a necklace over her head; from it hung a golden globe dotted by rubies representing every place she had landed, with a diamond for Columbus.

Then as he stepped back, she could feel his hand on her shoulder, guiding her toward the microphones. The best she could do was to stutter something about how flying was pretty easy, but she wished her autopilot could take over for the speeches.

"It's all been so wonderful. I just don't know what to say." The crowd and the microphones and the flashes from the cameras "dissolved into a blur," and then, suddenly, "it was all over."[774]

Russ took her by the hand. For the first time in thirty days, Jerrie got in the car with her husband and family to drive home. As soon as she clicked her seat belt, she slipped Gary's class ring off her finger, reached over the back seat, and handed it to him. "Thank you," she said. "It helped, especially over the Pacific."[775]

"What are you talking about?" Gary asked. "What happened over the Pacific?"

"Maybe that story should wait until things settle down," she said.

The crowd cheered and waved as they rolled slowly past.

The house and yard overflowed with hundreds more people, some familiar faces, many not. Once they got into the house and as soon as she could, this weary pilot finally slipped away to bed.

---

[774] Mock, *Three-Eight Charlie*, 274-275; Mock, interview, May 5, 2008.
[775] Vail and Edwards, "Winner Take All," 66.

Saturday, April 18 at dusk
HORN ISLAND, Australia

Horn Island looked dull and dreary, with no signs of life. "Worse yet, no coffee."[776]

Then Joan spotted Dave Robertson, the Cessna pilot she had talked to in the air. "This is the worst weather I've seen in this area in sixteen years," Robertson told her.[777]

Eventually Customs, consisting of one inspector, came over by boat from Thursday Island to pick up the two pilots and carry them back across the choppy sea.[778]

At the dock, Robertson said his goodbyes, leaving Joan alone to walk down the road and look over her first choice of hotels, the Royal. She needed a good laugh to lighten this "leaden" day, and the Royal provided it. The hotel was built in 1850; its walls had layers of grime, the kind that takes years to accumulate, and the sheets were "what American housewives call tattletale gray."[779]

"Well, any port in the storm," Joan figured, "and a refuge from the stares of the drunks sitting in a row outside the saloon on the main street."[780]

"Where's the bathroom?" she asked at the front desk, envisioning the luxury of a real bathroom after having to make do with sick sacks while flying.[781]

---

[776] Brown, *Fate*, 104.

[777] Ibid.

[778] Ibid.

[779] Ibid.

[780] Ibid.

[781] Ibid.

The proprietor looked surprised and nodded toward the rear. "Out back, half a block."[782]

No, thanks. She went in search of alternate accommodations. Down the muddy street she found another boarding place, the Grant. She would stay and write some letters.[783]

No writing paper available. Ok, then she'd send a wire.

"From here?" The man at the desk asked in amazement. "Not possible."

Ok, then a good hot meal.

The cook was gone for the day.

She ate a cold supper.[784]

For all the strikes against her in this "godforsaken place," she chanced to meet someone from the Australian Broadcasting Corporation with whom she had a nice chat.[785]

"They say that's a cyclone forming out there," she remarked.

"So that's what they're calling it now?" he said. "Hurricane, cyclone, tropical depression, or just plain old 'storm.' It all amounts to just one more thing that turns people's TV screens to snow, and they start calling us."

"Sounds about right," Joan said. She lifted her glass of cola. "A toast: To time, money, and tropical depressions."

---

[782] Ibid.

[783] Ibid.

[784] Ibid.

[785] Ibid.

The President Is Calling

Saturday, April 18
COLUMBUS, Ohio

In the morning, the phone and the doorbell rang early. From her bed, Jerrie heard something she had not heard in a month: Russ answering for her. He picked up the phone from the kitchen downstairs and she closed her eyes.

When the doorbell chimed again, she dressed and went downstairs. The kitchen table and countertops were filling fast with flower arrangements and telegrams. Russ was still on the phone, dictating, while his mother wrote furiously. She could hear Roger's voice as he answered the front door. Russ noticed Jerrie and he waved frantically, motioning for her to stay in the kitchen, then he went back to saying, "Uh-huh, yeah" into the phone. He snapped his fingers at his mother for a pen. Glancing out a window, Jerrie saw a photographer in the yard, so she was quite happy to stay in the kitchen, walking only as far as the coffeepot.[786]

She poured a cup of coffee, sat down, and picked up the morning newspaper. She skipped quickly over the headline, "Global Flight: Jerrie First Gal to Go It Alone," and down the page until she found what she was really looking for.

---

[786] Mock, *Three-Eight Charlie*, 276-277; Mock, interview, May 5, 2008.

Joan Merriam Smith took off today bound for Darwin, Australia. From there, she is headed for Lae, New Guinea, depending upon flying conditions.[787]

Joan was still in Australia? For three weeks, Russ had told Jerrie that Joan was right behind her. She looked up at her husband, a man who had bullied her, yelled at her, stretched the truth and outright lied to her, all the way around the world. Yet she was also looking at a man who had put everything else in his life on hold for two years to support her flight. She couldn't have made it without him, and it would be her name on the record books, not his. She reached for the sugar.

On the dining room table, along with the usual stacks of bills and daily mail, the newspapers were also piling up. Looking over the headlines, she spotted a name she didn't expect. She fought back tears as she read about an airliner that attempted an instrument approach at Dhahran during a sandstorm and went down into the Persian Gulf. Howard Lynch, the former TWA pilot who had stood with her in his kitchen in Saudi Arabia and warned her of sandstorms, was listed as a passenger on that flight.[788]

Jerrie looked out the window at the crowd in the yard. She had to pull herself back together and face the moment. She glanced at her name in a headline, then set the paper aside to pick up her phone messages. Dave Blanton had called, asking her to an event planned for her in Wichita. She picked up another one. Art Weiner had called to say the Pentagon was offering to give her a supersonic ride on a Voodoo jet. The

---

[787] "Global Flight," *Honolulu Advertiser*, April 18, 1964, A-4.

[788] Mock, *Three-Eight Charlie*, 147; Mock, interview, May 5, 2008.

Smithsonian Institution wanted to display Charlie in the National Air and Space Museum outside of Washington. Radio Italiana out of New York wanted to send a crew to film a documentary on Jerrie and her family. The producers of the TV show *To Tell the Truth* wanted to bring her to New York to be a guest on their show. She heard her husband say "no" into the phone at least once, but it was obvious she was going to have to get up in front of more microphones and give more talks.

The phone rang again. Russ picked it up. This time he didn't say anything, not even "Uh-huh." He didn't dictate anything or even look up at anybody. After what seemed like a lot of listening, he finally turned to Jerrie, cleared his throat, and said, "Uh, this one's for you."

"Who is it?"

Russ put his hand over the receiver. "It's the White House, dear."

"What do they want?"

Her husband raised his eyes at her as he sometimes did when he didn't like her questions. Putting his hand over the phone, he answered in a terse whisper, "President Johnson would like to present you with a medal in a ceremony in the Rose Garden. They want to know, would it be possible for you to come to Washington on May fourth?"

Out the kitchen window, a photographer climbed on a reporter's back, trying to get a shot of her. From the front of the house, a screech of brakes was followed by a yell, as somebody argued over parking in the street. Russ kept his hand over the receiver and his eyes on her.

"Yes, dear." She took another sip of coffee. "But I really don't know what to say to the president." Russ's eyes bulged at her again.

"But I suppose I can think of something," she added.[789]

Telegrams and letters kept coming in from around the world for weeks. Among them, one from Brigadier General R.H. Strauss, Commander, 81st Air Division, Lockbourne Air Force Base: "On behalf of professional aviation, I salute your ability and your courage."[790] Another came from Max Conrad, a pilot known as the "Flying Grandfather" who held the record for "Speed around the world, westbound" (a remarkable feat completed in eight and a half days).[791] Conrad wrote, simply, "Congratulations, wonderful woman."[792]

---

[789] Mock, *Three-Eight Charlie*, 277; Mock, interview, May 5, 2008.

[790] Vail and Edwards, "Winner Take All," 66.

[791] "Max Conrad," Wikipedia, accessed Jan. 2, 2023, https://en.wikipedia.org /wiki/Max_Conrad.

[792] Vail and Edwards, "Winner Take All," 66.

The Past is Calling

Sunday, April 19, 8:00 a.m. (Australian Eastern Time)
HORN ISLAND, Australia

Dave Robertson met Joan at the dock, and the two of them sat in the boat, taking the whipping wind and sea spray in the face on the shuttle back to Horn Island. Weather or not, she'd rather give the air a try than stay any longer in this place.[793]

They both took off for Port Moresby. The clouds began to gang up on her, and she dropped to 300 feet. That was just too low: low to the ground, hills, buildings; low to anything coming loose in this wind; even high waves. She turned around and flew back to Horn Island, where she was stuck for two more hours waiting on weather reports via Darwin. Darwin was sending out an advisory that a cyclone was forming out there. That must have been what she had come through the day before.[794]

The weather cleared up enough that she was off again at 2:00 p.m. and landed at Port Moresby around 5:00. There to meet her were Robertson, his wife, and their daughter Ann, who was learning to fly.

From Port Moresby north to Lae, flying over the Owen Stanley Mountains, would only take an hour, yet she couldn't take off. The mountain range rises to 15,000 feet, with heavy

---

[793] Brown, *Fate,* 105.
[794] Merriam, "Longest Flight," 47; Brown, *Fate,* 105.

storms building after 11:00 a.m. every day. An afternoon crossing was just too dangerous.[795]

Since her departure would have to wait until morning, she got a good hotel and hot meal–at last–with thanks, again, to Trans Australia Airlines.[796]

Monday, April 20, 7:00 a.m. (Australian Eastern Time)
PORT MORESBY, New Guinea

Back in the States, when she was planning her trip, Joan had worked out a few contingency plans. In case she had trouble refueling anywhere, she had packed a funnel, plus soft chamois cloths to drape over it, to filter out sand or debris. Yet, even here in New Guinea, she had found a Shell Oil facility equipped with a modern filtering system, where she could fill up just like at home.[797]

Now it was time for Joan to get on with the mission. At the airport, she received a kind offer. Colonel Bayet, who flew a DC-3 out of Moresby, said he'd be willing to fly ahead and relay weather updates to her. When she went on out to the airfield, she found out that she had been the first person to make a direct crossing from Darwin in eight months, which is why she hadn't been able to get any pilot reports on the weather.

She took off just after 7:00 a.m. and climbed until she was above the clouds at 12,500 feet, headed across the spine of New Guinea, and over the fourth rainforest of her journey.[798]

---

[795] Merriam, "Longest Flight," 47.

[796] Brown, *Fate*, 105.

[797] Smith, interview, 2017; Merriam, "Longest Flight," 47.

[798] Brown, *Fate*, 106; "Tribute to a Star," *Ninety-Nine News*, Aug.-Sept. 1964, 11.

As she flew, Joan's thoughts naturally turned to Amelia. Lae was the last place anyone had seen Earhart alive. It seemed to Joan that Amelia's spirit would be more present here than at any other spot along her route. The closer she got to the place, the closer she felt to her heroine, and the more anxious she became—about Amelia, and about her own quest, as well.[799]

Monday, April 20, 9:00 a.m. (Papua New Guinea Time)
LAE, New Guinea

When Joan touched down at Lae, she was greeted by "several hundred people,"[800] including six people who had met Amelia when she landed there in 1937. Over lunch, Joan interviewed them about their recollections of Amelia and looked over the photos they had taken of the famous aviatrix. She also posed for group photos with them herself.

Seeing that this part of the world hadn't changed much in the intervening years made her feel closer to Amelia. She would later write: "The strip, layout of the village, rugged mountain range, the steamy hot jungle, native huts, natives bare from the waist up . . . still the same. How glad I am that after twenty-seven years, this remote spot hasn't gone completely 'modern'!"[801]

One woman still owned the hotel where Amelia had stayed. Joan wanted to spend the night there, but it was closed for renovations, and her new-found friends fell into a polite disagreement over who got the honor of bringing her home.[802]

---

[799] Merriam, "I Flew," 81; Brown, *Fate,* 106.

[800] Merriam, "I Flew," 81.

[801] "Tribute to a Star," 12.

[802] "Tribute to a Star," 11.

Once they got that sorted out, she asked for a ride over to the Western Union office, to send a message to Ohio:

"'Sincere congratulations on your great achievement. Hoping the clear skies and tailwinds of your trip will always be with you," she wrote in a telegram to Jerrie.[803]

Meanwhile, back in the States, Joan's allies were doing what they could to plead her case about the race/not-a-race. John Sarver wrote to Ruth Deerman, President of the Ninety-Nines, the International Organization of Women Pilots. Joan "constantly hailed your group and sincerely hoped her achievement would bring glory to the Ninety-Nines. . . . She has lived for the day she could fly the Amelia Earhart route and become the first woman to completely circle the world."

Sarver listed the important differences between Joan's and Jerrie's flights: that Jerrie's flight was 4,600 miles shorter than Joan's, that Jerrie's flight included "no stops within 1,000 miles of the equator," and that all Jerrie's stops were "in big cities (full maintenance available)." While acknowledging Jerrie's accomplishment as "First to Fly Around Northern Circumference of the World-Feminine," Sarver urged Deerman to "flex your muscles" and call "attention to the true facts of this important record."[804]

Although Sarver insisted that an around-the-world record should consist of at least "24,950 statute miles,"[805] the circumference of the earth at the equator, Jerrie was complying

---

[803] Vail and Edwards, "Winner Take All," 66.

[804] John Sarver to Ruth Deerman, April 20, 1964, courtesy of Tiffany Ann Brown.

[805] Ibid.

with the FAI's requirement of 22,858 miles, the distance at the Tropic of Cancer, "for an official circling of the earth."[806]

Tuesday, April 21

Over breakfast and coffee the next morning, Joan's friends made a suggestion. Why not take the day off, and ride with a local pilot, whom Joan referred to as "Laurie," on his regular run, delivering groceries to villages in the mountains of New Guinea?

After all the hours of solitary flying, Joan enjoyed being "a passenger and to have the plane in the hands of such a capable pilot."[807]

At each stop, the locals ran out to greet Joan and Laurie and fill baskets with coffee and produce. Then Joan helped Laurie reload the plane with homegrown vegetables to take back to Lae. On the way back, Laurie pointed out one road that ran along the coast out from Port Moresby for fifty miles, and then just stopped; just one more local curiosity in the perpetual effort to civilize the jungle some day. Joan relaxed and enjoyed this landscape, every bit as "lush and green" as the Amazon.[808]

Wednesday, April 22

Joan would have loved to stay, but she had achieved her objective for this stay in Lae: collecting interviews of people who had known Amelia Earhart personally.

Finally, like it or not, it was time to depart. At the door of her plane, she stopped, held up her camera, and snapped

---

[806] Mock, *Three-Eight Charlie,* 263.
[807] Brown, *Fate,* 106.
[808] Ibid., 106-107.

pictures of the views north, south, east, and west, from the spot where Amelia's wheels last touched the runway. Then she got in, waved a sad goodbye to everyone, took off, and dipped her wings in a last farewell and salute to Lae.[809]

As she began her ascent, she turned her attention to her next challenge. This one coming up was similar to the situation Earhart once faced, and Joan's feelings associated with all of that were complicated.

In 1937, Amelia Earhart had been headed toward Howland Island, due east across the Pacific. Joan believed she had been headed there in part because a landing strip had been made especially for her. And yet, Amelia never found it.

By the time of Joan's flight in 1964, Howland Island was uninhabited, so she flew toward the next safe place to land, on the American military base at Guam, nine hours to the north, making her fourth and final equatorial crossing.

Joan concentrated on finding her target. Locating a continent was one thing. Picking out "pin-dot" islands left no margin for error.

She fought her anxiety by focusing on getting to Guam as fast as she could, for "the best possible motive,"[810] which was meeting up with her husband Jack. She picked up as much speed as the turbochargers would give her, but the plane was heavy with full gas tanks. She occupied her mind with providing "regular position reports. . . . There (was) nothing much to observe over water than water, and the instrument panel."[811] Still, 400 miles out of Guam, her thoughts returned to

---

[809] Ibid., 107.

[810] Ibid.

[811] Ibid.

the mystery of Earhart's last flight. Had she turned toward Guam, intentionally or otherwise? Joan planned to continue her investigations of the many unanswered questions when she reached Saipan. She hoped some of the local people would be willing to talk to a woman, particularly a woman who had followed Earhart's path.[812]

With one of her radios working better, it was fun to hear the man in the tower at Guam ask her, in regular old American English, "Apache three-two-five-one Poppa, how do you read?" and to give him the answer, "Loud and clear."

"Good to hear from you, Joan. Sending some boys out to say hello."

That comment made her laugh with relief, since she knew what it meant. As a Navy wife, she was receiving a triumphal escort to the island. Two hundred miles out of Guam, two Navy jets climbed up from the horizon, streaked straight toward her, then parted, leaving behind white contrails on either side of her flight path, announcing her arrival in the sky, before circling around from behind and settling in next to her, going much slower than their normal speed.

Recording her memory, Joan described it as "a bit of a shock to see something loom up out of the corner of my eye and turn to find a Constellation flying just off the left wing. Sort of like a minnow being escorted by a whale."[813]

Two more jets soon joined the formation, a Navy DC-4 to her right and another jet following behind. She described the experience–a minnow surrounded by a whale, a marlin, and a shark–as "one of the greatest highlights of the entire flight, an

---

[812] Ibid., 107-108.
[813] Ibid., 108.

occasion my grandchildren will hear told and retold, should I have grandchildren someday."[814]

They flew in such close formation that, when her camera case slipped off the top of the fuel tank, one of the pilots told her on intercom that something had fallen next to her.[815]

They passed over the field at Agana Navy Base, just 500 feet off the ground, thrilling a huge crowd below. Then the three large aircraft peeled off, leaving her to proceed with her landing.

As she put down her gear, she heard a hissing sound. Something was wrong with the gear flaps, and she would have to have that checked right away.

Her heart pounded as she rolled to a stop, looking for Jack's face in the crowd. People came milling around before she could get out of the plane, stringing leis around her neck, shouting their welcome. She was greeted by Rear Admiral and Mrs. T.A. Christopher, Captain Gerald Barlow, and Governor and Mrs. Manuel F. Guerrero of Guam. But where was Jack? Then Admiral Christopher handed her a telegram from the USS *Endurance*. After all her delays, "Jack was back at sea with his ship. We had missed the mid-Pacific reunion."[816]

As soon as her hosts could pull her away from the autograph signing and the flashbulbs, the Christophers took her to their home. The Navy presented her with a photo album showing the otherwise unbelievable flight formation of the big planes with her Apache that, as noted in a newspaper article, looked "like a bumblebee" by comparison.[817]

---

[814] Ibid.

[815] Ibid.

[816] Ibid., 108-109.

[817] "Joan Merriam's Bumble Bee Lands in Guam," *Desert Sun*, April 22, 1964.

After dinner, dessert arrived in the form of a "large and elaborate" cake, with the route of her flight in the icing. The note that came with the cake read, "Compliments and congratulations from the Thomas Bakery."[818]

It was good to be back on American soil. After all the places she had been, all the people she had met, and all their reactions to her, it was a relief to be surrounded by people who understood that she was on her way toward making history.

Yet it was also exhausting. She excused herself and went to bed early.[819]

Thursday, April 23
AGANA, Guam

Joan slept off and on for "a sweet ten hours,"[820] but woke up to a driving rain. The reports coming in from the typhoon hunter planes indicated a low-pressure system to the south that would ground her for a day before it moved out to the west.[821]

Joan needed a day for the mechanics to look at those gear flaps, anyway. She was introduced to the head mechanic, Chief Elbert. She explained what she knew, and he promised that the crew would get on it first thing. For her, it meant another day with the charts, coffee, and rain out the window.

Meanwhile, the malicious lies she had first heard about from John Sarver while she was in Singapore continued to follow her. Seems the FAA had received a telegram prior to her arrival on

---

[818] Brown, *Fate*, 109.

[819] Brown, *Fate*, 109.

[820] Ibid.

[821] Ibid.

Guam, claiming that she was flying with fuel tanks that were not airworthy. Pacific region FAA inspector Bob Gale had the tanks inspected by his associate on Guam, a Mr. Warner, who declared they were "perfect."[822] Joan told Warner about the vicious calls and named the source. She got the same response from him as she had received from Sarver: "Ignore it." Gale provided Joan with a letter to take with her saying, "We had an inspection."[823]

Yet no matter what was breaking down, no matter what accusations were being made, Joan stuck to her resolve. She would take no shortcuts; she would complete the Earhart route.[824] She had finally made it to the place where she was one day away from a journey of a lifetime. She had to pay a visit to an obscure island which had been pulling her, as if with an invisible, powerful magnet, for twelve years.

Friday, April 24

Joan took off at dawn for the tiny island of Saipan, less than two hours to the north. Until there was definite proof that Amelia was headed for Saipan, was held there and perhaps buried there, she would hold to her Howland Island theory. Until then, she would follow up on the Saipan theory, anyway.

But soon after takeoff, she discovered that the landing wheels weren't returning all the way to the closed position. The hydraulic gear that was supposed to hold them up wasn't holding pressure. If she let the wheels dangle, they might not go all the way back down and lock into place for a safe landing.

---

[822] Ibid., 115.

[823] Ibid.

[824] Gilbert, "The Loser," 84.

She had no choice but to turn around and fly back to Guam. She landed safely, but this issue had to be fixed.

Saturday, April 25

Next morning, she went back to visit with Warner, and together they went to see the guys in the shop. It sounded as if these mechanics knew jets and DC-3's better than a twin-engine, but she didn't have anyone else to work with. She hung around the shop until they had something to show her.

"Here's your problem, ma'am." The man held up a grimy flap, wiping off the grease. "See how this is worn out? Won't rotate any more. She'll have to be replaced, I'm afraid."

The FAA and Navy men did what they could do. She was given a ride back to the base with a promise that any repair work would be done at no charge. They showed her a phone she could use, but she didn't exactly get the answers she wanted.

It was heartbreaking enough to keep being reminded that the race was over, but it didn't help that her sponsors, who had heard the news too, didn't want to pay for replacement parts. There was no way to talk to Jack, either. After an hour or two, she found herself screaming into the phone. *"Are you just going to leave me out here in the middle of the ocean?"*

It took more yelling, but eventually some replacement parts were ordered, and she received a promise that they would be delivered on a commercial flight. She could only guess at how long it would actually take for the parts to arrive.

She tried to relax by walking around. Guam was one of many military bases in the Pacific, and the small community of Agana looked like other military bases she had seen and heard about. They had a miniature Statue of Liberty and a small radio dish pointed toward the sky. Somewhere underground, men were probably sitting at desks with headphones on, listening for conversations among Russian ships, planes, and submarines and trying to decipher them.

Back in Long Beach, the military men passionately debated the Cold War, at every dinner and cookout. Her job as a military wife was to act interested, without asking too many questions. As a pilot, her job was to show her gratitude for any assistance offered, without wandering into any restricted areas, either in the air, or on the ground.

By the next day, the FAA men told her that they were working out an arrangement. The parts she needed would be purchased in California and stored on a commercial airliner bound for Hawaii. The crew from one flight would hand the parts off to the crew for the next flight bound from Honolulu to Wake Island. From Wake, a military plane would bring them to Guam. It would take a few more phone calls to be sure the plan would work; the schedule was going to be tight. It was still going to take a day or two, and please don't tell anybody, but the parts would be on their way soon.[825]

Joan thanked everybody and went for another walk.

There were only so many lunches and parties that the nice people of Guam could keep inviting her to. One by one, they resumed their routines. Eventually, Joan had nothing much to do but pace up and down the beach. She watched a young couple spread out their picnic blanket on the sand. The girl wore a bright yellow bikini in that new style that seemed all the

---

[825] Ibid.

rage these days, based on the pictures Joan saw in *Life* magazine and the Sears catalogue. The boy wore a pair of cut-off jean shorts and a St. Christopher's medal. From his crewcut hair and cigarette, he looked to be career Navy. He was probably going to fly cargo planes around for the Navy for the next forty years. His wife would follow him from one clump of sand and weeds in the middle of the ocean to another, dragging along their one, two, three, four kids, and that life would probably be just fine for them all. As for Joan, she still had more flying to do.

By Monday night, after most of the offices and shops were all closed up, she found her way down one gravel road to the only sign that was still lit up, the neon glow blinking "Schlitz."

A guy in a T-shirt, jeans, white socks and penny loafers, smoking and shooting pool by himself, seemed to be the only other customer in the place. He paid no attention to her. The barroom was quiet except for the click of the cue ball hitting the eight and crowd noise on a small television. Behind the bar, an Asian woman wearing horn-rimmed glasses and a flowery print dress wiped the counter as she watched the TV. The tiny black-and-white screen held an image of a metal globe against a backdrop of skyscrapers. The World's Fair in New York. Joan's aunt and uncle were hoping to go, as soon as Joan's mom recovered from her surgery.

Joan took a seat at the bar. "I'll have a bourbon and cola, please." They didn't have the brand of cola Joan preferred, so she asked for the bourbon "on the side."

When the woman handed her the drink, along with a bottle of cola with a straw in it, Joan said, "You folks know how to throw a nice party."

The bartender smiled. "You famous."

"Must not get many visitors passing this way, do you?"

The woman smiled again and shook her head. "Nice lady last week."

"When did she stop here?"

The woman looked up at the calendar pinned to the wall and put her finger on the day: April 11. Jerrie had come and gone from Guam days ahead of Joan, just like the papers said. Joan put down her cola. She picked up the other glass, drained it, and set it on the counter. "Looks like this one's empty."

No matter what reporters wrote, and no matter what anyone accused her of, Joan was still determined to become the first person in history to complete Earhart's equatorial route.

Tuesday, April 28[826]

Finally, the parts had come in, everything had been installed, and the hydraulic gear flaps were ready, supposedly. By that afternoon, she was "off to see Saipan."[827]

From Guam she flew over Rota Island, then Tinian, where the world's "first atomic bomb was loaded on the airplane Enola Gay, bound for Hiroshima."[828]

Since she first read Amelia Earhart's book, Joan had always wanted to visit the place where Earhart was rumored to have been imprisoned by the Japanese. She tried to forget the

---

[826] By this point, discrepancies appear in Joan's recorded journal, between the dates she provided and her recall of the number of days between events. Discrepancies also appear between Joan's recorded journal and her articles published later, perhaps accounted for in part by the crossing of the International Date Line.

[827] Brown, *Fate,* 110.

[828] Ibid.

distractions, and turned her mind and heart toward this question.

The people on Saipan seemed interested in the Earhart story, too. Joan listened as a man in a white short-sleeved shirt gave her a tour through the coconut trees, telling her about the claims of eyewitness accounts of the "the two people who came from the sky." They walked through the trees to a small stone and concrete building with tiny windows covered by bars, almost invisible in the shadows. "Fred Noonan and Amelia Earhart were held prisoners here," the tour guide said. "Mr. Noonan was executed, and Amelia died a few weeks later. She is believed to be buried over there." He waved in the direction of some trees.

Joan didn't argue or say much. Nobody seemed to have proof of any of it, and the place left her uneasy. Flying back from Saipan, she tried to get used to the possibility that she might never know what became of her heroine. She recalled the rumors that Amelia's camera convinced the Japanese that she was a spy, and she began to wonder if the photos she had just taken could be a problem.[829]

She had another issue to deal with, anyway. Some of her dashboard instrument lights were clicking on and off, as if maybe the plane was running low on electricity. "Neither generator was putting out enough power."[830] The ADF might go out, or the radio. The plane still flew, but on her next flight, she might be looking for tiny Wake Island, out there in the endless

---

[829] Merriam, "I Flew," 82.
[830] Brown, Fate, 110.

ocean, without any help.[831] "It had to be corrected, no matter what the delay."[832]

She was "really beginning to feel jinxed,"[833] but all she could do was head back to Guam, "disgusted and discouraged,"[834] and take the plane back to the shop.

Once she dropped off the plane, she found the bar again, and headed inside for a cola. She took a seat, then spotted a newspaper. Jerrie Mock's smiling face stared up at her from an article about her record-breaking flight. Another photo showed the thousands of people who had come out to the airport to see her land in Columbus a few days before.

Joan gulped down her cola, discarded the newspaper, and headed back to the hangar to check on her plane.

"Technicians worked for two and a half more days" to correct the "insufficient electrical output"[835] before she was ready to try again.

---

[831] Merriam, "I Flew," 82; Merriam, "Longest Flight," 48; Brown, *Fate,* 110.

[832] Merriam, "I Flew," 82; Brown, *Fate,* 111.

[833] Merriam, "I Flew," 82.

[834] Ibid.

[835] Brown, Fate, 110-111.

Tape, Screwdriver, and Landing Gear

Friday, May 1, sunrise
AGANA, Guam

A crowd, including Governor Guerrero, mustered out before their coffee to say goodbye. Admiral Christopher handed Joan an honorary medal, and a representative of the Marianas Lions Club laid a bouquet of roses in her arms. The Navy band played as she boarded the plane and waved goodbye.[836]

Warner advised Joan about bad weather at Wake, but it was her decision whether to continue on or stay grounded. Well, there was nothing for it but to get moving. After filing her flight plan, she took off for a "long, lonely leg ahead"[837] of approximately eleven hours. Wake Island, the next outpost equipped with Navy infrastructure, was 1,500 miles away over "nothing but water."[838]

All instrument systems seemed A-OK. She got on the radio, looking for someone to talk to, and found two or three planes, all military. Next, she needed something to talk about with them, so she brought up her latest favorite subject: today's headwinds.

"Everything is fine up here at 30,000 feet," the pilot of a Navy plane responded.

---

[836] Brown, *Fate*, 109.

[837] Brown, *Fate*, 111.

[838] Ibid.

He was just showing off, of course. He knew she couldn't get up to 30,000 feet in an Apache. Even when not heavily loaded, the service ceiling of her plane was 25,000 feet. Her flight plan called for 9,000 feet. At the moment, she was almost up to 5,000 feet, climbing heavily and slowly, through a cloudless sky.[839]

Then, one and a half hours out, a warning light came on. Her landing gear was jammed. She shook her head. "I should be immune to trouble by now!"[840]

She radioed Guam. Chief Elbert thought the problem was hydraulic, and she should return to Guam. Joan thought the problem was mechanical, and she should keep going.[841]

"I don't like it," he said. "You might not be able to get your gear down. You'd have to chance it with a belly landing."

She glared at the radio speaker for about a minute before replying, "If I have to make a belly landing, I might as well do it closer to home!"[842]

She kept going.

She put her mind to work on how to solve the problem. With a screwdriver and a piece of tape, she manipulated the gear handle until she was able to push whatever had been blocking it out of the way enough to get the wheels up into the plane. After four hours of tinkering, the gear light went on again, meaning she had succeeded in getting the gear back into the wheel well.[843]

Guam radio wanted to know how she was doing.

---

[839] Merriam, "I Flew," 82; Brown, *Fate*, 111.

[840] Brown, *Fate*, 111.

[841] Merriam, "I Flew," 82; Merriam, "Longest Flight," 48; Brown, *Fate*, 111.

[842] Brown, *Fate*, 111.

[843] Ibid.

"No emergency," she radioed back. "Continuing on to Wake."[844]

She was determined to avoid turning back. But the wheels kept slipping, and the opening in the floor sent a roaring wind into the cabin. Her charts and crackers and teddy bears bounced around all over the place. The plane got harder to control, and it took more strength just to hold the wheel in place. In another hour, she had to follow the whole procedure all over again. Off and on for four hours, she "fiddled and pumped and cussed the slipping wheels back into position" into the wheel well.[845]

---

[844] Ibid.
[845] Merriam, "I Flew," 82.

"Come in High and Land Low"

WAKE ISLAND

Joan picked up the Wake beacon signal, nice and strong, and a big relief. But she could barely pick up the VHF omni signal at Wake. Not good. The sun inched on down behind her. As darkness fell, she spotted the first twinkle of runway lights.

Wake Island is a slender, V-shaped spit of land–actually three islands on a coral reef hugging a lagoon–all alone in the endless ocean. As Joan approached the runway, she was greeted by the local birds. "Never had I seen so many birds in one place at one time, as there were terns on Wake."[846]

The control tower warned her, "Beware of birds. Come in high and land low."[847]

A nice trick, she thought, *especially when you were not sure of whether the gear is going down on schedule or not.* Yet even after all her problems, she touched down only seven minutes after her estimated time of arrival.[848]

A small crowd had gathered at the airstrip. Joan was greeted by George La Caille, head of the FAA on Wake, his wife Janie, and Father Canice Cartmed, the island's chaplain. Cartmed's red hair, so different from most people she had encountered in the last several weeks, reminded her that she was finally getting closer to home.

---

846 Brown, *Fate*, 112.
847 Ibid., 113.
848 Merriam, "I Flew," 82; Brown, *Fate*, 111-112.

They promised to keep the plane under constant surveillance and escorted her on the grand tour of the island. It sounded as if each Quonset hut and structure they had to show her was the "FAA commissary" or the "FAA this" or the "FAA that," until they suddenly ran out of island to tour. "Wake Island is less than three miles square" was explained to her with pride. Well, it was time to turn into her FAA bed, anyway.[849]

---

[849] Brown, *Fate*, 113.

Alfred Hitchcock Wasn't Kidding

Saturday, May 2
WAKE ISLAND

Weather was deteriorating again. After a leisurely breakfast in the FAA mess hall, Janie La Caille drove Joan beyond the Quonset huts and out to the beach for a morning of bird-watching. As they walked down to the shore, Joan noticed that the beach seemed to be covered with large pebbles. "Look at those rocks," she said. "Almost perfectly round. How do they get that way?"[850]

"Those 'rocks' are tern eggs," Janie explained.

The birds came swooping in by the millions, chirping so loudly that Janie and Joan couldn't hear each other. Joan thought about the scenes of birds attacking people in the Alfred Hitchcock movie *The Birds*. "I had the eerie feeling that the birds would kill us if we trampled on their eggs," she recalled. Finally, she screamed to Janie, "Let's go!"[851]

Still grounded by the weather, Joan sat around talking about flying–known as "hangar-flying"—with Ken Sitton, the Pan Am station manager, and Ted Awana, who had worked on the airstrip on Howland Island that Earhart and Noonan were supposed to have landed on when Ted was a boy.[852] Ted's wife

---

[850] Ibid.
[851] Merriam, "I Flew," 82; Brown, *Fate*, 113.
[852] Brown, *Fate*, 113.

Lulaine, president of the Wake Island Woman's Club, arranged a dinner in Joan's honor.[853]

At dinner, Joan spoke with two search-and-rescue pilots. Their large amphibian planes were kept on 24-hour alert. Listening to the pilots, it sounded to Joan as if their operations were well-organized here in the American-occupied Pacific islands. Good to know.[854]

Tuesday, May 5

As the sun rose on Joan's third day on Wake Island, she was finally able to take off for Honolulu, 2,300 miles away. Although she had been on American soil since Guam, she wouldn't feel like she was in "the home stretch"[855] until she reached Hawaii.

The tough breaks with the plane had left her jumpy. The landing gear wasn't really fixed, she still couldn't count on the autopilot, and her intuition was needling her that something else wasn't right.

After a mere 200 miles in the air, a warning light bore out her hunch. The right engine was overheating. With more than 2,000 miles to go to Hawaii, there was no way she could risk having one of her two engines quit on her. "Sick with disappointment,"[856] she banked slowly around and headed back to those "dreary" metal Quonset huts. She would say later that she felt "down" and "cut off from the world."[857]

---

[853] Ibid.

[854] Ibid., 114.

[855] Merriam, "I Flew," 82.

[856] Ibid.

[857] Merriam, "I Flew," 82; Brown, *Fate,* 114.

The two mechanics on Wake humbly tried to explain that, like the crew on Guam, they were more accustomed to the larger military cargo planes. They weren't sure where to begin with a smaller twin-engine plane like hers, and couldn't guess what would cause one engine to overheat. They came up with a possible theory, so while they worked, Joan went for another walk along the shore.

When she returned, one of the men approached her wearing an ear-to-ear grin. "Ma'am? Let me show you something." He motioned her over to a worktable, where both engines of *The City of Long Beach* rested, their propellers removed. He lifted one of the engines off the table, while the other man pried the cover loose from the front end. Out poured a steady stream of dead, winged insects that formed a pile as big as a basketball. "Looks like these grasshoppers might be your problem," he said. "We've already emptied out one engine. It was full of 'em, too."[858]

Joan didn't argue. She might have flown through more than one swarm of flying bugs in Africa.

Another day of cleaning out the engines, oiling everything, and putting it all back together, and she was told the plane was ready to go.[859]

Wednesday, May 6

"Like a child counting the days before Christmas," Joan was counting down the "days and hours" until she would be headed back to California.[860]

---

[858] Merriam, "I Flew," 82.

[859] Merriam, "I Flew," 82.

[860] Brown, *Fate*, 114.

With just a glimmer of daylight making its way through ominous clouds, she took off. Below her, the sea was swelling; above her, the clouds didn't top out until 10,000 feet. Checking with some pilots in the air, she was told that the weather was better at 8,000 feet, but once again, her plane was too heavy with full gas tanks to climb that high. Her thermometer showed forty-five degrees outside, her heater wasn't working, and whenever she turned away from the sun it got colder in that cockpit. Still, as long as the two engines kept purring along and the tanks of fuel remained intact, she would just have to live with it.[861]

Passing the hours over that endless Pacific again, she recalled another Frank Sinatra song, "Around the World in Eighty Days," that she and Jack used to listen to in their San Diego apartment, back in 1962. Sinatra sang about traveling around the world "to keep a rendezvous," even "when hope was gone." Joan had been traveling in Amelia's world for fifty-two days so far, and she hoped it wasn't going to take her eighty days. What she had to achieve, above all, was to complete the journey that Amelia had not been able to complete.[862]

She continued to check her position routinely until, four hours out of Wake, she discovered that her jinx had returned. Her ADF and sun-line shots from her sextant told her that she had already fallen a full hour behind schedule. The headwinds weren't the worst she'd seen, but they were strong enough to

---

[861] Ibid.

[862] Merriam, "I Flew," 82.

slow her down. The wheels being down would slow her even further.[863]

She could hear pilots reporting a heavy overcast over the international dateline up ahead. When she could no longer see much sky or ocean in front of her, she knew she was approaching the overcast. Running an hour behind schedule meant she might not have enough gas to make it to Honolulu.

Okay, time for her *next* Plan B. Midway Island was five hours off course, and then it would be another ten-hour flight from there to Hawaii, but she didn't really have a choice. She radioed Midway and began dropping down from 9,000 feet. As she descended, she flew out of the lightning, and the break from bad weather was a relief while it lasted.

Then, almost as soon as she saw land, she was greeted by yet another flock of birds: not terns this time, but gooney birds. First one, then two, then another and another. Over the engines, she thought she heard a thump or two. All she could do was cross her fingers and hope none of them flew into one of her propellers as she touched down at Midway at 4:30 p.m. local time.[864]

Stepping down from the plane, she was welcomed with more leis. She signed autographs and shook hands with the base commander, US Navy Captain George Washington Davis V. She smiled for the photographers and the crowd that had gathered on learning her flight had been diverted to Midway. Captain and Mrs. Davis proudly gave her the tour.

Midway was home to 5,000 people, mostly government employees, and 8,000 gooney birds which made Midway their

---

[863] Merriam, "I Flew," 82; Merriam, "Longest Flight," 48.
[864] Brown, *Fate*, 115-116.

home year-round, except for October and November–mating season. "Only for these two months do they disappear from the island."[865]

Joan would recall, "The birds are graceful creatures in the air. But oh, their landings! They'd never pass proficiency tests, even in primary flight training. How they ever got their wings I'll never know."[866]

Although clumsy at landing, the gooney birds were elegant dancers. "They have a lovely, graceful, pecking dance. Sort of a two-step. I took many slides of the gooney birds dancing."[867]

Captain Davis said, "That's the mating dance."

"But it's only May," Joan protested, "and I thought you said–"[868]

It was a mystery for which Captain Davis had no answer.

Joan planned to get an early start in the morning, before the gooney birds woke up.[869]

Wednesday, May 6

After crossing the IDL, Joan experienced her second daybreak of May 6. The morning light was overshadowed by storm clouds coming in from different directions, and Joan didn't want to "play umpire"[870] with the feuding weather

---

[865] Ibid., 116.

[866] Ibid.

[867] Ibid.

[868] Ibid.

[869] Merriam, "Longest Flight," 48; Brown, *Fate*, 117.

[870] Brown, *Fate*, 117.

systems. She took the plane up anyway, but three hours out, she had to admit she was in trouble.[871]

A Navy pilot radioed that things were clear at 17,000 feet, but Joan couldn't take the Apache to that altitude carrying the weight of full tanks. She had to return, hoping the gooney birds wouldn't be hanging around, waiting to run into her. Hopefully they had gone "wherever gooney birds go when the weather isn't safe, even for birds."[872]

Thursday, May 7, 6:10 a.m. (Samoa Time)
MIDWAY ISLAND

By sunrise the clouds had only broken up a little, and a report from another pilot didn't promise much better. Joan tried again anyway. It was only another 1,300 miles to Hawaii.

At 9,000 feet she angled around "towering cumulus clouds,"[873] but her autopilot was still out, and so was her heater.

"Cold. Cold. Cold," she recorded in her journal. "My feet were numb."[874]

Finally, little green bumps of land broke the monotony of the open ocean. "How good Hawaii looked. ONE more hop after Hawaii and I'd be HOME."[875]

She brought the plane in for a landing at sunset in Honolulu, trying to get her lipstick on and her hair ready to face the next crowd, cameras, and reporters.

---

[871] Ibid.

[872] Ibid.

[873] Ibid.

[874] Ibid.

[875] Brown, *Fate*, 117.

Hawaii lived up to its reputation for hospitality. Joan's shoulders were draped with multi-colored leis, and carnations and roses were pressed into her arms. In the crowd, she saw familiar faces such as Sargent Cartwright, who was the Piper dealer when she worked for West Florida Gas in Panama City; Bob Gale, the regional head of the FAA who had provided her a letter stating that her tanks passed inspection on Wake; as well as a cadre of reporters.[876]

Still, when a reporter from the local television station asked when she thought she would arrive in Oakland, she was not ready to commit. Instead of giving him the succinct answer he wanted, she heard herself mumble something about, "Engines running fine right now, but we have to check."

She heard the reporter's wrap-up, as he turned back to face his cameraman. "Still weary from her long journey. And back to you, Dave, in our studio." His voice sounded distant, as if Joan was still out there between the clouds and the waves.

She was taken to a suite at the Hilton Hawaiian Village with a view overlooking Diamond Head. She was pleased to "hangar-fly" part of the evening away with the president of the Hawaiian Aero Club.[877]

She would have to stay in Hawaii until the 25-knot winds calmed. Meanwhile, both the plane and the pilot needed some rest and repair work. As long as she was grounded, she planned to make the most of it with a visit to Diamond Head. She wanted to visit the plaque overlooking the beach that recognized Amelia Earhart as the first pilot to fly solo from

---

[876] Ibid., 117-118.
[877] Ibid., 118.

Hawaii to California, a feat she achieved two years before her attempt at the world equator record.[878]

She loved Hawaii, but "couldn't linger longer in the land of leis" when the completion of her quest was so close. "ONLY ONE MORE LEG,"[879] was typed in uppercase.

The next morning, the forecast was not favorable for her 2,400-mile hop to California. At best, it would be a seventeen-hour flight, and she could only carry twenty hours of fuel, so she had to wait for the best possible wind conditions. That turned out to be another two-day delay. The entire trip had been an endless series of delays; an extra day or two here, then there, and having to get something repaired, not just once, but twice. Still, between all the trips to check on the plane, and all the interviews and invitations to lunch and dinner, she had gotten time to shop and to relax in the sun for two whole hours on Waikiki Beach.[880]

Sunday, May 10
HAWAII

Before dawn, it was back to the Apache for a smooth takeoff and into the blue. Almost immediately, that right engine started overheating, and she had to turn back to visit her mechanic friends, yet again.[881]

---

[878] Ibid.

[879] Ibid.

[880] Merriam, "I Flew," 82; Brown, *Fate,* 118-119.

[881] Merriam, "I Flew," 82.

Monday, May 11

The *next* day, Joan got away around noon and took the plane up to 11,000 feet. She was forced to hand-crank the landing gear again.

Still, the flight was going smoothly enough until, after she passed the point of no return, that right engine began to consume fuel just a bit too fast. To save gas, she flipped the switch to cut back on the mixture, and continued this way for the next fourteen hours. Even with that, the weakened engine exhausted its fuel supply from the right-wing tank and began drawing from the left side of the plane, fuel the left engine needed, as well.

This one was going to be close. As the last light of the setting sun gradually twinkled away, Joan searched up and down the radio dial for someone to talk to or even listen to, trying to get her mind on anything else *except* "A.E." this time, as the stars came out.

Hours later, after occasional chats on the radio, the black night was broken by a thin, bright line across the horizon. Dawn over the mainland. Better to keep looking at that horizon than at the needle on the fuel gauge. She was running out of gas, and running out of hope that she would make it.

A few minutes later, she was flying in bright sunshine. She switched from one radio frequency to another, listening to people congratulating her. After fifty-six days, including crossing the equator four times, she began to think that she just *might* make it.

With only one hour to go, another warning light appeared on the control panel. After all her careful attention, the right engine was overheating anyway. She flipped the switch to shut it down.

She would have to limp the rest of the way on half power. It was time to ask for some help, which, in eleven years of flying, she had never asked for before.

"San Francisco?"

"We read you loud and clear, Joan. Welcome to California."

"I'm down to one engine. Must request Coast Guard escort."

"Roger that. Coast Guard escort will be with you pronto."

Within minutes, a Coast Guard Search and Rescue plane was flying alongside her, which offered some comfort, even if they couldn't actually help her fly. Relying on one engine, she was forced to consider the very real possibility that she still might have to ditch in the Pacific, less than one hour from home.[882]

Tuesday, May 12, just before 9:00 a.m. (Pacific Time)
OAKLAND, California

The Oakland Airport coming into view meant Joan was down to her last few minutes of the flight. She switched the right engine back on to have full power for the landing and when it came on, some observers concluded she had been faking the trouble just for attention.

The wheels touched. The landing gear held, and she rolled the plane to a stop. At 9:12 a.m., after 27,750 miles and fifty-six and a half days, suddenly, it was over. She would go on record as having completed the longest solo flight around the world. By anyone, male or female, ever. Even if she did not win the "race," she had accomplished exactly what she had set out to do all along. With any luck, some people would take notice.[883]

---

[882] Ibid.
[883] Ibid.

She opened the door and set foot on the ground to be greeted with cheers, bouquets of roses, welcome-home speeches, and a telegram from President Johnson. Once again, she stepped out of solitude into almost more attention than she could handle.

"And then I thought of Amelia, and the flowers I was holding suddenly seemed a sort of tribute, not just to me, but to her, too. (Another) telegram was handed to me which said, 'In Amelia's name I thank you for your generous gesture in dedicating your flight to her. May this be the first of many triumphs in the air.' It was signed Muriel Earhart Morrisey, Amelia's sister. Now my dream was ended in joy."[884]

---

[884] Merriam, "I Flew;" Merriam, "Longest Flight," 47.

Taxiing Out of the Spotlight

Looking back, it isn't clear why the accomplishments of both pilots didn't bring them greater fame and fortune. With historical hindsight, we can only identify a few contributing factors.

On the one hand, in 1964, some dynamics were emerging in America that might eventually work in favor of women, at least, in a broad-brush sort of way. Our nation was entering a time of economic prosperity, the Baby Boom generation was emerging, and the trend toward gender equality was on the rise.

A new generation of American women would earn more money and climb farther in their careers than any before them. In the summer of 1964, *The Feminine Mystique,* by Betty Friedan, hit number two on the bestseller list and was discussed on talk shows. The book addressed women as they began to claim more power in a male-dominated society, and described the frustrations of women and "housewives" with Freidan's phrase "the problem that has no name."[885]

Yet at the same time, the attention of the nation was captured by a steady barrage of other news from multiple fronts. The growing unpopularity of the Vietnam War and the draft, racial tensions, civil rights, and social justice issues heated up throughout the country. During the time that Jerrie and Joan were on their flights, one of the NASA missions, Gemini 1, was launched, and the nation's attention was focused on astronauts

---

[885] "The Feminine Mystique," *Wikipedia,* https://en.wikipedia.org/wiki/The_Feminine_Mystique.

such as John Glenn and the space race between the US and the USSR. The era of the Sixties would later be described as a "busy news cycle."[886]

With the rise of commercial and private aviation, pilots in general, and women pilots in particular, could still find another adventure to embark upon and another record to break. But in an era before 24-hour streaming news became available anywhere and anytime via ubiquitous portable devices, the financial and media support that could have propelled Joan and Jerrie to immortality dissipated within a few years.

---

[886] Eric Capper, "Takeoff: Ode to a Legend-The First Woman of Flight." *Private Air*, August/September 2007, 30.

Last Flight

After Joan made it through the crowds and reporters and got the plane put away safely, she could finally share some of her struggles with her husband, albeit by long-distance telephone calls.

Getting to hear her story made Jack beyond proud. "If she hadn't had all that [prior] experience, she never would have made it."[887] Still, once she was finally free to talk to him in private, more or less, she also had to share her worries about the next little snag.

"They're calling me 'the loser.'"

"I know," Jack said. "We're going to see what we can do about that."[888]

The next day and a half went by too fast, trying to talk to reporters, find someone to fix that engine, and maybe even catch up on her sleep. On Thursday, May 14 she flew the short hop from Oakland back to her hometown. As the Apache landed, the Long Beach Municipal Band struck up the "American Eagle March," and 300 people shouted, "Welcome home, Joan!" She stepped down from the plane and was escorted up to the table and the microphone. A banner over everyone's heads read: **WELCOME HOME, JOAN! FIRST WOMAN TO COMPLETELY CIRCLE THE GLOBE,** then, in smaller lettering, her favorite part: *"Our* Amelia Earhart."

---

[887] Smith, interview, 2017.
[888] Ibid.

Mayor Edwin Wade presented her with a two-foot-tall, walnut-and-silver trophy and a speech congratulating her on being "the first woman to completely circle the globe." She was thankful that she didn't have to say much, except to raise the trophy over her head while everyone clapped and cheered some more. By the end of the flight, the plane had 800 signatures. Yet, she couldn't shake the feeling that, even now, she still missed Amelia.[889]

Still, she was able to come home to her husband. "He's a real easygoing guy, and he accepts me the way I am. He never made any objection to anything I ever wanted to do–including flying around the world."[890]

From that point forward, Joan evidently encountered trouble making ends meet and getting back into the air. Hints of publicity have been found, such as one video sequence which appears to be a press conference in which Joan is having fun placing a globe over her head.[891] Still, while there was talk of a book coming out and a movie deal, talk wasn't making the payments.[892] Joan wasn't sure if she cared about fame, but companies who had sponsored her flight, who got their names on her plane and were seen by the world in photos and on television, didn't seem to want to sponsor someone who wasn't viewed as the "winner," and they weren't offering to put her in their ads, despite her achievement.[893]

---

[889] Merriam, "I Flew;" Burnett, 174.

[890] Merriam, "I Flew," 78.

[891] Oddball Films, 1964, Clip (accessed April 7, 2017), http://www.oddball films.com/clip/13171_7557_aviation.

[892] Whitton, "Las Vegas Chapter," *Ninety-Nine News*, April, 1965, 14.

[893] Gilbert, "The Loser," 84.

The bills she owed on the plane and for the trip still added up to over $18,000, and after several months off, she didn't even have regular full-time work. Without enough offers coming in, Joan picked up some jobs she had done before, making charter flights. She looked into getting back on the schedule to teach flying students and re-build some of her routine.

Her irritation with her financial situation continued to chafe her. In her interview with James Gilbert of *Flying* Magazine, Joan noted, "It's been estimated by newspaper coverage and magazine coverage and so forth, that Piper, for instance, received in excess of $300,000 in publicity, and I have yet to receive the first nickel. Nor did I get any help from the factory, telegrams or anything."[894]

The controversy extended beyond finances. Gilbert described it as "the sinister affair of the medal." Joan was upset that Jerrie had received the gold medal from the FAA, while Joan's flight was longer, and more difficult. "It . . . mattered very much to Joan, and she was bitterly hurt and upset at this apparent slight."

Gilbert referenced "stories of pressure and persuasion applied to the FAA that . . . strengthened their determination not to give her (Joan) a medal." One example he cited was a phone call in which "one of (Joan's) advisers harangu(ed) the Assistant Administrator for General Aviation for over an hour. . . . 'If they ever thought of giving her the medal, why, that guy kind of cooked her goose,' said my informant."[895]

Najeeb Halaby wrote Joan a letter stating the FAA's position in the matter. He started out by praising the "originality and

[894] Ibid., 81.
[895] Ibid., 84.

example of [her] brave flight, but concluded "that the feat speaks for itself, has been recognized by me and my associates, and will be judged by history. This is more important than further action by the Federal Government."[896]

Within a week of the completion of Joan's flight, a "smoldering" dispute seems to have come to a head.[897]

Jerrie called Joan "a poor loser."[898]

Joan responded that Jerrie's remark was "the most ridiculous statement I have ever heard from a licensed pilot."[899] She insisted that she had achieved exactly what she set out to do: She had completed Amelia Earhart's equatorial route. She was not only the first woman, but the first person, to fly solo around the world at the equator, and she always would be. Yet in one story after another, what Joan *actually did* was always mentioned as a postscript to what she had *not* done.

In particular, Joan expressed irritation about the process that would determine who would be awarded the NAA sanction. She ran up $300 in long distance phone bills on that one issue alone.[900] She couldn't understand how Jerrie was granted sanction for an around-the-world record that didn't require her to cross the equator,[901] or how the two flights could be considered together. "The flights are unalike. How can you measure them as alike?"[902]

---

[896] Ibid., 83.

[897] Lee Craig, "Aviatrixes Fly at Each Other Over World Hops," Long Beach Press-Telegram, May 15, 1964.

[898] Ibid.

[899] Ibid.

[900] Gilbert, "The Loser," 81; Brown, *Fate*, 191.

[901] Gilbert, "The Loser," 82.

[902] Brown, *Fate*, 190.

Nor did she feel she could accept the offer to apply for sanction for a different weight class, which would require besting the existing speed record of eight days,[903] as that would have made it impossible to visit with those who remembered Amelia.[904]

Sarver confirmed that, to Joan, it was about more than a race. Not only did she intend to follow Earhart's route, but she also wanted "to completely research the Amelia Earhart story in New Guinea and Saipan."[905]

Yet the tension between the two fliers might have been invented, or at least over-emphasized, by the news media. One remembrance on Joan's Find a Grave memorial page presents a different picture: "While the press played up the supposed 'rivalry' between you two, Ms. Mock spoke very highly of you and offered up nothing but praise for you and your skills as a pilot."[906]

Jerrie was also complimentary of "Joanie" to this author, years later.[907] Maybe by that point, and in light of Joan's tragic death, Jerrie's opinions had softened.

After the world flight, Joan also considered other intriguing possibilities for earning a living, including collaborating with someone willing to help write her story.

Beatrice Ann "Trixie" Schubert loved adventure, and had published three books so far. Trixie's mother died when she was young. Her father abandoned Trixie and her brother to go to

---

[903] The record of just over eight days was set by Max Conrad in 1961.

[904] Gilbert, "The Loser," 82; Sarver to Deerman, April 20, 1964.

[905] Sarver, press release, April 17, 1964.

[906] "Joan Merriam Smith," Find a Grave.

[907] Mock, interview, Sept. 2, 2007.

Hollywood to pursue a chance at an acting career, and the two children were raised by their grandmother.[908] Trixie enjoyed a successful career as a journalist, including work as a freelance foreign news correspondent in America, Europe, Asia and Africa. She married Dr. Delwyn Schubert, who coordinated education programs for the US Air Force in Africa, Asia and Europe. They had three children, and in the 1950s they were stationed at Wiesbaden Air Base in Germany.[909]

Trixie earned her pilot's license, and studied German and Russian for an assignment with the Associated Press to travel behind the Iron Curtain. She was in Moscow to cover the trial of Francis Gary Powers, the pilot of the CIA's U-2 spy plane that was shot down over the Soviet Union, and she supplied information for Radio Free Europe in Munich. She flew in the All-Woman Transcontinental Air Race, or "Powder Puff Derby," and the All Woman's International Air Race, or "Angel Derby," and worked as the associate editor of an aviation newspaper.[910]

Also, like so many women who loved to fly, Trixie was aware of the risks, as evidenced by a letter to her children, whom she referred to with the opening, "Dear Monkeys Three–Patrice, Heide, Norman." The letter was believed to have been written before a solo flight Trixie took from Kansas to California

---

[908] Tiffany Ann Brown, interview by author, February 16, 2019.

[909] Brown, interview, Feb. 16, 2019; Brown, *Fate*, 11; "Dr. Delwyn G. Schubert," Find a Grave, accessed March 2, 2019, https://www.findagrave.com/memorial/9476931/delwyn-g-schubert.

[910] "Trixie-Ann Schubert: Lecture Titles," Gertrude Purple Gorham Management Agency, courtesy of Tiffany Ann Brown.

in January 1964, when she was forty-two years old.[911] In it, she wrote of being "somewhat of a fatalist," admitting that the flight would be challenging, but assuring her children of her faith in God: "You have nothing in life to fear, NOTHING, while you adhere to the magnificent faith bestowed on you in Baptism."

Trixie left a note with the letter, asking that it not be opened until at least February 20 of the same year. The letter would not be found until after her death in February 1965, almost a year to the day after the date on which she intended it to be opened.[912]

Trixie was also a member of the Ninety-Nines, and interested in Joan. In May of 1964, she recorded in her journal that she drove "to Redondo Beach's 'Plush Horse' for homecoming banquet for Joan Merriam Smith. Was seated at head table near Joan. Would most like to get a crack at writing her book."[913]

Then, on September 21, 1964, she wrote: "Joan Merriam Smith here. Gradually I'm building up enough data to get her book underway."

On October 14, 1964: "With Joan Merriam and her mother all day in Long Beach."

November 4, 1964: "Finally sent off the manuscript of Joan's flight. Worked all day yesterday with Joan at Long Beach. Jack took us to lunch."

Trixie was also interested in the Amelia Earhart story and the research into Earhart by Fred Goerner, one of the pilots who flew alongside *The City of Long Beach* to escort Joan on departure day from Oakland. Trixie attended a lecture by Goerner in

---

[911] Ibid.

[912] Brown, *Fate, xvi-xvii*; Brown, interviews, February-May, 2019.

[913] Brown, *Fate*, 12.

September 1964, and her granddaughter, Tiffany Ann Brown, believes that Fred, Trixie and Joan had notes to compare with each other after Joan's visit to Saipan.[914]

Joan was getting to travel around to air shows and lectures, but the money she received still wasn't covering insurance and other expenses for the plane. The Smithsonian and other museums expressed an interest in the plane, but "they wanted [51-Poppa] donated. . . . And I still owed $17,000-plus on the Apache, along other debts incurred during . . . the world flight."[915]

The *Long Beach Independent Press-Telegram* reported, "Due perhaps to Mrs. Mock's priority in the spotlight, Joan's anticipated revenue from speaking engagements and personal appearances failed to come through."[916]

But Joan did receive invitations to speak, travel, and have fun. Her journal includes the following recollection:

> [The plane] had her moments of grandeur and glory even after the world flight; as when I was invited to fly an Air Force F-106B in September. The little Apache flew me to Castle Air Force Base where, after two days of tests and orientation, I was able to fly at speeds of Mach II in the F-106. Then I flew officers and pilot of the F-106 for an orientation ride in 51-Poppa. Our speed? Mach .296.[917]

In October, Joan was "one of the stellar attractions" at the

---

[914] Brown, interview, Feb. 16, 2019.
[915] Brown, *Fate*, 122; Smith, interview, 2017.
[916] "L.B. Flier," Feb. 18, 1965.
[917] Brown, 128.

Aircraft Owners and Pilots Association (AOPA) Plantation Party[918] at Hollywood-by-the-Sea, Florida. She recalled, "Where no plane ordinarily was permitted, 51-Poppa was invited." Joan landed the plane on the Diplomat Hotel and Country Club golf course, Number 2 Fairway. "We taxied across highways, causeways, and through gas stations (without buying gas)."[919] A photo was taken of AOPA vice president Max Karant giving her a "special award" –a broken golf tee marker struck by her "famous Apache."[920]

Linda Alvord, a member of the Oregon chapter of the Ninety-Nines, published her memory of Joan's visit to Portland where she was honored at a luncheon and was the featured speaker at the chapter's banquet.[921] Joan arrived at Portland International Airport on a "typical rainy day in January."[922]

At the luncheon, Joan received "the coveted 'rose' award," presented to her "as a woman who has contributed an outstanding achievement in society."[923] Alvord said Joan was "in good spirits" at the banquet the next evening, where she took the audience "on a 'round the world' flight via colored slides. Among the most impressive was a picture of a gentleman, who in turn held a picture of himself shown with Amelia Earhart."[924]

Joan told Alvord that, far from being content to have achieved "her heart's desire" of flying Earhart's equatorial

---

[918] The AOPA Plantation Party is now called the AOPA Expo.

[919] "Longest Flight," photo and caption, 47.

[920] Ibid.

[921] Linda Alvord, "Oregon Chapter," *Ninety-Nine News*, April 1965.

[922] Ibid.

[923] Ibid.

[924] Ibid.

route, "she wanted to set altitude records as a test pilot. What a girl!"[925]

Despite the intermittent speaking fees she received, Joan was frantic for funds. "In a desperate last resort," she put the plane up for sale, but the only offers she received were too low. When she received a call from a "reporter who was appalled that I would even consider selling the historic little plane," she took 51-Poppa off the market.[926]

A story was published about Joan's financial hardships and "sentimental attachment" to the plane, and as a result, Joan received an avalanche of letters.[927] Joan wrote, "The letters that impressed me the most were those from children. It has always been my dual purpose to achieve the equator flight record to fulfill my own great dream . . . (and) to light the dreams of other young people" to pursue a career in aviation.[928]

Throughout the remaining months of 1964, Joan and her friends brainstormed several ideas that would keep Joan in the air, and pay the bills. One possibility was a flight around the world by "the polar route," over both the north and the south poles.[929] Another possibility was breaking the altitude record for a private plane and/or a solo pilot.

According to Joan, "There were other ideas, such as a group of coin collectors who suggested I have a commemorative coin struck and sold."[930]

---

[925] Ibid.

[926] Brown, *Fate*, 123; Smith, interview, 2017.

[927] Brown, *Fate*, 123.

[928] Ibid.

[929] Ibid., 121.

[930] Ibid., 124.

She did accept one offer from the Lorraine Limestone Company of Tehachapi, California. The company wanted to lease the plane and retain Joan to fly business executives in and out of Alaska, Ecuador, and Peru.[931] Jack wasn't sure if their representative, Bill Eytchison, was a "scammer" or a legitimate businessman. Yet $25,000 was invested into this new small company; the Smiths were told not to worry about making money for the first year, and there was a possibility that Jack could join his wife in the business. Joan liked Eytchison's attitude that "you must not lease that plane without you as a pilot. Some part-time flier might take it out and crack it up. After you fly it six months with us . . . it's yours again to put in some museum." Joan signed a six-month contract with him.[932]

Also, by the new year, negotiations appear to have been underway to preserve *The City of Long Beach* for all time in Paul Mantz's "Movieland of the Air" Museum in Santa Ana, California.[933]

On Saturday, January 9, 1965, Joan got a call from Eytchison. He was in Las Vegas where he had flown his plane for some repairs, and asked if she could fly up and ferry him back to Long Beach. Later, Eytchison claimed they were flying to a "business meeting" where Joan was to have discussed plans for circling the globe by flying the polar route.[934]

The day was clear and sunny, with ceiling and visibility unlimited, and she agreed to come get him. We

---

[931] Ibid.

[932] Smith, interview, 2017.

[933] Schubert and Smith, "World Flight;" Burnett, 174.

[934] Brown, *Fate*, 120.

have Joan's account of what happened that day, from the manuscript of a book she was writing with Trixie. The chapter describing the crash is entitled "Last Flight."[935]

When she met Eytchison at the Thunderbird Airport in Las Vegas, he pulled out $1,500 in $100 bills, and tried to hand her $800 in cash as an advance.[936]

She said, "That's a lot of cash to be responsible for. Why don't you keep it all until we get back to Long Beach?"[937]

He put the money back in his jacket pocket.
They had been airborne about an hour when Joan asked Eytchison, "Do you smell anything strange?" She thought she detected the odor of burning. Thinking it might be a gas leak in the electrical gas heater up front, she turned it off. But the odor became stronger, more like burning metal, until they both noticed smoke in the cabin. She shut off the automatic pilot, the radios, and all the electrical equipment. Still, the heat on the floor became intense, and she shut off the air ducts to the cabin and moved her seat back until her toes could just reach the rudder control.[938]

"We were at 8,500 feet, twenty miles past the last town, Daggett, still twenty-seven miles from Apple Valley Airport." Neither the town nor the airport was in sight, and to make either one. They would have to clear two mountain ranges and yet maintain their present altitude; not possible. No time to look for a landing area. They would get one chance to put the plane down. To Joan it looked as if they were "holding hands with

[935] Schubert and Smith, "World Flight;" Brown, *Fate*, 122-130.
[936] Brown, *Fate*, 124.
[937] Ibid.
[938] Ibid., 125.

fiery death."[939]

"Let's get down fast," she said, turning the radios back on and transmitting on the emergency frequency. "Mayday, Mayday, this is N3251-Poppa. Fire in forward cabin. Going down." She repeated the distress calls twice and then shut off the radios and all electrical equipment again, in case they were the source of the fire.[940]

They headed for a flat spot on a mountain ledge. As she skimmed low, she could see stumps of trees sticking up, so she headed instead into a valley on the other side.[941]

She reached behind her seat for her fire extinguisher, started to read the instructions, and then realized they were in Portuguese. She'd had to buy a new fire extinguisher in Brazil, and had meant to get that thing replaced. Well, okay, she would probably just follow the usual "PASS" protocol anyway: Pull the pin, Aim, Squeeze and Spread.[942]

Eytchison pulled off his jacket and took over flying, while Joan crawled under the panel to check for loose wiring, but the heat was unbearable. Smoke burned their eyes. They tried opening a window, but that only stirred the smoke around, so they had to close it.[943]

Eytchison grabbed their thermos of coffee. Joan took the flashlight, a rescue signal mirror, and a pair of pliers and jammed them all into her purse.

They descended until they were rabbit-hopping over boulders

---

[939] Ibid.

[940] Ibid.

[941] Ibid.

[942] Ibid.

[943] Ibid., 126.

and low hills. She didn't dare put the wheels down. On this rough terrain, a belly landing was their only hope. At fifty feet she opened the door so that it wouldn't be crushed or jammed on impact, and that made the plane shudder and vibrate even worse. "In my heart I knew there was no hope for 51-Poppa. I couldn't save my burning plane. I felt next to positive that this was curtains for 51-Poppa's occupants as well. I had had my big dream, and now it was over, and I was sorry only that I was taking another's life with me."[944]

They fastened their seat belts. Joan surveyed the ground and spotted their best chance. A pipeline road offered the clearest area in sight, even though it rose and fell as much as sixty degrees, and every 300 feet or so there were piles of dirt and rocks. They would just have to barrel into them.[945]

Eytchison called out the speed: "Eighty, seventy-five, seventy, sixty-five, sixty."[946]

The next reasonably level spot loomed ahead. Joan yelled "NOW" and dropped the plane in.[947]

The propellers hit first, setting off a shrill shriek like a buzz saw whining through metal as the props cut through rock, followed by an acrid odor, then a scraping and grinding as the fuselage beneath them ripped open. After that, Joan remembered "nothing more for a while."[948]

Eytchison would tell her later that when they hit, the plane slid straight ahead and then veered off to the left. His reflex was

---

[944] Ibid.

[945] Ibid.

[946] Ibid., 127.

[947] Ibid.

[948] Ibid.

to try to force the right rudder to work, but that was to no effect, since they were skidding on the fuselage. He yelled, "Out. OUT!" When Joan didn't move, he half dragged, half carried her away from the burning plane.[949]

The next thing she could recall was being on her knees and fighting for breath. As she turned to look at her plane, flames shot up from the forward section. She felt a "numb horror and pity for the plane. It was like seeing part of myself burn."[950]

There was a succession of muffled explosions and then Eytchison called out, "Run. Try to run."[951]

Joan's purse lay nearby on the desert floor. She picked it up and crawled away "as fast as my bruised body would permit."[952]

Then she remembered to ask, "The money?"

"It's in my jacket," Eytchison said. "Still on the seat in the cabin."[953]

They looked back at the plane. The seats, burned to metal skeletons, were in smoldering ruins. The signs Joan had made to display at airshows, which read, "Please do not autograph the plane," were destroyed along with the rest of the contents of the cabin.[954]

"Five-one-Poppa had not exploded on impact," Joan wrote, in a kind of eulogy for her beloved Apache, "as if the plane had somehow granted me a reprieve even though it would never fly

---

[949] Ibid.

[950] Ibid.

[951] Ibid.

[952] Ibid., 127.

[953] Ibid., 128.

[954] Ibid.

again itself."[955]

She also wrote, "In a situation that had all the earmarks of a final flight for us both, the broken plane let her life ebb away slowly by fire, giving me time to escape, giving my life continuance."[956]

She pulled things out of her purse. The flashlight wouldn't work. They might have to use the little mirror to try catching the eye of the pilot of a search plane.[957]

They had gone down in the desert at 1:30 p.m. It was now 2:15 p.m. as they "stared at the vast, barren land."[958] Her flight time had expired, and a search would be initiated. Pilots are supposed to remain with the aircraft, but how long would they last without food or water, and with lightweight clothing in this place at 4,000 feet, where nighttime temperatures could drop to 15 degrees Fahrenheit?[959]

The hills kept them from seeing a pickup truck approaching the plane until it started to drive away again. Eytchison jumped up and shouted until the truck came to a stop.[960]

The driver, John Thiede, had spotted smoke rising from the desert floor. He figured someone had set an old car on fire, and he had almost decided to continue on toward home, twenty-five miles away, figuring he would be coming back up to take a look the next day. Yet as he drove along, he got curious about this fire, and as he got closer, he could see that it wasn't a car. He wrote

---

[955] Ibid.

[956] Ibid., 122.

[957] Ibid., 128.

[958] Ibid.

[959] Ibid., 129.

[960] Ibid.

down the plane's tail number, which was still visible among the flames, along with the words, "Burned cockpit. No survivors." He was headed off again when he heard Eytchison yelling.[961]

Upon hearing what Thiede had initially meant to report, Joan "blanched at the thought of [her] husband receiving that 'no survivors' message on his ship."[962]

Eytchison asked Thiede to give Joan a ride to a hospital while Eytchison stayed behind to guard the plane.[963]

Still woozy from that bump on her head, Joan didn't argue. She got in the truck.

As they headed off, Joan looked over her shoulder at her beloved Apache. She had spent $35,000 preparing the plane for the world flight, including new parts, components, and extra equipment. The cabin was completely burned. The right wing slanted upward, with fuel seeping down, steadily feeding the fire. Two tanks still had fuel, perhaps as much as seventy gallons, so they could still explode. All that remained intact were the tail section and wings with some of the signatures still readable, offering only the faint hope that a few mementoes of the equatorial flight might be preserved.[964]

They drove into Lucerne Valley, where Joan called first the FAA and then Jack. Then the man drove Joan to the hospital in Apple Valley for X-rays, which would reveal a broken nose.[965]

Meanwhile, back in the desert, Eytchison was left on his own. At 4,000 feet, it was getting cold, and he had no way of

[961] Ibid.

[962] Ibid.

[963] Ibid.

[964] Ibid., 130.

[965] Ibid., 129.

knowing when anybody would be coming for him. Moving was slow and painful, but he managed to gather up some wood. He took off his shirt and dipped it in gasoline, used a cow chip for a torch, and eventually got a blaze going. Later, X-rays would reveal two chipped bones in his spine.[966]

Help arrived, and a sheriff's guard was stationed at the plane to keep gawkers away. Still, the plane was left to burn for twelve more hours before it was finally put out.[967]

The wreck put Joan back in the limelight, but not in the way she wanted. Her plane had been her livelihood. The wreckage was put up for auction, and a few signatured sections and the tail were purchased by Paul Mantz to be placed in the "Movieland of the Air" Museum. Joan was left to figure out how to pick up and start over again in aviation, while still wondering, "How do you replace the only asset you had?"[968]

Trixie submitted an article about the crash to the *Saturday Evening Post*, but did not get an immediate response. When the response from Hillel Black, Trixie's editor at the *Post*, finally arrived several weeks later, it was a rejection.

After the crash of 51-Poppa, perhaps Joan had not lost out on all opportunities to stay in business. Representatives for two air taxi service companies each offered to kick in $25,000 to help her buy another plane. The idea was that she could fly for them, and her name recognition would help promote the companies.[969]

Also, she was able to earn at least a little money working an occasional gig test-flying for the Riley-Rajay Corporation. Jack

---

[966] Ibid., 130.

[967] Schubert and Smith, "World Flight."

[968] Brown, *Fate*, 130.

[969] Smith interview, 2017.

also recalled Joan's desire to set an altitude record with Rajay's experimental equipment.[970]

Trixie also remembered test-flying with Joan. In Trixie's journal entry for January 27, 1965, she wrote: "Wednesday a.m. Joan called and asked if I'd like to fly with her. We were up three hours in a Cessna 182 experimental plane, at 15,000 feet putting time on the test plane equipped with turbochargers. She used computer and wrote data for turbos at various power settings, etc. WONDERFUL DAY."[971]

On the morning of February 17, 1965, Joan and Trixie took off in a plane which had been loaned out to Joan, a modified Cessna 182 Skylane.[972]

Joan had originally invited another friend, Joyce Dixon, to accompany her on the fateful flight, but Joyce declined because her house "was a bit dusty."[973] So Trixie joined Joan for another day of flying.[974]

Newspaper reports offer a range of reasons for the flight. By some accounts, Joan "borrowed" the plane for a "simple routine flight."[975] Shirley Thom, a member of the Ninety-Nines, remembered hearing they were on their way to Vegas.[976]

Bill Eytchison said that he believed the pair was headed to

---

[970] Brown, *Fate*, 153; Smith, interview, 2017.

[971] Brown, *Fate*, 153.

[972] Ibid.

[973] Ibid., 154.

[974] "The Fiery End of '51 Pops,'" *The AOPA Pilot*, March 1966.

[975] California Digital Newspaper Collection, "Famed Aviatrix Dies in Crash," *Madera Tribune*, February 18, 1965, https://cdnc.ucr.edu/?a=d&d=MT1965 0218.2.5&e=-------en--20--1--txt-txIN--------1, accessed Feb. 6, 2019; Graham, "Legend Down."

[976] Brown, *Fate*, 154.

the Lucerne Valley to view the crash site of 51-Poppa, in order to gather information for Trixie's book.[977] Eytchison later told the press that he was to have been Joan's co-pilot on the proposed flight over the North and South poles, planned for September 1965. Eytchison's recollection was that Joan had planned to give up flying and go into the business end of aviation after the "pole-to-pole" hop,[978] although Jack adamantly refuted that Joan had made any such plans, at least not with Eytchison.[979]

Aviation researcher and helicopter pilot Bryan Swopes says Joan was "conducting functionality and reliability tests on a modified Cessna 182C Skylane" and that she "intended to attempt an altitude record with the turbo-charged Skylane."[980]

Perhaps Joan hoped to check more than one item off her list that day.

The Riley-Rajay Corporation was continuing to experiment with turbocharging, and Joan had been able to use the new equipment on her around-the-world flight. Yet in that era, the technology was still "mostly a black art," according to an article in *Aviation News*.[981] The article stated that Jack Riley "takes credit for being the first person to produce a general aviation airplane that would deliver 100% of its sea level power at 29,000 feet."[982]

Joan and Trixie's route took them over the San Gabriel

---

[977] Ibid.

[978] Burnett, 174.

[979] Brown, *Fate*, 121.

[980] Swopes, *This Day in Aviation*.

[981] "Jack M. Riley and the Riley Aircraft Corp." *Aviation News*, http://www.twinnavion.com/jackriley.htm.

[982] Ibid.

Mountains, an area with a history of aerial mishaps.[983] Wind conditions in this terrain may be particularly treacherous, especially for small planes, conditions which may not have been well understood in 1965.[984] In the Sierra Nevada Mountains just north of the crash site of Big Pines, investigators have more recently discovered remnants of some 2,000 small plane crashes over a sixty-year period. In 1976, an unexpected downdraft brought down a Cessna 182P near Mt. Whitney, farther north.[985]

Pilots from Air Force bases nearby had been using the San Gabriel Mountains to practice combat maneuvers since World War II.[986] At least a dozen crashes have been documented there, dating back to 1943.[987]

We may never know what went wrong, but the plane went down, and Joan and Trixie did not survive. The crash, and the investigations that followed, leave some unanswered questions.

One eyewitness, Mr. Robert Jones, resident manager of the Southern California Bible Conference, outside of Wrightwood, California, gave a statement a few days after the crash. He stated that, while "out on the conference grounds [he] happened to look up at the sky and observed a jet stream and was following it with my eye when I noticed a small plane."[988]

Jones returned his attention to the contrail until he "heard

---

[983] Graham, "Legend Down."

[984] Brown, 161.

[985] Ibid., 162.

[986] Graham, "Legend Down."

[987] Swopes, *This Day in Aviation*; Graham, "Legend Down."

[988] Brown, *Fate*, 194. By "jet stream," we believe he meant a contrail.

the motor of the small plane rev up."[989] When he looked at the small plane again, he "noticed that the right wing had folded back against the plane. Then the plane went into a nose dive and crashed."[990]

Mr. Jones stated that the plane was not on fire in the sky. He also stated that he estimated that the length of time between when he heard the motor of the plane rev up and saw the right wing folded back against the plane until it nose-dived and crashed was about ten to twelve seconds. Mr. Jones called his wife to come and spot the smoke, so they would be certain of the location.[991]

By that afternoon, more reports were coming in of smoke rising over the mountains.[992]

"We were in port," Jack recalled in June 2017. "I was having lunch with the officers. Our sailors on deck heard it on the radio, and they decided they had to knock on our door to give me the news."[993]

Jack recounted these events in a steady, calm voice, as if he had shared them many times before. "Trixie's husband was a professor in Los Angeles. They asked Dr. Schubert to come out to identify the bodies, but he declined. Then they asked me. We flew over the sight, about 7,000 feet up on the mountainside. It was a wooded area, with steep slopes. The bodies were burned so badly, you couldn't tell which person was which. I had to go

---

[989] Brown, *Fate*, 194.

[990] Ibid.

[991] Ibid.

[992] Graham, "Legend Down."

[993] Smith, interview, 2017.

by their jewelry."[994]

Newspapers reported Jack's reaction. In the *Ogden Standard Examiner*, Jack was quoted, "I don't have any doubt (that Joan died), because the plane never came back."[995]

Reporters also recorded the reaction of Joan's mother, Anne Merriam. "I figured sooner or later she would go like this. . . . I just didn't think I would lose her yet."[996]

Coincidentally, on February 19, Eytchison was quoted as saying that he had "bought a $117,000 plane just two days ago." That means Eytchison bought the new plane on February 17, the date of the fatal crash.[997]

In another sad coincidence, Hillel Black's rejection letter to Trixie was written February 17.[998]

As to causes of the crash, the evidence available remains inconclusive. The Civil Aeronautics Board (CAB), which was later absorbed into the National Air Traffic Safety Board, investigated the crash and created a report.[999]

In the months following the crash, the articles published about the investigation and conclusions leave some questions unanswered. Two days after the crash, the *L.A. Times* reported, "Little of the plane, a borrowed single-engine Cessna 182,

[994] Ibid.

[995] "Plane Crash Kills Famous Aviatrix," *Ogden Standard Examiner*, Feb. 18, 1965.

[996] "Famed Aviatrix Dies in Crash," *Madera Tribune*, Feb. 18, 1965, https://cdnc.ucr.edu/?a=d&d=MT19650218.2.5&e=-------en--20--1--txt-txIN--------1 (accessed Feb. 6, 2019).

[997] Brown, *Fate*, 150.

[998] Brown, *Fate*, 189.

[999] Brown, *Fate*, 159.

remained intact after it crashed in a ball of flame."[1000]

Evidently, a "Final Report" was published within a month. Yet three months after the crash, in May 1965, the *CAP* (Civil Air Patrol) *Times* published an article entitled "Search for Aviatrix's Plane Ends on a California Peak," detailing a search organized several weeks after the crash for pieces of the aircraft which were scattered further away from the crash site and were more difficult to locate.[1001]

According to the article, four agencies–the US Forest Service, Civil Aeronautics Board (CAB), Civil Air Patrol (CAP), and FAA–were involved in the search. The article notes, "The debris was identified as part of Mrs. Smith's missing plane and the case was closed. However, one oddity of the case still remains . . . Civil Air Patrol being directly involved with the parts of the plane of the former CAP member."[1002]

Ordinarily, the CAP would conduct an internal investigation, and leave the physical search for the CAB. This additional search effort might suggest that, three months after the event, authorities were still searching for conclusive evidence about the cause of the crash.[1003]

Then, the following February, the CAB reported that the plane crash was caused when Joan "encountered turbulent air

---

[1000] "Experts Seek Cause of Women Fliers' Crash," *Los Angeles Times*, Feb. 19, 1965.

[1001] "Search for Aviatrix' Plane Ends on California Peak," *CAP* Times, May 1965.

[1002] Ibid.

[1003] Bob Dunlop, interview with author, September 3, 2020, Tallahassee, FL. Dunlop was a pilot who owned a Cessna similar to Jerrie's in 1964. He still owned the plane when he spoke with the author in 2020.

while flying at high speed."[1004] The plane is believed to have been flying in excess of 190 mph when it entered the area of turbulence.[1005]

The CAB determined that the "resultant violent upward and downward forces broke off the tips of both wings and part of the tail structure of the Cessna 182 . . . and sent it hurtling into a 7,200-foot-high ridge."[1006]

Brown was also able to track down an article by Joan published posthumously in the March 1966 issue of the *AOPA Pilot*. The article includes an editorial sidebar which quotes details from the CAB report of the fatal crash:

> Probable Cause: Pilot entered an area of light to moderate turbulence at high speed . . . during which aerodynamic forces exceeding the structural strength of the aircraft caused in-flight structural failure.[1007]

The AOPA sidebar goes on to state that, according to the CAB report, the purpose of the flight was to test the function and reliability of the "experimental turbocharged engine."[1008]

Was pilot error a factor as well? A medical journal article later referenced a forensic analysis: Joan "had a liver barbiturate level of 0.4 mg %, consistent with use of Dexamyl #2 for appetite

---

[1004] "Turbulent Air at High Speed Cause of Crash," *Reno Evening Gazette*, February 10, 1966; Brown, *Fate*, 159.

[1005] Swopes, *This Day in Aviation*.

[1006] "Turbulent Air," *Reno Evening Gazette*; Brown, *Fate*, 159.

[1007] Brown, 159; "'Probable Cause,'" *AOPA Pilot*, March, 1966, 46.

[1008] "'Probable Cause,'" *AOPA Pilot*, March, 1966, 46.

suppression for weight loss."[1009]

Dexamyl was the brand name for a blend of the stimulant dextroamphetamine and the sedative amobarbital. According to Linda Desue, a retired nurse in Tallahassee, Florida, it was called the "diet pill," and students often used it to help them stay up all night to write their term papers or cram for exams. It would help keep a person up for a long time, followed sometimes by the proverbial "crash."[1010] Dexamyl was eventually banned, but at the time, it was legal and available over-the-counter.

"Judgment may have been affected," J. Robert Dille, M.D., MIH, retired FAA, USAF, and Army National Guard (ARNG) Flight Surgeon, concluded in the journal *Aviation, Space and Environmental Medicine*.[1011] However, the only NTSB record available during research conducted by this author in 2019-2020 made no mention of any errors in judgment. It listed probable cause as "Pilot in command exceeded designed stress limits of aircraft." The report listed "Weather – turbulence in flight, clear air" as a factor, and under "Remarks," mentioned that the plane had "Experimental turbocharged engine installed to provide meto power to 25,000 ft."[1012]

"METO" stands for "Maximum-Except-Take-Off (the highest power setting an engine will endure for more than a few

---

[1009] J. Robert Dille, "Record and Around the World Flights Through Singapore by Women," *Aviation, Space and Environmental Medicine, Volume 70*, No. 10, Octobr 1999, 1039.

[1010] Linda Desue, interview by author, May 2008.

[1011] Dille, "Record and Around the World Flights."

[1012] NTSB (formerly the Civil Aeronautics Board, or CAB) Identification: LAX65A0069, https://www.ntsb.gov/investigations/AccidentReports /_layouts/15/ntsb.aviation/brief.aspx?ev_id=76485&key=0.

minutes without potential damage)."[1013]

The NTSB record that exists today reads, "Full narrative not available."[1014] Tiffany Ann Brown writes, "After repeated check-ins with the NTSB, the answer I received was simply, "There are no narratives for these cases. Accident dockets have been destroyed."[1015]

A possible source of the turbulence that Joan's plane encountered is revealed in the eyewitness statement. Mr. Jones, who observed the plane's last few minutes of flight, mentioned a "jet stream" from another plane in the area. In her book, *Fate on a Folded Wing*, Brown explains, "Similarly to boats on a lake creating wakes that can affect other boats in their proximity, passing planes also can leave behind turbulent wakes that have the capacity to affect nearby planes."[1016] Brown also describes other cases of "turbulent wakes" affecting aircraft.

Joan's widower, Captain Jack Smith, remembered that mechanical damage was found that Joan didn't know about. "Turns out, the plane had been damaged in a storm on the ground. It had been rebuilt and checked out, and it was supposed to be okay, but it wasn't. They had encountered clear air turbulence. A top air fitting snapped, the racket broke, and one wing folded back against the fuselage."[1017]

Jack filed a lawsuit against "Rajay Corp., Z.E. Kuster Co.,

[1013] CalClassic Forum, https://calclassic.proboards.com/thread/7937/high-low-blower-meto-power, accessed August 29, 2022.

[1014] Ibid.

[1015] Brown, *Fate,* 154.

[1016] Ibid., 165.

[1017] Smith, interview, 2017.

Cessna Aircraft Co., Belmont Aviation Corp., West Coast Propeller Sales and Service Co., and Banning Aviation Co."[1018] seeking $500,000. "But nothing came of it," Jack said.[1019]

"Neither crash was pilot error," he added, sadly. "Both crashes were mechanical failure."[1020]

The bits of evidence available suggest a "perfect storm" of contributing factors. The inability to obtain a full narrative of the original report is puzzling.

G. Pat Macha, an aviation archaeologist who has been investigating plane crash sites in the mountains of California for fifty-five years, shared helpful insights about Joan's fatal crash. "I don't know if she checked the weather prog (prognosis) that day or she just looked at the sky and decided it was a good day to fly," Macha said.[1021] "Normally, in that area, pilots would fly through Cajon Pass (which would have afforded lower altitude and less turbulence), but she simply flew a direct line over the mountains."

Macha added, "There have been conversations about modifications made to the Cessna she was flying that day, and whether or not attachments were properly fastened down."

He also explained the hazard of clear air turbulence. "Clear air turbulence can occur when a wave of air moves up from the ocean or a basin, and goes up, over and down the other side of the mountains, potentially interacting with high winds at higher altitudes over the high Sierras. You can get sucked down, and the catch is, you can't see it. There are a few cases of crashes

---

[1018] "Aviatrix's Husband Files $500,000 Suit, *Santa Ana Register*, Feb. 10, 1966.

[1019] Smith, interview, 2017.

[1020] Ibid.

[1021] G. Pat Macha, telephone interview by author, February 17, 2022.

attributed to CAT, and this could be one of them."

Macha was amused at the suggestion that proximity to a military base, or the crashes of military planes in the area, had anything to do with Joan's crash. "Military flights have other risk factors – training missions, flying in formation – so, no."

Macha believes the full narrative of the investigation report exists, somewhere. Finding it, he said, is "not impossible, but it might be difficult... In those days we were losing hundreds of light aircraft monthly in this country. People who were smart in some ways were not always so smart in the air, and it was common for planes to go down on flights from LA to Palm Beach, for instance. Today we're losing 5% of what we were [losing] then." The reports are probably "in cardboard boxes in DC,"[1022] Macha said, evoking the final scene in the movie *Raiders of the Lost Ark*.

Bryan Swopes clarified some aspects of the crash, as well.[1023] Swopes explained how a turbo-supercharger adds thrust by pushing more air and fuel into the engine, which becomes more valuable as the plane climbs into higher altitudes and thinner air.

The engineers with Riley-Rajay would have developed a test plan for Joan's flight. "Test flying is actually very boring," Swopes said. Ordinarily, pilots conduct tests off the shoreline, where the air is smooth. However, this flight was taken over the mountains, where clear air turbulence can indeed be unpredictable and unseen. Swopes directed readers to his website, *This Day in Aviation*, for accounts of clear air turbulence bringing down even commercial airliners. Once Joan's plane

---

[1022] Ibid.

[1023] Bryan Swopes, interview with the author, Feb. 17, 2022.

went into a dive, the air would have spun the propeller faster than it had been spinning as initially powered by the engine, which would have caused the revving sound that an observer heard. As the plane was coming apart, the pilot would have been incapacitated by the g-forces; according to Swopes, both Joan and Trixie would have lost consciousness prior to impact.[1024]

The funerals for Joan and her friend Trixie were held the same day. Trixie's remains were buried at Holy Cross Cemetery in Culver City, California. The remains of her widower, Dr. Delwyn G. Schubert, joined Trixie's in 2004.[1025]

An obituary in the *Long Beach Independent Press-Telegram* on February 21, 1965 noted Joan's historic accomplishment with a nod to her idol: "Mrs. Smith won fame last spring by flying the 1937 route of the ill-fated Amelia Earhart, becoming the first person to solo around the earth at the equator."[1026]

Joan's remains were buried at Forest Lawn Memorial Park (Cypress) in Orange County, California. A favorite poem of Joan's, "High Flight," by John Gillespie Magee, Jr., was printed on cards handed out at the funeral. The poem reads in part:

> Oh, I have slipped the surly bonds of Earth
> And danced the skies on laughter-silvered wings;
> Sunward I've climbed and joined the tumbling mirth

[1024] Swopes, interview.

[1025] "Beatrice Ann 'Trixie' Gehrung Schubert," Find a Grave, accessed March 2, 2019, https://www.findagrave.com/memorial/196037594/beatrice-ann-schubert; "Dr. Delwyn G. Schubert," Find a Grave.

[1026] Mark Clutter, "Simple Funeral Conducted for Joan Merriam Smith," *Long Beach Independent Press-Telegram*, Feb. 21, 1965.

of sun-split clouds – and done a hundred things…
I've topped the wind-swept heights with easy grace,
Where never lark, or even eagle flew
And, while with silent, lifting mind I've trod
The high, untrespassed sanctity of space,
Put out my hand, and touched the face of God.[1027]

The poem is especially poignant because Magee was a young pilot who died at age nineteen in a collision between two military aircraft less than four months after he wrote the sonnet, in December 1941.

Many of Joan's friends expressed their sorrow at her untimely death. The April 1965 issue of *The Ninety-Nine News* included tributes from several fellow female pilots.

Linda Alvord, who met Joan at a Ninety-Nines banquet in Oregon, wrote in the *Ninety-Nine News*, "All eagerness for flying has, for the moment, ceased to exist." Alvord referenced a favorite poem of Joan's:

I'd rather find an island in the Sky,
Than stay below and only wonder why.
I'd rather feel the cool tempestuous air,
Than only felt of earthly cares.
Oh Lord, lift up a gentle hand
To guide me to a certain land;
You know, the one we oft describe
As a special "Island in the Sky."[1028]

[1027] John G. Magee, "High Flight."
[1028] Alford, *Ninety-Nine News*, April 1965.

Carole B. Dunn, from the Long Beach Chapter of the Ninety-Nines, attended funeral services for both Trixie and Joan. She wrote in the *Ninety-Nine News*, "Joan had a beautiful blue casket and many lovely flower arrangements in the shapes of the 99 emblem and propellers, and the Civil Air Patrol flew by the grave in the military formation of one plane missing."[1029]

In the same issue, Gerry Whitton, from the Las Vegas Valley Chapter, wrote about the memorial service held for Joan in Las Vegas. "It was an especially sad occasion as Joan lived here for two years and even after she moved away she was a frequent visitor at the home of Fran and Tom Johnson where she planned a great deal of her around the world trip."[1030]

When asked by a reporter, Jerrie Mock answered that she was "deeply shocked" by the news of Joan's death.[1031]

Joan's tombstone reads:

Joan Merriam Smith
1936–1965
Flew 1937 Amelia Earhart route. First person to fly solo
around the world at the equator. Longest solo flight in history.
First woman to fly twin-engine aircraft around the world.
Awarded Harmon Trophy posthumously 1965. An inspiration
to women everywhere.[1032]

Captain Smith talked about these chapters of his life in his living room in Prattville, Alabama in 2017. He spoke with clear

---

[1029] Dunn, "Long Beach Chapter," *Ninety-Nine News*, April 1965, 16.
[1030] Whitton, "Las Vegas Chapter," *Ninety-Nine News*, April 1965, 14.
[1031] "L.B. Flier," Feb. 18, 1965.
[1032] "Joan Merriam Smith," Find a Grave.

recall, and without remorse, only resignation. "Here we were, getting set up for a life together… I was planning to retire from the service, and go into business with her. Our future was assured–and then I lost her. It was tough."[1033]

The Ninety-Nines continued to honor Joan. Jack also honored his late wife's memory by attending events hosted by the Ninety-Nines and by announcing plans to set an altitude record that Joan had wanted to set.

On April 25, Jack attended a reception at the American Newspaper Women's Club in Washington, DC. The reception honored both Amelia Earhart and Joan Merriam Smith with the theme, "Flying Salute to World Friendships." Fellow members of the Ninety-Nines flew in from countries in which both pilots had made landings, including Malaysia and Indonesia.

Jacqueline M.C. Smith of the Washington, DC Chapter of the Ninety-Nines reported in the June 1965 issue of *The Ninety-Nine News*, "Ruth Deerman, International President (of the Ninety-Nines), presented the Amelia Earhart Stamp Album to Vice Admiral Paul Ramsey, USN, for Admiral David MacDonald, Chief of Naval Operations, in appreciation for the Navy's part in the search for Amelia Earhart and the honor they accorded Joan Merriam Smith when they sent the military escort to greet her when she flew in to Guam."

Two plaques commemorating the flights were presented at this reception, one to be installed on Guam and the other on Midway. Jacqueline Smith further noted, "The money raised at this reception is to go for the Amelia Earhart Scholarship Fund." She also commented that everyone who met Jack Smith at the

---

[1033] Smith, interview, 2017.

event "were quite taken by him."[1034]

After visiting with Jack, Fran Johnson from the Las Vegas Valley Chapter of the Ninety-Nines commented, "He sure looks like an 'outer space man' when he dons the attire he will wear for (the altitude record) flight."

The Ninety-Nines set up scholarship funds in honor of both Joan and Trixie. The Tucson Chapter erected a plaque in the "Volador Room" (flyer in Spanish), the room for flying guests of the Tucson Aviation Authority (TAA) in honor of Joan's stop in Tucson on her around-the-world flight. The idea was expressed to erect a plaque at each stop that Joan made on her trip.[1035]

The Riley-Rajay Corporation suggested that Jack set an altitude record with their turbocharger, as Joan had wanted to do. On July 20, 1965, Smith took off from the Long Beach Municipal Airport in a turbo-charged Rajay Cessna 210, setting out to break the world altitude record for a light piston aircraft of 32,540 feet. Smith reached 35,700 feet, without benefit of a pressurized cabin, and dedicated the flight as a tribute to his late wife. The record stood for three months.[1036]

In those months following the crash, Jack also responded in a different way.

By 1965, the American people were beginning to argue against continued involvement in the Vietnam War. Yet in his grief, Jack went off to war by choice. "I decided, I'll just volunteer to go 'in country' (active combat) for a year. I said I don't care if I don't come back. Can you imagine?" he asked as

---

[1034] Smith, "Washington DC Chapter," *Ninety-Nine News*, June 1965, 21.

[1035] Shock, "Tucson Chapter," *Ninety-Nine News*, April 1965, 21.

[1036] "FAI records received by Marvin G. Smith," *World Air Sports Federation*.

he looked back on those days. "You shouldn't let anybody go like that. But they did."[1037]

He was sent to Saigon. Even though he was stationed at the military headquarters, the city wasn't safe. People were getting "fragged" with grenades, and it could happen at any time. Smith walked around in the middle of the street, even at night. He just couldn't find a reason to care anymore.[1038]

In December, 1965, Joan was posthumously awarded the Harmon Trophy for Outstanding Aviatrix of 1964 by Vice President Hubert H. Humphrey, saluting her as one of the nation's most outstanding women pilots.[1039] The Navy granted Jack leave from his tour of duty in Vietnam to fly in to Washington, DC to attend the ceremony held in the Indian Treaty Room of the Executive Office Building on December 15, 1965, where he accepted the award on her behalf. "I had to have blues made by a local tailor there in DC," Jack recalled. "It was fun. There were other people accepting an award that day. There was a balloonist, and other categories." He remembered Vice President Hubert Humphrey as "a nice guy!"[1040]

The Ninety-Nines petitioned Congress for special recognition of both Amelia and Joan.[1041] The aviation pioneers are mentioned side-by-side in the US Congressional Record, dated March 17, 1969. The resolution declared in part:

[1037] Smith, interview, 2017.

[1038] Ibid.

[1039] Hubert Humphrey, "Harmon International Aviation Trophies," speech, December 14, 1965.

[1040] Smith, interview, 2017.

[1041] Ruth Deerman and Pat Lambert, "Joint Resolution in Honor of Joan Merriam Smith," *Ninety-Nine News*, June 1965.

The deeds and courage of these two women stand out as shining examples of the kind of service and dedication which individuals can render in the cause of their country.[1042]

May 12, 1968 was proclaimed Amelia Earhart-Joan Merriam Smith Day by Spiro T. Agnew, at the time the Governor of Maryland; John Chafee, Governor of Rhode Island; John Reading, Mayor of Oakland, California; and Edwin Wade, Mayor of Long Beach, California.[1043]

Over the years, Smith found ways to recover, such as throwing himself into community service. The town of Prattville, affectionately nicknaming him "Captain Jack," recognized him with a 2016 Citizen of Character Award. Smith was praised on the Prattville-Autauga Character Coalition's website:

"If Captain Jack is not at home with his wife Martha, you'll find him in the Prattville community at his church, the golf course or at Habitat for Humanity in Prattville. . . . We are grateful for all he has done!'[1044]

Jack still keeps photos and articles about Joan, her plane, and her flight in his home.

[1042] "Senate Joint Resolution 81," *Congressional Record-Senate*, March 17, 1969, 6571.

[1043] *Congressional Record*, 6572.

[1044] "2016 Citizen of Character-Mr. Jack Smith," *News Prattville-Autauga Character Coalition*, June 6, 2016, accessed Sept. 18, 2022, https://www.pachar acter.org/award-recipients. The quote has since been removed from the website.

Life on the Ground for Jerrie

After the crowds and reporters and cameras faded away, Jerrie went back to working with her husband and raising their children. Russ and Jerrie also made time for fun trips in the plane. In December of 1965, Jerrie, Russ, her sister Barbara Saar, and their friend Al Baumeister embarked on an excursion from Columbus, Ohio, to Texas, Mexico, Guatemala, Belize, Grand Cayman, Jamaica, the Bahamas, Florida, and back to Columbus.[1045]

The ripple effects from the historic flight would continue to be a part of her life.

In the summer of 1964, Jerrie received a visit from two men from the CIA. They showed her pictures of missile bases in the United States and asked if she had seen anything that looked like an American base, anywhere on her trip, particularly in the UAR.[1046]

Throughout the Cold War era, both the United States and the Soviet Union attempted to draw nations into alliances, against the opposing power.[1047] In 1964, President Gamal Nasser was in power in the UAR, and he strove to maintain a policy of neutrality, which is reported to have created some tension between the UAR and the United States.

[1045] "Famous Aviatrix Stops at Cayman," *The Caymanian*, December 5, 1965; Mock, interview, Feb. 28, 2008.

[1046] Mock, interview, July 1, 2007.

[1047] "Cold War," *Wikipedia*, accessed Jan. 3, 2023, https://en.wikipedia.org/wiki/Cold_War.

These dynamics were beyond Jerrie's interest, and she was happy to tell her visitors the truth, that she had not seen anything more than what she had already reported.

For Jerrie, the expectation was that she and her achievement would naturally become world famous; however, she found celebrity to be a mixed blessing.

Russ, the advertising man, worked diligently to help get his wife and her achievement widely recognized, intending it to be a source of future income. Back when Russ first began supporting this project, he wrote letters to friends, expressing his dreams of follow-up ventures.

A letter he wrote to "Ralph" on December 9, 1963, included this hope:

"If all goes well, I am sure we can use this (flight around the world) as a stepping stone to additional projects with Jerrie behind the stick. I think, for instance, that she should be the first girl to fly to Antarctica."[1048]

It was imperative, Russ believed, to "keep her name hot enough to knock off a second record." He told "Ralph" that achieving subsequent records would help establish Jerrie as "a good commercial property," complete with sponsorships.[1049]

Even though she found celebrity intimidating, Jerrie made the effort to step into the spotlight. Some events were fun for her. In 1965, the Cessna Corporation flew Jerrie and Russ to the Paris Air Show. At the US Embassy in Paris, they met two of the original "Mercury Seven" NASA astronauts. They flew from

---

[1048] Russ Mock, letter, Dec. 9, 1963.
[1049] Ibid.

Paris to England where they got to do a little sightseeing together, before heading back to Columbus.[1050]

She also made appearances on television programs, such as the *Today* show and *To Tell the Truth*, that delivered her personality directly into the living rooms of our nation.[1051] In 1964, *To Tell the Truth* was one of the most popular programs in America. An individual who had an unusual occupation or experience and two imposters were seated on one side of a screen with a panel of four celebrities on the other side. The panelists asked questions and had to guess which of the three contestants was not a phony. The two imposters were allowed to lie, but the authentic person was sworn to "tell the truth." After the person's true identity was revealed, the screen was removed, and all three guests joined the celebrities for a follow-up talk.

When Jerrie appeared on *To Tell the Truth*, panelist Orson Bean commented, "She has All-American looks, and I think when they make the film, Doris Day will play her part." Doris Day, an A-list actress of the time, was known for her own All-American looks and personality.[1052]

Yet the story of the woman pilot who flew solo through sandstorms, overcame sabotage, and averted an onboard fire has never been made into a movie.

Jerrie did not thrive during the grind of the speaking tour demands. "The kind of person who can sit in an airplane alone," Jerrie told one reporter many years later, "is not the type of

---

[1050] Mock, interview, May 5, 2008.

[1051] Saunders, "How an Ohio Housewife Flew Around the World."

[1052] Mock, *Three-Eight Charlie*, 277; *To Tell the Truth*, episode aired on April 27, 1964; Mock, interview, Feb. 17, 2009.

person who likes continually to be with other people."[1053] Her sponsors expected her to pay back their investment with her speaking fees, even though she didn't enjoy facing the crowds and the questions. When the phone rang with invitations, she accepted as many as she and Russ could schedule. During one stretch, she gave nine talks in ten days. She played her part without allowing her distaste for it to show, and sent the proceeds to the *Dispatch*, while still having to spend her own money on babysitters for daughter Valerie.

When they flew commercially, Russ proudly asked the flight crew to make an announcement about the celebrity on board, never comprehending why Jerrie didn't enjoy the fame. Jerrie compared the spotlight on her to being an animal on display in the zoo, and compared profiting from her dream to selling her soul. She wanted to return to normal life, to be left alone, to fly her plane. "I'd rather go to an island where there are no phones or TV," she said, "and never talk to anyone again."[1054]

Whenever possible, Jerrie went back to doing exactly what she was doing before Russ first suggested the around-the-world idea: flying her plane, seeing the world, keeping in touch with other pilots, and exploring other possibilities.

In 1965, Jerrie considered setting another distance record, flying a closed course in a different weight class, C-1B. She met Frank Hearn, the man who was awarded the sanction for this distance record before her. His flight plan would have been to fly from Fort Barrow, Alaska, to Key West, Florida. Jerrie and Frank got along fine, but then she didn't hear from him for

---

[1053] Saunders, "How an Ohio Housewife Flew Around the World."

[1054] Mock, *Three-Eight Charlie*, 206; Saunders, "How an Ohio Housewife Flew Around the World;" Mock, interview, Feb. 17, 2009.

some time. Months later, his remains and the wreckage of his plane were found. He had flown into a mountain.

Subsequently, Jerrie was given the sanction for that particular distance record, but again, someone else wanted it. Rather than make it difficult for the other pilot, Max Conrad, Jerrie simply handed over the sanction. Conrad set that record. Light aircraft pilots "were sort of a club," Jerrie explained. "Mostly we worked together."[1055]

Jerrie continued to break barriers and set records. A few months after her worldwide journey, an Air Force pilot gave her a ride in a McDonnell F-101 Voodoo jet fighter. The jet reached a speed of 1,038 mph (Mach 1.7), and Jerrie briefly handled the controls, making her one of the few women at the time to fly at supersonic speeds.

In 1965, she broke the speed record for a closed course of 312 miles and another record, with a plane weighing 2,200 pounds, flying 205 mph in an Aero Commander 200. In 1966, she broke the nonstop distance record for a woman with a 4,550-mile flight from Honolulu to Columbus in thirty-one hours; and Governor Rhodes greeted her at the airport once again. Overall, Jerrie set twenty-one speed and distance records.[1056]

Meanwhile, Russ and Jerrie were unable to keep pace with paying the bills. Jerrie never flew Charlie again. Instead, she was given a Cessna 206 by the manufacturer in exchange for displaying Charlie at its factory.[1057] But in 1969, the

---

[1055] Mock, interview, May 5, 2008; Saunders, "How an Ohio Housewife Flew Around the World."

[1056] "Jerrie Mock: Record-Breaking American Female Pilot," Laurel M. Sheppard, *Aviation History*, July 2005.

[1057] Saunders, "How an Ohio Housewife Flew Around the World."

Internal Revenue Service demanded $6,000 in taxes on the new plane. Jerrie hired a lawyer to fight the tax bill. Although she won, the legal fees were the same amount as she would have paid in taxes.[1058] As a result, she could no longer afford to fly. Her dreams of further world travel would go unfulfilled.

She made her last solo flight in 1969, to sell and deliver her last plane, her new Cessna 206, to the Missionaries of the Sacred Heart in New Guinea.[1059] Years later, she received a letter from a man named Jerrie Mock, living in New Guinea. Her plane had been used to fly his mother to the hospital in time for her to give birth to him.[1060]

In 1972, Jerrie received a visit from a Mr. El Gabre from the UAR. He explained that, when she had accidentally landed at Inchas, he had been the person on the other end of the line when she watched it ring on the wall. The Russians were indeed there, but at the time, the Soviet presence in the United Arab Republic was unknown to the United States. El Gabre confirmed Jerrie's fear that many of the men on the base at Inchas, who served Jerrie cider by the King's pool, were killed in an Israeli bomb strike during the Six-Day War of 1967.[1061]

Peter Barker, the man who, along with his wife Marlin, had taken such good care of her in Egypt, emigrated to Australia. When he retired, he visited Jerrie in Columbus. Only then did he feel free to explain to Jerrie why he had not sent the film she had entrusted him to mail back home to her. He believed it was

---

[1058] Ibid.

[1059] Rev. Bernard Jakubco, interview by the author, Aug. 10, 2022.

[1060] Mock, interview, May 5, 2008; Saunders, "How an Ohio Housewife Flew Around the World."

[1061] Mock, interview, May 5, 2008.

his duty to turn over the film to the CIA. Evidently, the CIA kept her photographs of the church that Christopher Columbus had visited in the Azores, her camel ride, and the King's pajamas. The photographs were never returned to Jerrie.[1062]

At home, the "jet-setting and dinner parties" inevitably faded away, replaced by ordinary life and the usual struggles.[1063] Russ and Jerrie had some arguments over money, and their daughter Valerie grew up hearing her mom threaten more than once to make "the island escape."[1064]

Russ eventually met a woman with enough money to take Russ on "trips to Morocco and China." Years later, Jerrie would recall, "He fell in love with her money. . . . He got rid of me so he could go with her."[1065]

Russ and Jerrie were divorced in 1979.

For the next decade, Jerrie wandered "between an apartment in Columbus, her parents' home in Newark, and the homes of her sons in Columbus and Michigan."[1066] The only work she could find was a part-time job as a greeter at a bank—more public relations, never her strong suit.

Although Russ had remarried, he and Jerrie spent a lot of time together. The possibility of a reconciliation emerged, at least in Jerrie's view. In 1991, Russ mailed Jerrie a check, a gesture that perhaps added momentum to that possibility. But soon after, Russ suffered a heart attack, and in the blink of an

---

[1062] We have not been able to find any corroborating record of Peter or Marlin Barker.

[1063] Saunders, "How an Ohio Housewife Flew Around the World."

[1064] Ibid.

[1065] Ibid.

[1066] Ibid.

eye, he was gone, along with any hope of rekindling their relationship.[1067]

Over the next year, it became clear that there was not much to keep Jerrie in Ohio. Not only had Russ died, but their younger son, Gary, who had moved to Florida, had also passed away.[1068] She moved with her son Roger and his family to Quincy, Florida, a small town about twenty-five miles from the capital city of Tallahassee. Jerrie invested $68,500, almost all of the money she had left, in a four-bedroom home on East King Street, in a quiet neighborhood with large trees, plenty of shade, and a small airport for private planes just down the road. Jerrie settled into a quiet chapter of life, almost as if the large oaks and bushes of her yard and neighborhood helped her disappear.[1069]

On one occasion, a man seeking an autograph had to wander from door to door before finally encountering someone who knew a Jerrie Mock. The owner of a bed-and-breakfast recognized the name. The innkeeper said that she lived just a block away, but even after she had been in Quincy for thirteen years, he had never heard about his neighbor being a pilot.

On another occasion, this author attended a flying show at the Tallahassee airport. A young woman in line at the gate to enter the event asked the women at the registration table to point out Jerrie Mock to her. They didn't know who she was asking about, so she whispered, "She was the first woman to fly a plane around the world!" At that, one of the women at the registration

---

[1067] Ibid.

[1068] "Gary Timothy Mock," Find a Grave, accessed Feb. 15, 2023, https://www.findagrave.com/memorial/236086667/gary-timothy-mock.

[1069] Mock, interview, Feb. 17, 2009; Saunders, "How an Ohio Housewife Flew Around the World."

table said, "Oh," and motioned toward Jerrie, who was sitting under an awning a few feet away, watching the show.

Although more than half a century has passed since Jerrie flew around the world in a tiny Cessna airplane, movies, fame, and legends have yet to materialize. The *On This Day* website included a single sentence to commemorate the fiftieth anniversary of Jerrie's accomplishment; it was listed after entries about a baseball game, the opening of a musical that ran for three performances, and the introduction of the Ford Mustang at the 1964 New York World's Fair.[1070]

Still, the fiftieth anniversary brought forth more notice and gestures of support. Wendy Hollinger, the publisher who re-issued *Three-Eight Charlie* in 2014, invited fellow fans of Jerrie to "Join us to celebrate this historic accomplishment" on Facebook and Twitter.[1071] The Ohio State University College of Engineering honored the "50th anniversary of historic flight by a Buckeye" on its website.[1072] In honor of the anniversary, the Udvar-Hazy Center, part of the Smithsonian's National Air and Space Museum, set up a "display of selected paperwork, photographs, and [Jerrie's] sunglasses" in the General Aviation section, near the

[1070] "What Happened on April 17, 1964," *On This Day*, accessed Jan. 7, 2023, https://www.onthisday.com/date/1964/april/17.

[1071] Wendy Hollinger, "50th Anniversary Celebration," *Three-Eight Charlie*, posted March 20, 2014, accessed Nov. 7, 2022, https://38charlie.com/2014/03/20/celebrate-the-50th-anniversary-of-jerrie-mocks-record/.

[1072] "50th Anniversary of Historic Flight by a Buckeye," The Ohio State University College of Engineering, posted April 17, 2014, accessed Nov. 7, 2022, https://engineering.osu.edu/news/2014/04/50th-anniversary-historic-flight-buckeye.

airplane that Jerrie flew.[1073]

In 2008, Jerrie was added to the Pioneer Hall of Fame List of the Women in Aviation International organization.

A gentleman named Bill Kelley, 85 at the time, a native of Newark, Ohio, and a fan, offered to mortgage his house to pay for a statue of Jerrie in her honor in her hometown. Jerrie's sister, Susan Reid, took up the cause, helping to raise the $48,000 for a bronze statue that, in September 2013, was dedicated at a museum in Newark.

Three of Jerrie's grandchildren took her to a bed-and-breakfast near her home in Quincy, where they crowded around a laptop to watch the statue dedication via Skype. On the screen, Jerrie watched a gathered assembly of 400 people and heard the tributes, including two young women who spoke of how Jerrie's flight helped make their careers possible. "To me, Jerrie Mock is what America is all about," one of the women said. "An ordinary person who has extraordinary dreams and turns them into reality."[1074]

A similar statue was unveiled on April 17, 2014, at the Port Columbus International Airport (now John Glenn Columbus International Airport). As part of the commemoration, a "lady pilot" landed a Cessna 180 at the same time and place that Jerrie landed fifty years prior.[1075]

[1073] "Celebrating Jerrie Mock, the First Woman to Fly Around the World," The National Air and Space Museum, posted March 11, 2014, accessed Nov. 7, 2022, https://airandspace.si.edu/stories/editorial/celebrating-jerrie-mock-first-woman-fly-around-world.

[1074] Saunders, "How an Ohio Housewife Flew Around the World."

[1075] Ibid.

September 15, 2014
QUINCY, Florida, 9:09 p.m. (Eastern Time)

Jerrie rested at home with her daughter Valerie by her side. She had one more journey to make.

September 30, 2014

Geraldine "Jerrie" Mock died in her sleep at her Quincy home. She was 88 years old.[1076] At her request, there was no funeral service. Instead, her final wish was for a plane to disperse her ashes over the Gulf of Mexico.

April 22, 2015

On a breezy spring day, Jerrie's friends and family members gathered at Bald Point State Park in Alligator Point, Florida, for a memorial for Jerrie. The family members included Jerrie's daughter, Valerie Armentrout; her daughter-in-law; four grandchildren; and two of the grandchildren's spouses.

The memorial was planned for April 17, the 51st anniversary of the completion of Jerrie's flight around the world, but bad weather delayed the gathering until April 22. An hour or so before sunset, three planes took off from the Tallahassee Regional Airport, some thirty miles to the north. Soon they were over the Gulf of Mexico, flying along the coast near Bald Point. This was a special location for Jerrie, whose son Gary used to take her on boat rides in the area.

The first plane was a replica of *The Spirit of Columbus*, a Cessna 180 Skywagon that was built the same year as Charlie,

---

[1076] Dan Sewell, "Mock, 1st female pilot to circle globe, dies at 88," *Tallahassee Democrat*, Oct. 2, 2014.

1953. The plane's owner, Dick Merrill, had the plane painted with Charlie's red-and-white colors.

The second plane, also a Cessna 180 Skywagon, was silver and red. The owner, Dr. Tom Navar, runs a company called Final Passage which provides a service for commemorations such as this one. Dr. Navar flew the plane, and was responsible for dispersing Jerrie's ashes over the Gulf of Mexico.

The third plane was a 1966 Cherokee with pilot Dale Ratcliff and two passengers aboard. One of the passengers was Wendy Hollinger, herself a member of the Ninety-Nines, who worked with Ratcliff to publish the 50th anniversary edition of Jerrie's autobiographical account, *Three-Eight Charlie*. Also on board was American aviator Shaesta Waiz, the first woman born in Afghanistan to earn a civilian pilot's license. After meeting Jerrie, Shaesta was inspired to fly solo around the world. In October 2017, at 30 years old, she became the youngest woman to do so in a single-engine plane.[1077]

The service included three special flyovers along the coast. The first flyover included all three planes in a greeting to the family members on the beach. On the second flyover, also involving all three planes, Jerrie's ashes were dispersed over the Gulf.

On the third and final flyover, the "missing man" formation was performed. Ratcliff's plane peeled off from the others and flew into the clouds.

The following week, Jerrie's granddaughter-in-law, Rachel Mock, published a story about the service in the *Havana* (Florida) *Herald*. Rachel wrote, "Jerrie often signed her books,

---

[1077] At 27, Joan held the record for youngest woman to complete the round-the-world solo flight in a twin-engine plane.

'Blue skies always, Jerrie Mock.' This memorial service was an ideal way to honor her life and achievements, a grand signature across blues skies."[1078]

The Spirit of Columbus, a.k.a. "Charlie," is now suspended in perpetual flight at the Smithsonian Institution's National Air and Space Museum in Washington, DC.[1079]

The legacy of women in aviation lives on, with new pilots continually reaching new heights, both literally and figuratively. From hearing the phrase "lady pilot" spoken in 1964 by fighter pilots in Egypt who were fascinated when a civilian woman managed to land on their supposedly invisible air base, to Zara Rutherford, a nineteen-year-old Belgian-British pilot who in 2019 became the youngest woman to fly solo around the world,[1080] women will never be tied to the ground.

Like Joan and Jerrie, every woman aviator is a Queen of the Clouds.

[1078] Rachel Mock, "Jerrie Mock's Memorial Service in the Sky," *The Herald of Gadsden County*, April 30, 2015.

[1079] Lucia Cheng, "Who Was the First Woman to Fly Solo Around the World?" *Smithsonian Magazine*, Aug. 12, 2022 (accessed Feb. 28, 2023) https://www.smithsonianmag.com/smithsonian-institution/who-was-the-first-woman-to-fly-solo-around-the-world-180980542; Judy Blair, "Three-Eight Charlie moves to Washington, DC," *Three-Eight Charlie*, posted May 16, 2022, https://38charlie.com/news-and-events/.

[1080] "Zara Rutherford," *Wikipedia*, https://en.wikipedia.org/wiki/Zara _Rutherford, accessed Feb. 6, 2023.

Notes about Geography

Agana, Guam, is now Hagåtña.

AID stood for the Agency for International Development. It is now the USAID.

Bône, Algeria, is now Annaba.

Burma is now Myanmar.

Calcutta is now Kolkata.

Djakarta is now Jakarta.

Tripoli, Libya, is now Tarabulus.

Fort-Lamy is now N'Djamena, the capital of Chad.

Massawa is now Mitsawa; Assab is now Aseb. Both cities are in Eritrea, a country in the Horn of Africa.

Port Aden is now in Yemen.

The United Arab Republic (UAR) was a sovereign state in the Middle East from 1958 to 1961. Egypt continued to be known officially as the UAR until 1971. The UAR is now Egypt.

Vishakhapatnam is now also spelled Visakhapatnam or Vizag.

Bibliography

2016 Citizen of Character Mr. Jack Smith." *Prattville Autauga Character Coalition.* June 6, 2016. https://www.pacharacter .org/award-recipients (accessed September 18, 2022).

Agnew, Spiro T., Governor of Maryland, C. Stanley Blair, Secretary of State, "Senate Joint Resolution 81-Introduction of a Joint Resolution in Honor of Amelia Earhart and Joan Merriam Smith," *US Congressional Record – Senate,* 6571, March 17, 1969.

"Alcor Goes 'Round the World." *Flying Magazine,* July 1964: 57.

Alvord, Linda, "Oregon Chapter." *Ninety-Nine News,* April 1965, 23.

"Amelia Earhart, 1897-1937/American Experience/Official Site /PBS" https://www.pbs.org/wgbh/americanexperience/ features/earhart-timeline/ (accessed May 19, 2022).

"Around the World in 30 Days." *Columbus Dispatch.* March 19, 1964.

"Aviatrix On Flight's Finale." *Honolulu Star-Bulletin.* April 17, 1964: 3.

"Aviatrix's Husband Files $500,000 Suit. *Santa Ana Register.* February 10, 1966.

Baumeister, A.J. and Russell Mock. "$1,000,000 Bodily Injury and Property Damage excluding Passenger Liability." *Certificate of Insurance.* Chicago: Underwriters at Lloyd's London and Certain English Companies, March 13, 1964.

Bevins, Vincent. "What the United States Did in Indonesia," *The Atlantic,* October 20, 2017, https://www.theatlantic.com/ (accessed October 18, 2018).

"Bexley Aviatrix Takes Off on Flight-First Stop Scheduled in Bermuda." *Columbus Evening Dispatch.* March 19, 1964: 1.

"Biography of Geraldine 'Gerry' (sic) Mock." *Women in Aviation.* n.d. http://library.thinkquest.org/21229/bio/gmock.htm (accessed February 2, 2008).

Blair, Judy. "Three-Eight Charlie moves to Washington, DC." *Three-Eight Charlie.* Posted May 16, 2022. https://38charlie .com/news-and-events/.

Bosworth, Adrienne. "Housewife Jerrie Mock, Newark Is to Circle Globe in Drip-Dries," *Newark (Ohio) Advocate,* March 16, 1964.

Brown, Tiffany Ann. *Fate on a Folded Wing: The True Story of Pioneering Solo Pilot Joan Merriam Smith.* Lucky Bat Books, 2019.

Burnett, Claudine. *Soaring Skyward: A History of Aviation in and around Long Beach, California,* 169-172. Bloomington, IN: AuthorHouse, 2011.

Capper, Eric. "Takeoff: Ode to a Legend-The First Woman of Flight." *Private Air,* August/September 2007, 30.

Chaffee, John H., Governor, Rhode Island. "Proclamation: Amelia Earhart-Joan Merriam Aviation Day," *US Congressional Record – Senate,* 6572, March 17, 1969.

Cheng, Lucia. "Who Was the First Woman to Fly Solo Around the World?" *Smithsonian Magazine.* Aug. 12, 2022 (accessed Feb. 28, 2023) https://www.smithsonianmag.com/ smithsonian-institution/who-was-the-first-woman-to-fly-solo-around-the-world-180980542.

Cleeland, Terri. "Quincy resident was first woman to fly solo around the world." *Tallahassee Democrat*, May 25, 2014.

Clutter, Mark. "Simple Funeral Conducted for Joan Merriam Smith." *Independent Press-Telegram,* Long Beach, California, February 21, 1965.

"Columbus Welcomes Flier." *Columbus Dispatch.* April 19, 1964, 51A.

Congressional Record, US. "Senate Joint Resolution 81-Introduction of a Joint Resolution in Honor of Amelia Earhart and Joan Merriam Smith." Washington, DC: US Senate, 1969, 6571-6572.

Craig, Lee. "Aviatrixes Fly at Each Other Over World Hops," *Long Beach Press-Telegram*, May 15, 1964. Accessed March 25, 2022. https://fateonafoldedwing.com/2021/03/29/joan-jerries-1964-post-world-flight-feud/.

Cunningham, James. "Mrs. Mock Makes It: Woman Flier Can Still Set New Speed Records." *Honolulu Advertiser*, April 14, 1964, 1.

Deerman, Ruth, and Pat Lambert, "Joint Resolution in honor of Joan Merriam Smith." *Ninety-Nine News*, June 1965.

Dille, J. Robert, M.D., M.I.H. "Record and around the world flights through Singapore by women." *Aviation, Space, and Environmental Medicine. Volume 70, No. 10.* October 1999: 1038-1040.

Dole, Office of US Senator Bob, Press Release, "Co-sponsored resolution 'Amelia Earhart-Joan Merriam Smith Aviation Day,'" March 17, 1965, Washington, DC. http://dolearchive.ku.edu/ask

Dunn, Carole B. "Long Beach Chapter." *Ninety-Nine News*, April, 1965, 15-16.

Earhart, Amelia. *Last Flight.* New York: Harcourt, Brace and Company, 1937.

Editors of Encyclopedia Britannica. "Wake Island." *Encyclopedia Britannica.* Last modified October 14, 2022. https://www.britannica.com/place/Wake-Island-Pacific-Ocean.

"Famed Aviatrix Dies in Crash." *Madera Tribune.* February 18, 1965. https://cdnc.ucr.edu/?a=d&d=MT19650218.2.5&e=-------en--20--1--txt-txIN--------1 (accessed February 6, 2019).

"Famous Aviatrix Stops at Cayman." *The Caymanian.* December 8, 1965.

Fenimore, Jeanne and Paula Sandling. "Trixie Ann Schubert." *Aux Tank: Newsletter of the San Fernando Valley Chapter of the Ninety-Nines*, June 2015.

"Final Results All Woman Transcontinental Air Race." *The Ninety-Nines, Inc. News Letter.* Accessed September 1, 2020. https://www.ninety-nines.org/pdf/newsmagazine/196008.pdf. August 1960, 12.

Find a Grave. "Beatrice Ann "Trixie" Gehrung Schubert." Memorial page 196037594, maintained by Peggy Dougherty (contributor 49251912); citing Holy Cross Cemetery, Culver City, Los Angeles, California, USA. Accessed March 2, 2019, https://www.findagrave.com/memorial/196037594/beatrice-ann-schubert.

_. "Dr. Delwyn G. Schubert." Memorial page 9476931, maintained by William Barritt (contributor 46493296), citing Holy Cross Cemetery, Culver City, Los Angeles, California, USA. Accessed March 2, 2019, https://www.findagrave.com/memorial/9476931/delwyn-g-schubert.

_. "Joan Merriam Smith." Memorial page 17235826, maintained by Find a Grave, citing Forest Lawn Memorial Park

Cemetery, Cypress, Orange County, California, USA. Accessed September 30 and November 20, 2013, https://www.findagrave.com/memorial/17235826/joan-smith.

"First Time in Air, She Was Afraid." *Long Beach (California) Independent.* Feb. 18, 1965. https://www.newspapers.com /image /719786428 (accessed Feb. 6, 2023).

Flight Magazine. "Around the World Solo in Her Family Airplane." 1964: 32.

Friedan, Betty. *The Feminine Mystique,* W.W. Norton, 1963.

Gale, Robert I., Director, Pacific Region. *Mrs. Jerrie Mock: Guam.* telegram, Washington, DC: Federal Aviation Agency, 1964.

Gant, Kelli. "Women in Aviation." http://www.ninety-nines.org /wia.html (accessed October 7, 2007).

Geiger, Stephanie Calondis, and Donna Nesbitt. *What Took You So Long, Jerrie Mock? A learning game for high school students.* student curriculum, Columbis, Ohio: The Columbus Council on World Affairs, n.d.

Gilbert, James, Associate Editor. "The Loser: An Epitaph to Joan Merriam Smith." *Flying* Magazine, August 1965: 80-84.

"Girl Fliers Slowed by Setbacks." *Honolulu Advertiser.* April 1, 1964.

"Global Flight: Jerrie First Gal To Go It Alone" (including sidebar). *Honolulu Advertiser.* April 18, 1964: A-4.

Graham, Terry. "A Piece of History: Legend Down" from *The History of Big Pines, WrightwoodCalif.com Forum* July 3, 2007. http://www.wrightwoodcalif.com/forum/index.php? (accessed November 20, 2013).

"Highest altitude achieved in a piston engine aircraft?"
Jetcareers.com. December 3, 2011. https://forums.jetcareers
.com/threads/highest-altitude-achieved-in-a-piston-engine-
aircraft... (accessed December 3, 2018).

History of the Bureau of Diplomatic Security of the US
Department of State: "Richard J. Griffin…164, folder…Aden
1-1-67." (accessed February 9, 2021).

Hollinger, Wendy. "50th Anniversary Celebration," *Three-Eight
Charlie.* Posted March 20, 2014. Accessed November 7, 2022.
https://38charlie.com/2014/03/20/celebrate-the-50th-
anniversary-of-jerrie-mocks-record/.

—. "About." *Three-Eight Charlie.* Accessed October 16, 2018.
https://38charlie.com/about/.

—. "Year End: Blue Skies Jerrie Mock." *Three-Eight Charlie.*
Posted December 31, 2014. Accessed October 16, 2018.
https://38charlie.com /news-and-events/.

"Honolulu Next For Lady Flier." *Honolulu Advertiser.* April 13,
1964.

"Housewife Jerrie Mock, Newark is to Circle the World in Drip
Dries." *Newark Advocate.* March 16, 1964.

Humphrey, Hubert H. "Remarks: Vice President Hubert
Humphrey: Harmon International Aviation Trophies,
December 14, 1965," p. 2-4. Minnesota Historical Society,
mnhs.org, provided by Tiffany Ann Brown.

"Jerrie Off on World Flight." *Newark Advocate.* March 19, 1964.

"Joan Merriam's Bumble Bee Lands in Guam." *Desert Sun,*
Volume 37, Number 223. April 22, 1964. https://cdnc.ucr.edu
/cgi-bin/cdnc?a=d&d=DS19640422.2.6&e-------en—20--1
--txt-txIN-------1. California Digital Newspaper collection,
accessed 12/19/2018.

"Joan Merriam Smith Dies in California Air Crash." Los Angeles (AP). February 18, 1965, provided by Tiffany Ann Brown.

Johnson, Fran. "Las Vegas Valley Chapter." *Ninety-Nine News.* April, 1965.

"July 1937: The Round-the-World Flight: Amelia Earhart 1897-1937." Public Broadcasting Service. https://www.pbs.org /wgbh/americanexperience/features/earhart-timeline. (Accessed May 19, 2022.)

"L.B. Flier Joan Merriam Smith, Writer Killed in Mountain Crash." *Long Beach Independent*, February 18, 1965. Accessed March 15, 2018, https://www.newspapers.com/image /17695322.

Levy, Felice D. "Obituaries on file." *Facts on File.* 1979. http://www.worldcat.org/title/obituaries-on-file/oclc/4933813 (accessed October 21, 2018).

Lovinger, Paul W. "Aviatrix: The Flying's Easy." *Honolulu Star-Bulletin*, April 14, 1964.

"Max Conrad." Wikipedia, September 25, 2021. https://en.wikipedia.org/wiki/Max_Conrad.

Merriam, Joan. "The Fiery End of '51 Pops'." *The AOPA Pilot.* March 1966.

—. "I Flew Around the World Alone." *The Saturday Evening Post,* July 25, 1964: 77-82.

—. "The Longest Flight." *The AOPA Pilot*, November 1964: 44-47.

—. "Tribute to a Star: Flying the A.E. Route." Long Beach Chapter, *Ninety-Nine News.* August-September 1964: 11-13.

Meunier, Claude. "Joan Merriam Smith: 2. The Flight." *SoloFlights Around the World.* Accessed October 1, 2013. http://www.soloflights.org/smith_text_e.html.

Mock, Geraldine L. *Summary of Arrival and Departure Times: Timetable*. Columbus, Ohio, 1964.

Mock, Jerrie. *Three-Eight Charlie*. Philadelphia/New York: J.B. Lippincott, 1970.

—. *Three-Eight Charlie*. Granville, Ohio: Phoenix Graphix Publishing Services, 2014.

Mock, Rachel. "Mock Marks 50th of historic flight." *Tallahassee Democrat*, October 10, 2013: 4E.

—. "Women Making History-Jerrie Mock: The First Woman to Fly Solo Around the World." *Tallahassee Woman* Magazine. February/March 2014: 36-39.

—. "Famous pilot's ashes spread over Gulf." *The Herald of Gadsden County*, April 30, 2015.

Mock, Russell C. "Invoice: Customs Carnet Fee and Deposit." Washington, DC: National Aeronautic Association, March 12, 1964.

"Mrs. Mock May Leave Tonight." *Honolulu Star-Bulletin*. April 14, 1964: 1A.

"Mrs. Mock's Dream." *Columbus Dispatch*. March 19, 1964.

"Mrs. Mock Lands in Azores." *Columbus Evening Dispatch*. March 27, 1964: 1.

"Mrs. Mock Sets Down At Oakland." *Honolulu Advertiser*. April 16, 1964: A-11.

"Mrs. Mock to Land in Isles Today." *Honolulu Star-Bulletin*. April 13, 1964.

"Mrs. Smith in Senegal." *Columbus Dispatch*. April 5, 1964.

"Mrs. Smith Is Forced To Land." *Palm Beach Post*. March 19, 1964.

"MSO-435 *Endurance.*" NavSource Online: Mine Warfare Vessel Photo Archive. n.d. http://www.navsource.org/archives/11/02435.html (accessed March 17, 2014).

Munguia, Hayley. "Team rediscovers how a 1964 Long Beach woman was the first to pilot a solo trip around the equator." *Press-Telegram.* Last updated December 18, 2019. Accessed December 19, 2019. https://www.presstelegram.com/2019/12/16/a-long-beach-pilot-made-history-55-years-ago-but-she-and-her-beloved-plane-faded-from-memory-until-now/.

"National Affairs-Aviation: Shades of Amelia." *Newsweek Magazine.* March 30, 1964: 20-21.

NTSB Identification: LAX65A0069 Aircraft: CESSNA 182C, registration N8784T 65/2/17. https://www.ntsb.gov/_layouts/ntsb.aviation/brief.aspx?ev_id=76485&key=0 (accessed June 12, 2020).

"Oops!! Wrong Airport." *Honolulu Advertiser.* April 2, 1964.

O'Brien, Keith. *Fly Girls: How Five Daring Women Defied All Odds and Made Aviation History.* Boston/New York: Eamon Dolan/Houghton Mifflin Harcourt, 2018.

Oddball Films, 1964 Clip. http://www.oddballfilms.com/clip/13171_7557_aviation. (Accessed April 7, 2017.)

"Piper Apache: Overview" https://www.aopa.org/go-fly/aircraft-and-ownership/aircraft-fact-sheets/piper-apache. (Accessed August 4, 2020.)

Piper Aztec Service Manual, "Combustion Air Blower Motor," 5D8, Piper Aircraft Corporation. (Accessed August 4, 2020.)

"Piper PA-23 Apache/Aztec," https://en.wikipedia.org/wiki/Piper_PA-23. (Accessed August 4, 2020.)

"Probable Cause." *AOPA Pilot.* March 1966.

"Project Gemini." Wikipedia. https://en.wikipedia.org/wiki /Project_Gemini (Accessed August 20, 2019).

Randleman, M. J. M.J. Randleman to Russell Mock, Washington, DC, January 8, 1963.

_. M. J. Randleman to William A. Ong, Washington, DC., July 10, 1964. Shared by Tiffany Ann Brown, February 27, 2019.

Reading, John, "Oakland, Calif., Apr 29, 1968. To: The Citizens of Oakland," *US Congressional Record – Senate*, 6572, March 17, 1969.

"Rountree, William M." *Wikipedia* https://en.wikipedia.org/wiki/ William M. Rountree (accessed July 12, 2022).

Sarver, John S. "Sarver & Mitzerman Press Release," April 9, 1964, courtesy of Tiffany Ann Brown.

_. Press release, dated April 17, 1964, shared by Tiffany Ann Brown, August 27, 2020.

_. John S. Sarver to Ruth Deerman, April 20, 1964. Shared by Tiffany Ann Brown, February 27, 2019.

Saunders, Amy K. "How an Ohio Housewife Flew Around The World, Made History, And Was Then Forgotten." *BuzzFeedNews*, April 12, 2014. http://www.buzzfeed.com /amyksaunders/the-untold-story-of-the-first-woman-to-fly-around-the-world (Accessed March 3, 2016).

Schubert, Beatrice Ann and Joan Merriam Smith. "World Flight: Joan Merriam Smith." Unpublished manuscript, 1965. Shared by Tiffany Ann Brown, March 15, 2019.

Schudel, Matt. "Jerrie Mock, First Female Pilot to Fly Solo Around the World, Dies at 88." *Washington Post*, October 1, 2014.

"Search for Aviatrix' Plane Ends on a California Peak." *CAP* (Civil Air Patrol) *Times*. May, 1965.

Sewell, Dan. "Mock, 1st female pilot to circle globe, dies at 88." *Tallahassee Democrat*, October 2, 2014.

Sheffield School of Aeronautics. "About Sheffield School of Aeronautics." Accessed September 23, 2020. https://www .sheffield.com/about-sheffield.

Sheppard, Laurel M. "Jerrie Mock: Record-Breaking American Female Pilot." *The HistoryNet Women's History.* https://www.historynet.com/jerrie-mock-record-breaking-female-pilot/# (Accessed October 7, 2007).

"Ships Bound for Far East." *San Pedro News-Pilot* (San Pedro, California). December 30, 1963. Provided by National Naval Aviation Museum, Pensacola, Florida, July 17, 2020.

Simmons, Dr. Martha Poole. Honoring Our Heros (sic), "Captain Marvin G. Smith-96." *Alabama Gazette,* December 1, 2019. https://www.alabamagazette.com/story/2019/12/01 /news/honoring-our-heros/1799.html (accessed July 6, 2020).

Smith, Jacqueline M.C. "Washington, DC Chapter." *Ninety-Nine News,* June 1965.

Sunday Star-Bulletin & Advertiser (Honolulu). "Mock in Guam; Next Stops Wake, Honolulu." April 12, 1964, A-2.

Swopes, Bryan. "17 March-12 May 1964: Joan Merriam Smith," *This Day in Aviation*: Important Dates in Aviation History. https://www.thisdayinaviation.com/17-march-12-may-1964-joan-merriam-smith/ (accessed February 24, 2022).

"Team Discovers How Long Beach Woman Was the First to Pilot a Solo Trip Around the Equator." *Long Beach Press Telegram.* December 16, 2019 (accessed June 19, 2020).

"Turbulent Air at High Speed Cause of Crash." *Reno Evening Gazette.* February 10, 1966.

"Two Women Fliers Killed in Crash." *Los Angeles Times.* February 18, 1965, 1.

"Two Women Fliers Remain Grounded." *Honolulu Star-Bulletin.* March 24, 1964.

TwinNavion.com. "Jack M. Riley and the Riley Aircraft Corp." http://www.twinnavion.com/jackriley.htm. (Accessed June 24, 2020.)

"US Woman Flier Reaches P.I. in Globe-Circling Trip." *Honolulu Star-Bulletin.* April 8, 1964.

USS *Dahlgren (DLG-12) Muster List Directory.* https://www.uss dahlgren.com/db/mldir.php (Accessed July 7, 2020).

USS *Endurance (AM-435). Wikipedia.* n.d. http://en.wikipedia.org/ wiki/USS_Endurance_(AM-435) (Accessed March 3, 2014).

USS *Hoel (DDG-13). Wikipedia.*n.d. https://en.wikipedia.org/wiki /USS_Hoel_(DDG-13) (Accessed July 7, 2020).

USS *Valor (AM-472). Wikipedia.* n.d. http://en.wikipedia.org/wiki /USS_Valor_(AM-472) (Accessed July 7, 2020).

USS *Vital (MSO-474). Wikipedia* https://en.wikipedia.org/wiki/ USS_Vital_(MSO-474) (Accessed June 26, 2020).

Vail, Betty and Dixon Edwards. "Winner Take All." *Flying* Magazine, July 1964: 33-66.

Wade, Edwin. "Proclamation." *Congressional Record - Senate,* 6572, March 17, 1969.

"Wake Island." *Wikipedia.* Last modified January 17, 2023. https://en.wikipedia .org/wiki/Wake_Island.

"What Happened on April 17, 1964." *On This Day.* Accessed January 7, 2023, https://www.onthisday.com/date/1964 /april/17.

Whitton, Gerry. "Las Vegas Valley Chapter." *Ninety-Nine News,* April 1965: 14-24.

"Woman Flier Can Still Set New Speed Records." *Honolulu Advertiser*. April 14, 1964: A-2.

"Woman Flier Reaches Libya." *Honolulu Star-Bulletin*. April 1, 1964.

"Women in Aviation." Wikipedia. https://en.wikipedia.org/wiki (Accessed June 9, 2022).

World Air Sports Federation. "FAI Records received by Marvin G. Smith (USA)." *Records*. https://fai.org/records?record= marvin+smith (Accessed December 19, 2018).

"Zara Rutherford." *Wikipedia*. https://en.wikipedia.org/wiki /Zara_Rutherford (Accessed February 6, 2023).

Appendix A

The following references indicate Jerrie at some point accepted that she was, in fact, in a race with Joan.

Russ to Jerrie: Joan's left San Juan, on her way to South America, so get going.[1081]

Jerrie to Russ: If you call me again about Joan, I'll come home on an airliner.[1082]

Karachi was where Joan Merriam Smith's and my routes met and then ran together for a few thousand miles. . . . We had both left the U.S. on the same day and I, despite my one-week delay in Bermuda, had evidently reached Karachi at least two days sooner. But her flight had started officially in Oakland, 2,000 miles west of Columbus. Even if I were the first to get back to the U.S., she could still be the first to circumnavigate the globe. I would have to keep on the move.[1083]

[A] gentleman from a wire service . . . wanted some extra help. He handed me a cable from his boss in Europe. It said, 'Please report on the sad progress of Joan Merriam Smith.' He wanted me to tell him where she was. I wondered how he expected me to know.[1084]

My going to Calcutta and Bangkok brought . . . accusations

[1081] *Three-Eight Charlie*, 34.

[1082] Ibid., 90.

[1083] Ibid., 154.

[1084] Ibid., p. 164.

that I had shortened my route in order to get home before Joan Smith. Actually, I flew my originally planned route.[1085]

I didn't know how far back Joan Smith might be, and *I didn't intend to lose a race around the world* because of a stupid burned-out motor.[1086]

Russ to Jerrie: You're way ahead so far, but Joan might still catch up with you.[1087]

Russ to Jerrie: [F]or a few days, Joan was really making time. It looked like she might catch up with you. Jerrie to Russ: Remember back . . . in January . . . when we first heard about Joan. . . . I said I didn't think anyone could get a plane in shape that quickly unless they had a lot more advice and money than I. It was a little like the tortoise and the hare.[1088]

Russ to Jerrie: I take credit for getting her off in a rush by announcing to the press that you were leaving any day.[1089]

Mrs. Mock's husband Russell says Miss Merriam's flight is not sanctioned by the Federation Aeronautique Internationale and can't be classified for any speed records.[1090]

[1085] Ibid., p. 175.

[1086] Ibid., p. 191, emphasis added.

[1087] Ibid., p. 206.

[1088] Ibid., p. 248.

[1089] Ibid., p. 248.

[1090] Adrienne Bosworth, "Housewife Jerrie Mock, Newark Is to Circle Globe in Drip-Dries." *Newark (Ohio) Advocate*, March 16, 1964.

Index

About the Author

Taylor C. Phillips serves as the chaplain at Westminster Oaks Retirement Community in Tallahassee, Florida, collecting life stories and sharing them with upcoming generations. Taylor earned degrees in philosophy, theology, and psychology from Rhodes College, Columbia Seminary, and Pacifica Graduate Institute.

In 2015, he led a series entitled A Whirlwind Tour of the History of Women in Aviation through the Osher Lifelong Learning Institute at Florida State University. He has published articles in the *Leading Age* internet magazine, the *Presbyterian Older Adult Ministries Newsletter*, and the *Mission Yearbook* of the PCUSA. High school students working with Taylor have developed History Fair projects which have placed first in district, second in state, top ten nationally, and top twenty worldwide in the annual Florida History Fair/ National History Day competition.

Taylor tells stories on stage at Florida Storytellers events, The Moth storytelling events, churches, schools, and conference centers. He leads a group engaging in dream interpretation from a Jungian perspective. Taylor lives in Tallahassee, Florida, with his beloved wife Pam, their sons Colin and Isaac, and their Belgian Malinois, Chuck. They enjoy drinking coffee at the Black Dog Café at Lake Ella. Learn more about Taylor at https://rekindledstories.wixsite.com/taylorphillips.

Photo by Debbie Bass

Made in the USA
Coppell, TX
16 December 2023

25461323R00252